Surveys in the
Economics of Uncertainty

Surveys in the Economics of Uncertainty

Edited by
John D. Hey and Peter J. Lambert

Basil Blackwell

First published 1987
First published in paperback 1989

Basil Blackwell Ltd
108 Cowley Road, Oxford OX4 1JF, UK

Basil Blackwell Inc.
432 Park Avenue South, Suite 1503
New York, NY 10016, USA

British Library Cataloguing in Publication Data
Surveys in the economics of uncertainty. –
    (Uncertainty and expectations in economics).
    1. Economics – Decision making
    2. Uncertainty
    I. Hey, John D.   II. Lambert, Peter J.
    III. Series
    330   HB199
    ISBN 0-631-15335-7 (hb)
          0-631-16891-5 (pb)

Library of Congress Cataloging-in-Publication Data
Surveys in the economics of uncertainty.
    Includes index.
    1. Uncertainty.   2. Economics.   I. Hey, John Denis.
    II. Lambert, Peter J.
    HB615.S97   1987   330   87-10366
    ISBN 0-631-15335-7 (hb)
          0-631-16891-5 (pb)

Typesetting by Unicus Graphics Ltd, Horsham
Printed in Great Britain by TJ Press Ltd, Padstow

CONTENTS

EDITOR'S INTRODUCTION

This volume began life when we took over as Editors of the *Bulletin of Economic Research* and initiated a series of survey articles on various aspects of economics. Our initial strategy was to compile a list of active eminent economists and invite those on the list to survey an area of economics in which they were currently involved in research. Our editorial control over the subject matter was relatively passive. Nevertheless, a series of useful surveys emerged – indicating the diversity and vitality of ongoing economic research.

Interestingly some half-dozen of the earlier surveys were all concerned with various aspects of what might broadly be termed the Economics of Uncertainty. On reflection, it is clear that this accurately identifies one of the key concerns of economists, both then and now.

While one of our initial intentions had always been to collect together periodically sets of surveys in book form, we were pleasantly surprised to see these half-dozen surveys forming the core of a cohesive volume. To complete the volume we invited a further four contributions in areas specified by us – thus enabling us to fill in various gaps and resulting in the present volume.

One matter over which we did exercise editorial influence was that concerning the *purpose* of these surveys. We felt very strongly that these surveys were to inform non-specialist economists about developments in the various specialisms. Whether necessary or not, the latest research developments in economics are almost invariably reported in the leading academic economics journals, usually in a technically rigorous (difficult?) form and often involving specialist language. To the majority of economists, this medium of communication is simply too difficult. This inevitably means that it takes a long time for new developments to filter through to the general reader.

The primary purpose of these surveys was to get round this communication problem by getting specialists to communicate the new ideas in their specialisms in non-technical language. We feel that all the authors have achieved this primary aim: the essays in this volume should be accessible to the intelligent second- or third-year undergraduate economist, as well as to the postgraduate economist and specialists in other areas. While the reader will have to invest some intellectual effort, the careful writing of these surveys should mean that this effort is minimized.

Additionally, the various authors – because they are writing about developments in areas which excite them – have conveyed this excitement in their writing. The reader should quickly be convinced that this volume is concerned with important developments in an important discipline.

The ten essays consist of 5 pairs of essays written on the same topic. Generally, our idea was that the first of the pairs would be a broad theoretical overview of recent developments in a particular area, while the second would explore the empirical or policy implications of that theory or the various extensions, generalizations and applications of the theory, though there are some minor variations on this general theme.

The first pair of essays is addressed to the very foundations of the Economics of Uncertainty: the modelling of rational behaviour under uncertainty. From the 50s, through the 60s and into the 70s the Subjective Expected Utility (SEU) paradigm had become increasingly established as *the* paradigm for modelling such behaviour. Even now, this paradigm reigns virtually unchallenged amongst practitioners – as the rest of the book bears witness. However, through these post-war decades, and increasingly so in the 80s, some economists – most notably those using experimental methods – had been building up a large body of empirical evidence which indicated that individual behaviour often departed consistently and significantly from that predicted (or assumed) by the SEU paradigm. At first, the temptation was to dismiss such evidence, but by the late 70s and early 80s the sheer volume of such evidence was hard to ignore. This led a group of economists – originally few in number, but latterly much larger – to explore the development of new theories of behaviour under uncertainty which were not contradicted by the empirical evidence. These new theories are the concern of chapter 1, written by Robert Sugden, himself the co-originator (with Graham Loomes) of two of these new theories: Regret Theory and Disappointment Theory. Chapter 2, the second in this pair, written by Lynda Appleby and Chris Starmer (research associates of Loomes and Sugden respectively), gives more detail on the experimental evidence giving rise to these new theories. Taken together, these first two chapters give fascinating insight into a dynamically new area of economics, and one that gives the lie to the notion that theoretical economists ignore the accumulation of empirical evidence.

For practitioners within the SEU paradigm, one of the key members of this new school of economists is undoubtedly Mark Machina, who, in a famous 1982 *Econometrica* paper (cited by Sugden at the end of chapter 1) showed that many of the key propositions of applied SEU theory would still be valid even if individuals did not behave in accordance with SEU theory, but rather in accordance with (Machina's) *Generalised* Expected Utility theory (or 'Expected Utility theory without the independence axiom'). This profound result 'saves the bacon' of many SEU-practitioners, and gives them justification for continuing to operate within the SEU paradigm. This is just as well – since the remaining 8 chapters of the book operate within that paradigm!

The second pair of chapters were both written by Ray Rees, and indeed were the first pair of surveys to be published in the *Bulletin of Economic Research*. They both concern the theory of Principal and Agent, an important (relatively) new branch of economics, and one that has given a whole new insight into a class of problems involving *delegated choice*. This is where 'one individual has the responsibility for taking decisions supposedly in the interests of one or more others, in return for some kind of payment' (to quote Ray Rees). Uncertainty is inherent in this problem. In the first of the pair, Rees sets up a general framework for its analysis, and in the second extends and applies that framework to a whole range of phenomena.

The third pair of chapters were both written by Chris McKenna and concern *search theory*, another (relatively) new area of the Economics of Uncertainty and one which has led to many insights into real world situations – including unemployment. Until the advent of search theory, economists used to assume, for example, that in atomistic markets (those with large numbers of buyers and sellers) there would be a *unique* price. A glance at the real world suggests that this is not, in fact, the case, with, for example, the same colour TV available at different prices in different shops, or with (apparently identical) workers being paid different wages. (An extreme case, of course, being where one worker is paid – being employed – while another is not – being unemployed.) The purpose of search theory in its original form is to describe how rational agents should react to such a dispersion of prices; for example, how should you search for a colour TV which you know is sold at different prices in different shops? Clearly, the longer you search, the more likely you are to find low prices; but the longer you search the more costly it is to you (unless you like shopping!). A classic trade-off problem exists – but one confounded by uncertainty. In chapter 5, the first of the pair, McKenna, solves this problem, and various generalizations. Then, in chapter 6, he explores the *market* implications of such behaviour – in particular, asking whether, in the face of such rational reaction, the original dispersion will persist, and, if so, what implications the dispersion will have for the nature of the market equilibrium. The answers have interesting repercussions.

Chapters 7 and 8 are both written by Mark Taylor and concern Implicit Contract theory – as applied to the labour market. Initially, this theory was developed to explain certain stylized facts concerning the real world which were not explicable with other labour market theories. Of particular concern was the desire to explain why it is the 'normal practice in most western economies to lay off workers as product demand [falls], paying the rest of the workforce a fairly unchanged wage'. Intuitively, one might expect that the firm would simply lower the wage paid to all its existing employees. Taylor shows why this intuition may be incorrect, and explores a number of implications flowing from this demonstration. In chapter 8, further implications are explored, most notably those which have useful things to say about Keynesian economics and the existence – and persistence – of unemployment.

The final pair of chapters should, perhaps, not appear in a serious academic book – since they are concerned with an illegal activity, that of tax evasion. However, if the material is considered as positive, rather than normative, our consciences are clear! Alternatively, we could argue that this material provides useful ammunition for the tax authorities in their efforts to reduce (or eliminate) tax evasion. The first of the pair, chapter 9, is written by Frank Cowell and begins by examining the simple problem of the optimal amount of tax evasion by the SEU-maximizing individual. It then broadens the analysis, and concludes by examining the very issue we noted above. In particular, this chapter sheds useful light on whether tax authorities should deter by frequent auditing or by high punishments. The second of the pair, chapter 10, is written by Massimo Marrelli who comes from a country where tax evasion is almost a national pastime – rivalling football for popularity. He discusses attempts to estimate the magnitude and importance of tax evasion in a number of countries.

Overall we feel that this book provides important evidence of the vitality of ongoing economic research – not just as intellectual activity, but more importantly as a light to illuminate many problems of the real world and as a weapon to rectify some of those problems.

We hope you get as much out of reading this book as we did.

John D. Hey
Peter J. Lambert

NEW DEVELOPMENTS IN THE THEORY OF CHOICE UNDER UNCERTAINTY[1]

Robert Sugden

For many years almost all economic analysis of choice under uncertainty was based on expected utility theory. The validity of this theory, both as a prescription as to how people ought to choose and as a description of how they do choose, was hardly questioned. The few sceptics, led by Maurice Allais, were generally perceived as eccentrics, outside the main stream of economic thought. Now it seems that their time has come. There is a rapidly-growing literature criticizing expected utility theory and suggesting alternative approaches. Let me say at the outset that this paper does not purport to be a general survey of this literature. (Two excellent surveys are available, written by Schoemaker (1982) and Machina (1983).) Rather, it describes one *class* of alternative theories that has been developed in the last few years by, among others, Bell, Chew, Fishburn, Hagen, Loomes, MacCrimmon, Machina and myself. I believe that this work provides *one* promising avenue for progress, but it is certainly not the only one.

1. EXPECTED UTILITY THEORY

It is generally agreed that expected utility theory, in its modern form, was initiated by von Neumann and Morgenstern (1947, 1953) who showed that an individual whose preferences satisfied certain axioms would choose as though maximizing expected utility. For some years following the publication of von Neumann and Morgenstern's proof, there was doubt about how their axioms should be interpreted (see Samuelson, 1952 and Malinvaud, 1952) and various alternative systems of axioms were proposed. As a result of these debates it became recognized that expected utility theory rested on three essential axioms, *ordering*, *continuity* and *independence*. Possibly the simplest formulation of these axioms was provided by

[1] Many of the ideas presented in this paper developed in discussions with Graham Loomes and Mark Machina.

1

Herstein and Milnor (1953); the following discussion is loosely based on this presentation of expected utility theory.

I shall define a *prospect* as a list of *consequences* with an associated list of probabilities, one for each consequence, such that these probabilities sum to unity. Consequences are to be understood as *mutually exclusive* possibilities; thus a prospect comprises an exhaustive list of the possible consequences of a particular course of action. Consequences may themselves be prospects. For my present purposes, the concept of probability must be taken as unproblematic. It may be interpreted either in terms of relative frequency (as proposed by von Neumann and Morgenstern, 1953, p. 19) or in terms of subjective degrees of belief.

An individual's preferences are defined over the set of all conceivable prospects. This set is taken to be a *mixture set*. This means the following. Suppose that p and q are any two prospects belonging to the set of conceivable prospects. Let λ be any probability between 0 and 1. Then we may construct a third prospect yielding p with probability λ and q with probability $1 - \lambda$, and this prospect will also be a member of the set of conceivable prospects.

The *ordering* axiom requires that the individual should have a preference ordering over the set of all conceivable prospects. Letting $\succcurlyeq$, $\succ$ and $\sim$ stand for the relations of weak preference, strict preference and indifference, this axiom requires that $\succcurlyeq$ should be complete, reflexive and transitive on the set of conceivable prospects. The *continuity* axiom can be formulated in various ways, but its spirit is captured in the following version. Let p, q, r be any three prospects such that $p \succ q \succ r$. Then there must be some compound prospect, constructed by mixing p and r in some probabilities λ and $1 - \lambda$, that is indifferent to q. The *independence* axiom can also be formulated in various ways; here is one version. Let p, q and r be any three prospects, such that $p \succcurlyeq q$. Then a $\lambda : (1 - \lambda)$ probability mix of p and r must be weakly preferred to a $\lambda : (1 - \lambda)$ mix of q and r, for any value of λ in the range $0 < \lambda < 1$. (Herstein and Milnor show that a weaker version of this axiom is sufficient, but this is a technical detail.)

If these axioms hold, it is possible to assign a real-valued utility index $U(p)$ to every prospect p such that the utility function $U(\cdot)$ represents the individual's preference ordering. (That is, higher utility numbers correspond with more preferred prospects.) Further, the utility function has the property that the utility of any compound prospect (i.e. any probability mix of prospects) is the probability-weighted sum of the utilities of its component prospects. Thus if prospect p yields $x_1, \ldots, x_n$ with probabilities $\pi_1, \ldots, \pi_n$ (where $\pi_1 + \ldots + \pi_n = 1$), $U(p) = \pi_1 U(x_1) + \ldots + \pi_n U(x_n)$. In other words, if the individual chooses according to his preferences, he chooses as if maximizing expected utility. The *von Neumann–Morgenstern utility function* $U(\cdot)$ is unique up to a positive linear transformation: that is, utility is measured on a cardinal scale for which both the origin and the unit are arbitrary.

For the purposes of exposition, I shall take the case in which there is a finite number of *pure* (monetary) consequences – that is, consequences experienced with certainty. Then the set of conceivable prospects comprises all those prospects that can be formed by probability mixtures of these pure consequences. To allow a diagrammatic presentation, I shall (wherever possible) limit myself to the case in which there are only three pure consequences, although the arguments I shall put forward apply more generally. The three consequences will be written x_1, x_2, x_3, where for the individual whose preferences are being analysed, $x_1 < x_2 < x_3$. A typical prospect may be written as (π_1, π_2, π_3) where π_1, π_2, π_3 are the probabilities associated with x_1, x_2, x_3. Since $\pi_2 = 1 - \pi_1 - \pi_3$, we may suppress π_2 if we wish. This is convenient for a diagrammatic presentation: prospects may be represented in (π_1, π_3) space, the set of conceivable prospects being the set of points at which $0 \leqslant \pi_1 + \pi_3 \leqslant 1$.

Suppose that the individual's preferences over this set of prospects satisfy the axioms of expected utility theory. Then there must exist von Neumann–Morgenstern utility indices $U(x_1)$, $U(x_2)$ and $U(x_3)$ – or, in short, u_1, u_2 and u_3 – such that the utility index for any prospect (π_1, π_3) is given by

$$V(\pi_1, \pi_3) = \pi_1 u_1 + (1 - \pi_1 - \pi_3) u_2 + \pi_3 u_3 \tag{1}$$

(For my purposes it is convenient to distinguish between a utility index assigned to a pure consequence and one assigned to a prospect; from now on I shall use $U(\cdot)$ to denote the former and $V(\cdot)$ to denote the latter.) Now consider the set of all prospects that generate the same expected utility, say v^*: this is a typical indifference class, or an indifference curve in (π_1, π_3) space. The equation for this indifference curve is

$$\pi_1 u_1 + (1 - \pi_1 - \pi_3) u_2 + \pi_3 u_3 = v^*$$

or

$$\pi_1(u_1 - u_2) + \pi_3(u_3 - u_2) = v^* - u_2 \tag{2}$$

Notice that this is the equation for a line with gradient

$$\left. \frac{d\pi_3}{d\pi_1} \right|_{V = v^*} = \frac{u_2 - u_1}{u_3 - u_2} \tag{3}$$

So we know that indifference curves are positively-sloped lines in (π_1, π_3) space. (Since $x_1 < x_2 < x_3$ by assumption, it is clear that $u_1 < u_2 < u_3$.) We also know that the gradient of these indifference lines is independent of v^*; so all indifference lines must be parallel. Notice also that the common gradient of these indifference lines can be taken as an index of risk-aversion (in the von Neumann–Morgenstern sense) over the three consequences x_1, x_2, x_3. (Given any arbitrary utilities u_1, u_3 – where $u_1 < u_3$ – assigned to x_1 and x_3, the individual is more risk-averse the greater is the utility associated with u_2; and the greater is u_2, the greater is the slope of the indifference lines.) The existence of a family of indifference curves is a product of the ordering and continuity axioms; that these indifference curves are parallel lines follows from the independence axiom.

These implication of expected utility theory are displayed in Figure 1 – a *triangle diagram* borrowed from Machina (1982, 1983). The triangle encloses the set of conceivable prospects, its corners representing the three consequences x_1, x_2 and x_3 with certainty. The parallel lines are indifference classes. The arrow in the middle of the triangle shows the *direction of preference* (from less-preferred to more-preferred prospects).

One implication of all this is that if we know an individual's preferences in the neighbourhood of *any one* prospect, we can construct his preferences over *all* prospects. (Here a 'neighbourhood' is to be understood in terms of probability space; the neighbourhood of a prospect defined for a given set of consequences contains prospects involving slightly different probability-mixes of the *same* consequences.) This result follows immediately from (3): if we know the slope of an individual's indifference curve at any point, the von Neumann–Morgenstern utility indices u_1, u_2, u_3 are defined up to an increasing linear transformation. In other words, we can construct a

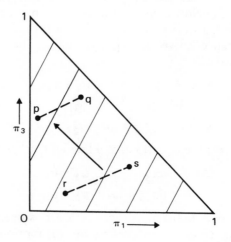

Fig. 1. Expected utility theory

von Neumann–Morgenstern utility function by observing preferences *locally*. Similarly, if we know an individual's preference between one pair of prospects, we can construct his preferences between many other pairs. Consider the pairs (p, q) and (r, s) in Figure 1; the gradient of the line pq is equal to the gradient of the line rs. Since indifference curves are parallel lines, $p \succ q \Leftrightarrow r \succ s$ (the case illustrated in Figure 1), $p \sim q \Leftrightarrow r \sim s$, and $p \prec q \Leftrightarrow r \prec s$. This implication of expected utility theory is particularly easy to test. Unfortunately, however, such tests tend *not* to support the theory.

2. VIOLATIONS OF THE INDEPENDENCE AXIOM

Possibly the first, and still the best known, test of expected utility theory was suggested by Allais (1953). Here I shall discuss a version of this test carried out experimentally by Kahneman and Tversky (1979). Kahneman and Tversky's subjects were asked to choose between two prospects. The first prospect, p_1, gave 2400 Israeli pounds with certainty. The second prospect, p_2, gave 2500 with probability 0.33, 2400 with probability 0.66, and nothing with probability 0.01. Then the subjects were asked to choose between two further prospects, p_3 and p_4; p_3 gave 2400 with probability 0.34 and nothing with probability 0.66; p_4 gave 2500 with probability 0.33 and nothing with probability 0.67. Notice that all four prospects involve different probability mixes of the same three pure consequences (0, 2400 and 2500); Figure 2 locates these prospects

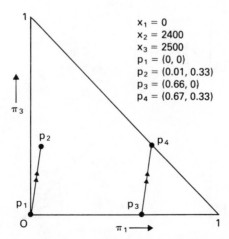

$x_1 = 0$
$x_2 = 2400$
$x_3 = 2500$
$p_1 = (0, 0)$
$p_2 = (0.01, 0.33)$
$p_3 = (0.66, 0)$
$p_4 = (0.67, 0.33)$

Fig. 2. The common consequence effect (Allais paradox)

in a triangle diagram. Since the gradients of the lines p_1p_2 and p_3p_4 are equal, expected utility theory entails $p_1 \gtreqless p_2 \Leftrightarrow p_3 \gtreqless p_4$.

In fact, however, subjects responded very differently to the two choice problems. In the first problem, 82 per cent chose p_1 while in the second, only 17 per cent chose p_3. This tendency of people to 'reverse' their preference from $p_1 \succ p_2$ to $p_3 \prec p_4$ has been observed in many experiments; it is known as the *Allais paradox* or *common consequence effect*.

Now consider another test. Kahneman and Tversky asked their subjects to choose between p_5, which gave 3000 with certainty, and p_6, which gave a 0.8 chance of 4000 (and a 0.2 chance of nothing). Then they asked them to choose between p_7, which gave a 0.25 chance of 3000 and p_8, which gave a 0.2 chance of 4000. Again, these are four prospects involving different probability mixes of three pure consequences (0, 3000 and 4000); Figure 3 locates them in a triangle diagram. Expected utility theory entails $p_5 \gtreqless p_6 \Leftrightarrow p_7 \gtreqless p_8$. In fact, 80 per cent of subjects chose p_5 in the first problem while only 35 per cent chose p_7 in the second. This tendency of people to reverse their preference from $p_5 \succ p_6$ to $p_7 \prec p_8$ has also been observed in many experiments; it is known as the *common ratio effect*.

Intuitively speaking, these two violations of expected utility theory seem to be closely related to one another. In each case, people seem to be attracted to a certain gain (p_1 or p_5) rather than a gamble with a slightly higher actuarial value (p_2 or p_6); but when it comes to a choice between two gambles in each of which the chance of winning anything is relatively small, they are attracted to the gamble with the larger prize (p_4 or p_8). This intuition, however, does

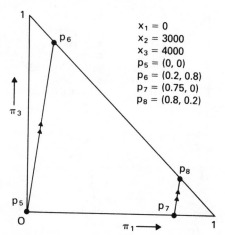

Fig. 3. The common ratio effect for gains

not account for the following variant of the common ratio effect. Kahneman and Tversky's subjects were asked to choose between the certainty of *losing* 3000 (p_9) and a 0.8 chance of losing 4000 (p_{10}), and then to choose between a 0.25 chance of losing 3000 (p_{11}) and a 0.2 chance of losing 4000 (p_{12}). Figure 4 locates these prospects in a triangle diagram. Again expected utility theory entails an equivalence between the two choice problems: $p_9 \gtrless p_{10} \leftrightarrow p_{11} \gtrless p_{12}$. And again there was a systematic tendency for subjects to behave contrary to the theory: 92 per cent chose p_{10} in the first problem while only 42 per cent chose p_{12} in the second. Notice that subjects are choosing an actuarially unfair gamble (p_{10}) in preference to a certainty (p_9); when it comes to a choice between two gambles, in each of which the chance of losing anything is relatively small, they are attracted to the gamble whose worst outcome is less bad (p_{11}). In some ways this is a mirror image of the previous form of the common ratio effect. (Indeed, Kahneman and Tversky coin the term 'reflection effect' for this type of relationship between choice problems.) It is tempting to compare the behaviour of the 92 per cent who chose p_{10} with that of the racegoer who, having lost small amounts of money on every race until the last, tries to recoup his losses in the last race by putting a large bet on the favourite.

3.   MACHINA'S 'GENERALIZED EXPECTED UTILITY ANALYSIS'

Nevertheless, as Machina (1982, 1983) has shown, the common consequence effect and *both* forms of the common ratio effect can

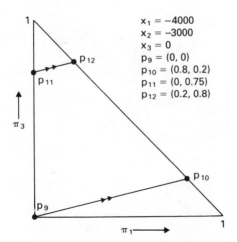

$$x_1 = -4000$$
$$x_2 = -3000$$
$$x_3 = 0$$
$$p_9 = (0, 0)$$
$$p_{10} = (0.8, 0.2)$$
$$p_{11} = (0, 0.75)$$
$$p_{12} = (0.2, 0.8)$$

Fig. 4. The common ratio effect for losses

all be characterized in the same way. Suppose we abandon the independence axiom but retain the ordering and continuity axioms. Then there will be a family of indifference curves in any triangle diagram, but these curves need be neither linear nor parallel. Now consider the common consequence effect as shown in Figure 2. For an individual with the pattern of preferences that constitutes this violation of expected utility theory, p_1 must lie on a higher indifference curve than p_2 while p_4 lies on a higher curve than p_3. This is consistent with the hypothesis that the indifference curves 'fan out' in the way shown in Figure 5. Notice that the fanning-out hypothesis does not entail that an individual *must* have the conjunction of preferences $p_1 \succ p_2$ and $p_3 \prec p_4$. The conjunction $p_1 \succ p_2$ and $p_3 \succ p_4$ and the conjunction $p_1 \prec p_2$ and $p_3 \prec p_4$, both of which are consistent with expected utility theory, are also consistent with the fanning-out hypothesis. What is *not* consistent with that hypothesis is the conjunction $p_1 \prec p_2$ and $p_3 \succ p_4$. In other words, the fanning-out hypothesis implies a *tendency* for expected utility theory to be violated in a particular direction; and this is exactly what is observed. It is easy to see that the fanning-out hypothesis is also consistent with the two forms of the common ratio effect illustrated in Figures 3 and 4.

The fanning-out hypothesis can be formulated more precisely in the following way. First we require that indifference curves in the triangle diagram should be *upward sloping*, movements north or west being preferred. (Recall that $x_1 \prec x_2 \prec x_3$.) Such movements involve reductions in the probability weights attached to less-preferred consequences and corresponding increases in the probability weights

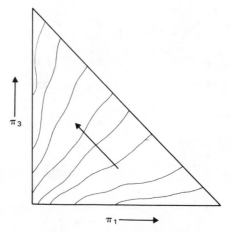

Fig. 5. Machina's 'fanning out' hypothesis

attached to more-preferred consequences; in other words, these are movements from stochastically dominated to stochastically dominating prospects. So the essential assumption is that if one prospect stochastically dominates another, the former is preferred. The second requirement is that as we move north or west, the indifference curves become steeper (or at least, no less steep).

Recall that under expected utility theory it is possible to construct a von Neumann–Morgenstern utility function by observing preferences locally; in terms of the triangle diagram, it is possible to assign utility indices to the three consequences by observing the slope of an indifference curve at any point. Thus, so long as indifference curves are smooth – and irrespective of whether they are linear or parallel – it must be possible to construct a *local utility function* by observing preferences in the locality of a particular prospect. Such a function may be written as $U(x;p)$ where x is a consequence and p is the given prospect. *In the neighbourhood of prospect p*, an individual chooses as though maximizing expected utility, $U(x;p)$ being his von Neumann–Morgenstern utility function. In expected utility theory proper, the local utility function is the same for every prospect, that is $U(x;p) = U(x;q)$ for all p, q. If instead the independence axiom is dropped, different prospects may have different local utility functions. Then the fanning-out hypothesis can be described in terms of properties of these local utility functions.

Machina (1982) formulates two such properties. He considers the case in which consequences are measured in units of wealth; the set of possible consequences is an interval (all values of wealth in a given range) and thus local utility functions can be assumed to be continuous and smooth. In this context a prospect is a probability distribution over the set of consequences; a local utility function is written $U(x;F)$ where F is a probability distribution. Machina's first property is that each local utility function should be increasing in x. This ensures that stochastically dominating distributions are always preferred. (In terms of the triangle diagram: indifference curves slope upwards.) The second property, which Machina calls Hypothesis II, is as follows. Let $R(x;F)$ be the Arrow–Pratt measure of risk aversion at x on the local utility function $U(x;F)$ (i.e.

$$R(x;F) = -[\partial^2 U(x;F)/\partial x^2]/[\partial U(x;F)/\partial x])$$

Then for any two distributions F_1, F_2, where F_1 stochastically dominates F_2: $R(x;F_1) \geqslant F(x;F_2)$. In other words, as we move towards stochastically dominating distributions, the degree of *local* risk aversion associated with any given level of wealth increases (or at least, does not decrease). Recall that in the triangle diagram, steeper indifference curves denote greater risk aversion; thus the effect of Hypothesis II is to require that as we move north or west, indifference curves become steeper (or at least, do not become less steep): they tend to fan out.

Recall that the starting point for Machina's approach is the rejection of the independence axiom and the retention of the ordering and continuity axioms. Given this approach, it is possible to represent an individual's preferences over prospects by a utility function. Machina has formulated very general properties that such utility functions might be assumed to have − in particular, a preference for stochastic dominance and Hypothesis II. An alternative, closely related, approach is to suggest particular mathematical forms for this utility function with the object of accommodating observed violations of expected utility theory. To simplify the presentation I shall return to my original device of assuming a finite number of pure consequences $x_1, \ldots, x_n$ measured in money units; a prospect is then a list of probabilities $(\pi_1, \ldots, \pi_n)$. Conventional expected utility theory is described by the functional form

$$V(\pi_1, \ldots, \pi_n) = \sum_i \pi_i U(x_i) \tag{4}$$

I shall now consider two alternative functional forms, both of which encompass expected utility theory as a special case.

4.1 Chew and MacCrimmon's 'Ratio Form'

Chew and MacCrimmon (1979) suggest the following functional form:

$$V(\pi_1, \ldots, \pi_n) = \frac{\sum_i \pi_i U(x_i)}{\sum_i \pi_i W(x_i)} \tag{5}$$

where $U(\cdot)$ and $W(\cdot)$ are two *different* functions, each assigning a 'utility' index to every consequence. Then the utility assigned to a prospect as a whole is the ratio of two 'expected utility' measures, one based on $U(\cdot)$ and the other on $W(\cdot)$. Notice that if $W(x_i) = 1$ for all i, (5) reduces to (4).

The value of this formulation can be seen by considering the special case in which there are just three pure consequences. Writing $U(x_i)$ as u_i and $W(x_i)$ as w_i, it is straightforward to deduce from (5) that the set of prospects for which $V(\pi_1, \pi_2, \pi_3) = v^*$ is defined by

$$\pi_1[v^*(w_1 - w_2) - (u_1 - u_2)] + \pi_3[v^*(w_3 - w_2) - (u_3 - u_2)]$$
$$= u_2 - v^*w_2 \quad (6)$$

This is the equation of an indifference curve in the triangle diagram. Since the consequences x_1, x_2, x_3 are being held constant, the only variables in (6) are π_1 and π_3. So it is clear that (6) is the equation for a line: *indifference curves are linear*. In addition, it can be shown that only two such equations – say for $V(\pi_1, \pi_2, \pi_3) = v^*$ and $V(\pi_1, \pi_2, \pi_3) = v^{**}$ – can be linearly independent. In other words, (6) defines a family of linear indifference curves *all of which intersect at the same point*. (In the limiting case corresponding with expected utility theory these lines are parallel.)

This may seem paradoxical, since the idea that indifference curves can intersect seems to contravene the axiom of transitivity, while the whole idea of the utility function $V(\cdot)$ presupposes transitivity. (If preferences over prospects can be represented by a utility function that assigns a real number to every prospect, those preferences *must* be transitive.) This paradox can be resolved, however, by recognizing that (6) is defined for all *mathematically possible* values of π_1 and π_3 while the logic of the problem is such that the only *meaningful* values are those consistent with the condition $0 \leqslant \pi_1 + \pi_3 \leqslant 1$. Thus the indifference lines may intersect at a point in (π_1, π_3) space *outside* the triangle of meaningful prospects.

Figure 6 shows how Chew and MacCrimmon's theory can generate indifference lines that satisfy both of the requirements of Machina's 'fanning-out' hypothesis: all that is needed is that the indifference lines should intersect at a point south-west of the origin. Where these lines intersect depends on the nature of the two functions $U(\cdot)$ and $W(\cdot)$. So Chew and MacCrimmon's theory offers a reasonably simple and tractable functional form that can encompass the common consequence and common ratio effects.

Chew and MacCrimmon (1979) show that their ratio form for $V(\cdot)$ follows from a particular set of axioms; a rather similar derivation is given by Fishburn (1983). Among the axioms used, naturally enough, is transitivity. Later I shall discuss what happens if this axiom is dropped.

4.2 Hagen's 'three moments of utility' model, and disappointment theory

In expected utility theory every consequence x_i has a utility $U(x_i)$, and then the utility of a prospect is given by the (probability-weighted) mean, or *first moment*, of the utilities of its component

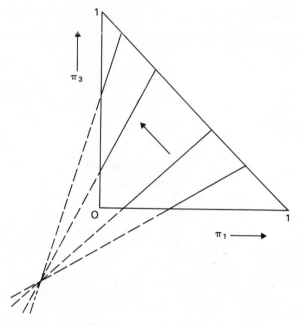

Fig. 6. 'Fanning-out' indifference lines for the Chew–MacCrimmon theory

consequences. Allais (1979) has suggested that the utility of a prospect might also depend on the variance, or *second moment*, of utility. Hagen (1979) takes this a stage further, suggesting that the utility of a prospect is a function of the first *three* moments of utility. He proposes an additive function of the form:

$$V(\pi_1, \ldots, \pi_n) = \bar{u} + f(M_2, M_3) \tag{7}$$

where $\bar{u}$ is the mean value of utility and M_2 and M_3 are the second and third moments; $f(.\,,.)$ is some real-valued function.

For the purposes of exposition it is convenient to consider the following simplified form of (7):

$$V(\pi_1, \ldots, \pi_n) = \bar{u} + \alpha M_2 + \beta M_3 \tag{8}$$

where α and β are constants. This expression can be expanded and rearranged to give:

$$V(\pi_1, \ldots, \pi_n) = \sum_i \pi_i [u_i + \alpha(u_i - \bar{u})^2 + \beta(u_i - \bar{u})^3] \tag{9}$$

Here, as before, I use u_i as a shorthand for $U(x_i)$. I shall assume that $\alpha < 0$ and $\beta > 0$. The first of these assumptions corresponds with Allais' (1979) intuition that the variance of utility is a measure of the riskiness of a prospect and that individuals are typically averse to such riskiness. Setting $\beta > 0$ has the effect of reducing the individual's aversion to risk in relation to *good* consequences (i.e. ones above the mean) and increasing it in relation to *bad* consequences (i.e. ones below the mean).

We may generalize (9) as follows:

$$V(\pi_1, \ldots, \pi_n) = \sum_i \pi_i [u_i + D(u_i - \bar{u})] \qquad (10)$$

Here $D(\cdot)$ is a real-valued function. We may now construct a Machina-style local utility function. In order to find the local utility index $U(x_i; p)$ for any consequence x_i, given any prospect p, we must differentiate (10) with respect to π_i. (Notice that under conventional expected utility theory, $V(\pi_1, \ldots, \pi_n) = \sum \pi_i U(x_i)$, and so $\partial V / \partial \pi_i = u_i$; thus the von Neumann–Morgenstern utility index for any consequence x_i can be arrived at by differentiating $V(\pi_1, \ldots, \pi_n)$ with respect to π_i. The procedure for arriving at a *local* utility index is a generalization of this.) It follows that

$$U(x_i; p) = u_i [1 - \sum_j \pi_j D'(u_j - \bar{u})] + D(u_i - \bar{u}) \qquad (11)$$

As it stands, this local utility function need not be increasing in its first argument; thus we may have $x_i \succ x_j$ but $U(x_i; p) < U(x_j; p)$. Recall that local utility functions must be increasing in this sense if we are to ensure that stochastically dominating prospects are always to be preferred to stochastically dominated ones. One way of ensuring this is to require that $D(\cdot)$ is a non-decreasing function whose gradient is always less than 1. Strictly, this assumption is not compatible with the simplified functional form (9), which *can* allow dominated prospects to be preferred to dominating ones. But, I think, the economically significant features of Hagen's proposal can still be captured if we assume in addition that $D(\cdot)$ is concave for negative values of $u_i - \bar{u}$ and convex for positive values (see Figure 7). Graham Loomes and I have explored the implications of assuming a $D(\cdot)$ function of this kind (Loomes and Sugden, 1985a). We have called our theory one of *disappointment*, for reasons that I shall explain later; the notion of disappointment was borrowed from Bell (1985).

It is useful to consider the simple case of a prospect p_0 that gives one particular consequence, x_0, with certainty. Then (11) reduces to:

$$U(x_i; p_0) = u_i [1 - D'(0)] + D(u_i - \bar{u}) \qquad (12)$$

If consequences are measured in money units, the set of possible consequences being taken to be an interval, and if the 'basic' utility-of-wealth function $U(\cdot)$ is assumed to be linear, it is not difficult to work out the following: the local utility function $U(x_i; p_0)$ must

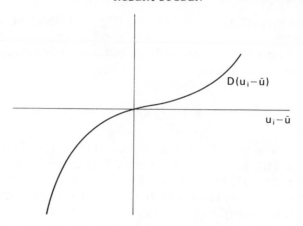

Fig. 7. A possible form for the $D(\cdot)$ function

have a point of inflexion at x_0, being concave for $x_i < x_0$ and convex for $x_i > x_0$.

Now consider another prospect, p_1, giving a different consequence x_1 with certainty, where $x_1 > x_0$. By exactly the same argument as before, the local utility function $U(x_i; p_1)$ must have a point of inflexion at x_1, being concave for $x_i < x_1$ and convex for $x_i > x_1$. Now compare the local utility functions $U(x_i; p_0)$ and $U(x_i; p_1)$. Clearly, p_1 stochastically dominates p_0. And in the range of values $x_0 < x_i < x_1$, $U(x_i; p_0)$ is convex while $U(x_i; p_1)$ is concave. In other words, the local utility function associated with the stochastically dominating distribution shows greater local risk aversion at each value of x_i. This corresponds with Machina's Hypothesis II. This seems to establish an affinity between Hagen's approach and Machina's; we might expect a theory based on (10) to be able to account for the common consequence and common ratio effects. Loomes and I (1985a) show that this is indeed the case. Our assumptions about the form of the function $D(\cdot)$ *tend* to generate 'fanning-out' indifference curves in the triangle diagram, although this is not *invariably* the case. In other words, our formulation does not necessarily satisfy Hypothesis II. Strictly speaking, then, neither Hagen's theory nor disappointment theory are special cases of Machina's, in the way that Chew and MacCrimmon's theory is. Nevertheless, there is a very close affinity between all these theories.

5. RATIONALITY AND THE INDEPENDENCE AXIOM

Expected utility theory is often presented as being not merely *descriptive* but also *prescriptive*; its axioms are supposed to have intuitive appeal as principles of rationality, and behaviour that violates these axioms is viewed as irrational. Given that the independence axiom is frequently and systematically violated by ordinary people, we seem forced to conclude *either* that ordinary people are irrational *or* that the independence axiom is not, after all, a necessary property of rational choice.

In appraising the independence axiom, it is useful to think about a possible analogy with consumer theory. Let p, q and r represent bundles of goods such that a consumer prefers p to q. Does it follow that he must also prefer a 50–50 *physical* mix of bundles p and r to a similar mix of bundles q and r? Clearly not. Let p stand for a fruit cake, q for a loaf of bread and r for a pack of butter. I may prefer the cake to the loaf while preferring half a loaf and half a pack of butter to half a cake and half a pack of butter. The explanation, of course, is that bread and butter are complementary goods. So if the independence axiom is to be justified it is necessary to show why this analogy fails – why there can be complementarity for *physical* mixtures of commodity bundles but not for *probability* mixtures of prospects.

The most persuasive answer is that given by Samuelson (1952, pp. 672–3): while the commodity bundles in the physical mixture are consumed *simultaneously*, the prospects in a probability mixture are *mutually exclusive*. Thus (says Samuelson) there is no reason why an individual's preference between two *prospects p* and *q* should be 'contaminated' by the nature of any third prospect *r* with which they are (probabilistically) combined.

The fact that people *do* systematically violate the independence axiom strongly suggests that some kind of complementarity effect is at work – that mutually exclusive prospects are, after all, 'contaminating' one another. At a psychological level, such contamination can occur in various ways; here I shall consider just one of these.

Bell (1985) suggests that individuals feel *disappointment* when, some uncertainty having been resolved, they end up with a consequence worse than they had expected. Conversely, they feel *elation* if they end up with something that is better than they had expected. Disappointment is painful; elation is pleasurable. (Suppose you have a 0.99 chance of winning £50,000. How do you feel when the 0.01 chance comes up? Disappointed.[2] Compare this with the situation in which you have a 0.99 chance of *losing* £50,000, and the 0.01 chance comes up. In each case the actual consequence is the same –

---

[2] This feeling of disappointment cannot be incorporated into conventional expected utility theory by allowing disappointment to count as part of the description of a consequence. This is because in the conventional theory the set of conceivable prospects is a mixture set (see p. 2). 'Winning nothing and being disappointed one didn't do better' is an intelligible state of affairs. So is 'winning nothing and being relieved one didn't do worse.' But a 50–50 probability mix of these two states of affairs does *not* make sense.

no change in your wealth – but your psychological response is very different.)

This intuition suggests a possible interpretation of the theory summarized in (10). We may interpret u_i as the utility of the consequence x_i *in itself*, that is, independently of its relation to other consequences; and $\bar{u}$ may be interpreted as an index of the individual's expectations prior to the resolution of the uncertainty in the prospect $(\pi_1, \ldots, \pi_n)$. Then we may interpret $D(u_i - \bar{u})$ as the disappointment (if $u_i < \bar{u}$) or elation (if $u_i > \bar{u}$) the individual feels if he ends up with a consequence whose 'basic' utility is u_i. There seems no particular reason to suppose that disappointment and elation should be such as to make $D(\cdot)$ linear; and if it is *not* linear, violations of the independence axiom may arise. This is how Loomes and I interpret our 'disappointment theory'. (Bell (1985) starts from the same intuition – indeed, it was from him that we drew the idea – but models disappointment and elation rather differently.) I leave it to the reader to decide whether disappointment can be considered to be part of a theory of *rational* choice; Loomes and I argue strongly that it can (Loomes and Sugden, 1985a) while Bell (1985, pp. 26–7) is more doubtful.

6. REGRET

You feel disappointment when 'what is' compares unfavourably with 'what might have been'; here 'what might have been' refers to other consequences you might have experienced, *had you been more fortunate*. It provides a route by which the utility you derive from one consequence of a prospect is influenced (or 'contaminated') by other consequences of the same prospect. But there is another sense in which you may compare 'what is' with 'what might have been'. Suppose you consider betting £5 on a 50–1 outsider in the Grand National. You decide not to bet, but the horse wins. You cannot feel *disappointment* (in Bell's sense) since, not having bet, you had no expectation of winning. But you may feel *regret* when you reflect on the fact that, *had you chosen differently*, you would now be £250 better off. Regret, then, is a route by which the utility you derive from a particular consequence of one action may be influenced by a consequence of a *different* action.

The possible significance of regret occurred at much the same time to David Bell and to Graham Loomes and me.[3] Independently we arrived at almost the same conclusion: regret theory (Bell, 1982;

---

[3] In a Yorkshire journal a little chauvinism may be permitted. David Bell, although now based in Harvard, is a native of Doncaster; and I am a native of Morley. Graham Loomes, though a Londoner by birth, has settled in York. Is the psychology of regret a peculiarly Yorkshire phenomenon? Further research is clearly called for.

Loomes and Sugden, 1982). Even more surprisingly, Peter Fishburn (1982, 1984) independently produced a very similar theory, but without making use of any psychological intuitions about regret. His approach was entirely axiomatic; he arrived at his theory by weakening the axiom system that generates the Chew–MacCrimmon 'ratio form'. It turns out there is a close similarity between the formal structures of Chew and MacCrimmon's theory and regret theory. I shall begin by outlining regret theory, as presented by Loomes and me (1982, 1985b).

Consider an individual who faces a choice between two courses of action. (Regret theory, at present, is essentially a theory of pairwise choice; how it should be generalized is an open question.) Suppose he chooses a particular action and as a result he receives the consequence x_i. With the benefit of hindsight, he knows that, had he chosen the other action, he would have received the consequence x_j. There is a composite experience: 'having x_i and missing out on x_j'. This experience may involve the pain of *regret* (if x_i is worse than x_j) or the pleasure of the inverse of regret, which we call *rejoicing* (if x_i is better than x_j). We may define a function $M(.,.)$ so that $M(x_i, x_j)$ is the (cardinally measurable) utility of this composite experience. Regret theory is based on the assumption that an individual seeks to maximize the mathematical expectation of utility, defined in terms of $M(.,.)$. (We call this *modified utility*: it is the intrinsic utility of 'what is', modified by regret or rejoicing.)

Suppose that the individual is choosing between two prospects, $p = (p_1, \ldots, p_n)$ and $q = (q_1, \ldots, q_n)$, each defined in terms of the consequences $x_1, \ldots, x_n$. And suppose that these prospects are *statistically independent*. This assumption is not necessary for regret theory, but it is useful as a way of highlighting certain similarities between it and other theories. Suppose the individual chooses p. Then the probability that he will receive any consequence x_i is p_i. If he had chosen q, the probability that he would have received any consequence x_j would have been q_j. Since the prospects are statistically independent, the probability that (having chosen p) he will receive x_i *and* miss out on x_j is $p_i q_j$. Thus the expected modified utility of choosing p *rather than* q is:

$$\sum_i \sum_j p_i q_j M(x_i, x_j) \tag{13}$$

Thus:

$$p \gtreqless q \Leftrightarrow \sum_i \sum_j p_i q_j M(x_i, x_j) \gtreqless \sum_i \sum_j p_i q_j M(x_j, x_i) \tag{14}$$

We may now define a new function $\Psi(.,.)$ by:

$$\Psi(x_i, x_j) = M(x_i, x_j) - M(x_j, x_i) \tag{15}$$

Notice that $\Psi(.,.)$ is a *skew-symmetric* function (i.e. $\Psi(x_i, x_j) = -\Psi(x_j, x_i)$). Then (14) may be rewritten as:

$$p \gtreqless q \Leftrightarrow \sum_i \sum_j p_i q_j \Psi(x_i, x_j) \gtreqless 0. \tag{16}$$

This formulation of regret theory corresponds exactly with Fishburn's *skew-symmetric bilinear utility theory* – *SSB theory* for short (Fishburn 1982, 1984). In our original paper, Loomes and I (1982) used a particular functional form for $M(.,.)$, so that

$$M(x_i, x_j) = C(x_i) + R[C(x_i) - C(x_j)] \tag{17}$$

Here $C(\cdot)$ is a 'basic utility function' assigning a cardinal utility index to every consequence; $R(\cdot)$ is another function which assigns an increment or decrement of utility – representing rejoicing or regret – according to the difference between the basic utilities of 'what is' and 'what might have been'. We assumed $C(\cdot)$ and $R(\cdot)$ to be increasing functions with $R(0) = 0$. Following a more recent paper by Loomes and me (1985b) I shall not use the functional form (17) but instead use the more general notion of a function $\Psi(.,.)$.

To show the links between regret theory and Chew and Mac-Crimmon's theory, I shall again analyse the case in which there are just three pure consequences: x_1, x_2, x_3. Let $p = (p_1, p_2, p_3)$ and $q = (q_1, q_2, q_3)$ be any two statistically independent prospects. Then $p \sim q$ if and only if

$$\sum_{i=1}^{3} \sum_{j=1}^{3} p_i q_j \Psi(x_i, x_j) = 0 \tag{18}$$

Expanding this expression and rearranging

$$q_1[(1-p_3)\,\Psi(x_2, x_1) + p_3\{\Psi(x_3, x_1) - \Psi(x_3, x_2)\}]$$
$$-q_3[(1-p_1)\,\Psi(x_3, x_2) + p_1\{\Psi(x_3, x_1) - \Psi(x_2, x_1)\}]$$
$$= p_1\Psi(x_2, x_1) - p_3\Psi(x_3, x_2). \tag{19}$$

This equation may be interpreted as defining the set of prospects q that are indifferent to a *given* prospect p. On this interpretation, q_1 and q_3 are the only variables. (The three consequences are being held constant.) Notice that this interpretation makes (19) into the equation for a line. So if p is any point in the triangle diagram, *the set of points indifferent to p is a line.*

We may construct equations like (19) for every possible prospect p. It is not difficult to prove that no three such equations can be linearly independent of one another. This means that *all indifference lines must intersect at a single point* (or, as a limiting case, be parallel to one another).

Have we therefore reproduced Chew and MacCrimmon's theory? Not quite, because so far there has been no assumption of transitivity. But it would be quite natural (particularly if consequences are defined in terms of wealth) to assume that, *under certainty*, preferences *are* transitive. In other words, we might assume that an individual has an *ordering of pure consequences* (OPC): in the three-consequence case, that the individual has a preference ordering over $\{x_1, x_2, x_3\}$ – say $x_1 \prec x_2 \prec x_3$ (as in the previous triangle diagrams). If there is a family of linear indifference curves in the triangle diagram, all of which intersect at a single point, and if the individual has a preference ordering over the three corners of the triangle, then it is easy to prove that the point of intersection must be *outside* the triangle. And this entails a preference ordering over all points in the triangle – i.e. over all probability-mixes of x_1, x_2, x_3.

In order to reproduce the 'fanning-out' indifference lines of Figure 6, the point of intersection must be to the south-west of the origin. This will be true if two conditions hold. First, the gradient of (19), i.e. dq_3/dq_1, must be positive (ensuring a preference for stochastic dominance). Second, for the family of lines defined by (19), dq_3/dq_1 must increase as p_3 increases (with p_1 held constant).

Since $x_1 \prec x_2 \prec x_3$, it is clear that $\Psi(x_2, x_1)$, $\Psi(x_3, x_1)$ and $\Psi(x_3, x_2)$ are all positive. So in order to guarantee that dq_3/dq_1 is positive it is sufficient that $\Psi(x_3, x_1) > \Psi(x_3, x_2)$ and $\Psi(x_3, x_1) > \Psi(x_2, x_1)$. And this in turn would follow from the intuitively-appealing assumption of *increasingness* (I): that for any x_i, x_j, x_k, $\Psi(x_i, x_k) \gtreqqless \Psi(x_j, x_k)$ $\Leftrightarrow x_i \gtreqless x_j$. Why is this assumption appealing? Because it is an implication of the following natural assumption about regret and rejoicing: the experience of 'having x_i and missing out on x_j' is more desirable, the more desirable is x_i and the less desirable is x_j. (As a limiting case, the possibility that this experience is unaffected by the desirability of x_j can be allowed.) Notice, incidentally, that OPC and I are both properties of the functional form (17).

Differentiating dq_3/dq_1 with respect to p_3:

$$\frac{\partial}{\partial p_3}\left[\frac{dq_3}{dq_1}\right] = \frac{\Psi(x_3, x_1) - \Psi(x_3, x_2) - \Psi(x_2, x_1)}{(1 - p_1)\Psi(x_3, x_2) + p_1[\Psi(x_3, x_1) - \Psi(x_2, x_1)]} \quad (20)$$

Given the assumptions of OPC and I, this derivative will be positive if and only if

$$\Psi(x_3, x_1) > \Psi(x_3, x_2) + \Psi(x_2, x_1) \quad (21)$$

So the general property of the $\Psi(.,.)$ function that generates 'fanning-out' indifference lines is the following property of *convexity* (C): for any x_i, x_j, x_k where $x_i \succ x_j \succ x_k$: $\Psi(x_i, x_k) \geqslant \Psi(x_i, x_j) + \Psi(x_j, x_k)$. I must confess that I have no intuition about this property; all I can say is that, empirically speaking, it works. (In terms of the functional form (17), the equivalent requirement is that for any x_i, x_j where $x_i \succ x_j$: $R''[C(x_j) - C(x_i)] \leqslant R''[C(x_i) - C(x_j)]$ – see Loomes and Sugden (1982).)

Thus if we assume OPC, I and C, regret theory generates an indifference map of the kind shown in Figure 6 – the kind that is also generated by Chew and MacCrimmon's theory. So in the case of pairwise choice over statistically independent prospects defined for three pure consequences, the two theories are formally identical. Admittedly, this is a very special case; but it encompasses the common consequence and common ratio effects.

The theories diverge if there are more than three pure consequences. Suppose we retain the assumption of statistically independent prospects, so that regret theory is encapsulated in (16), but allow four or more pure consequences. Then preferences over pairs of prospects may be non-transitive, even though there is a perfectly conventional ordering over the consequences themselves. (For examples, see Fishburn (1984) and Loomes and Sugden (1985b).) Indeed, as far as statistically independent prospects are concerned, the transitivity or non-transitivity of preference is the only real difference between regret theory and Chew and MacCrimmon's theory. Chew and MacCrimmon's axiom system includes an axiom of transitivity; if this is dropped, the result is regret theory (or SSB theory), as expressed in (16) (see Fishburn, 1982).

The theories diverge further if prospects are not required to be statistically independent. Consider the following example. Suppose there are three equally-probable states of the world. (Perhaps a fair die is to be rolled; state S_1 occurs if the die falls 1 or 2, S_2 occurs if it falls 3 or 4, and S_3 if it falls 5 or 6.) Suppose there are three distinct consequences, x_1, x_2, x_3 such that an individual has the preference ordering $x_1 \prec x_2 \prec x_3$. (Perhaps these are three money prizes, with $x_1 < x_2 < x_3$.) Now consider the three *actions* (i.e. lists of state-contingent consequences) set out in Table 1.

TABLE 1
State of the World and Probability

Action	S_1 (1/3)	S_2 (1/3)	S_3 (1/3)
A_1	x_1	x_2	x_3
A_2	x_3	x_1	x_2
A_3	x_2	x_3	x_1

Notice that all three actions give the same *probability distribution* of consequences (i.e. x_1, x_2 and x_3, each with a probability of $1/3$). In other words, they all correspond with the same prospect. So any theory based on a preference ranking of prospects must imply $A_1 \sim A_2$, $A_2 \sim A_3$ and $A_1 \sim A_3$. But regret theory does not imply this. Suppose the individual has to choose between A_1 and A_2, A_3 not being feasible. If he maximizes expected modified utility,

$$A_1 \gtreqless A_2 \Leftrightarrow \Psi(x_1, x_3) + \Psi(x_2, x_1) + \Psi(x_3, x_2) \gtreqless 0. \qquad (22)$$

It is easy to see that property C (convexity) entails $A_1 \preccurlyeq A_2$; *strict* convexity would entail $A_1 \prec A_2$. So regret theory can allow a strict preference between two stochastically equivalent actions. Further, the structure of Table 1 is such that if $A_1 \prec A_2$ is true, then by regret theory, $A_2 \prec A_3$ and $A_3 \prec A_1$ must be true too. So regret theory can allow a cycle of strict preferences over pairs of stochastically equivalent actions.

This may seem surprising, but it is in accord with the underlying logic of regret and rejoicing. These are experiences that arise when an individual compares what he has with what he would have had, had he chosen differently; if these experiences are significant, then the subjective value of choosing any one action cannot be independent of the nature of the action that has to be rejected in order to choose the first one. In other words, actions cannot be evaluated independently of the feasible set from which they might be chosen. And the intuitive appeal of the transitivity axiom seems to rest precisely on the presupposition that actions *can* be evaluated independently of feasible sets: to admit that 'might have beens' have a place in the theory of choice is to call the transitivity axiom into question.

There is a good deal of evidence of systematic non-transitivities in people's choices (e.g. Lichtenstein and Slovic, 1971; Grether and Plott, 1979), and at least some of this evidence can be accounted for by regret theory (see Loomes and Sugden, 1983). There is also some evidence of individuals *not* treating stochastically equivalent actions as equivalent to one another, and this too can be accounted for by regret theory. (See the 'isolation effect' discovered by Kahneman and Tversky (1979), and the explanation offered by Loomes and Sugden (1982).) So the idea that individuals always have preference orderings over prospects, however familiar it may be to economists, is open to question on both theoretical and empirical grounds.

At the same time it must be admitted that the evidence is not wholly in favour of regret theory. Consider the four actions set out in Table 2, consequences being measured in money units. Notice that the actions $A_1, \ldots, A_4$ correspond with the prospects $p_1, \ldots, p_4$ in Kahneman and Tversky's example of the Allais paradox (see p. 5); but in this case the prospects are *not statistically independent*.

TABLE 2
State of the World and Probability

Action	S_1 (0.33)	S_2 (0.01)	S_3 (0.66)
A_1	2400	2400	2400
A_2	2500	0	2400
A_3	2400	2400	0
A_4	2500	0	0

It is not difficult to work out that regret theory predicts $A_1 \gtrless A_2$ $\leftrightarrow A_3 \gtrless A_4$. Essentially, this is because regret theory does not allow any kind of complementarity between consequences in different states of the world; if two actions have a common consequence in one state of the world, then the ranking of those actions must be independent of the nature of that consequence.

This, of course, is Savage's sure-thing principle, which is contained in regret theory (see Loomes and Sugden, 1982, p. 813). So in a case like the one illustrated in Table 2, the Allais paradox pattern of preferences – $A_1 \succ A_2$ and $A_3 \prec A_4$ – is incompatible with regret theory, but compatible with the theories of Machina, Chew and MacCrimmon and Hagen, and with theories based on disappointment. Preferences of this kind – systematically violating the sure thing principle and thus running counter to the predictions of regret theory – *have* been found in experiments (e.g. Moskowitz, 1974; Slovic and Tversky, 1974).

7. CONCLUSION

Experiments show that human beings, choosing under uncertainty, behave in systematic and predictable ways. It would be extremely satisfying to discover a simple theory that was compatible with all of this evidence – only a tiny fraction of which I have discussed in this paper. No such theory has yet been found. Perhaps one is waiting to be discovered by an Isaac Newton of economics; perhaps not. I suggest that it is worth carrying on the search, and that the theories I have described in this paper, however imperfect, represent valuable first steps.

School of Economic and Social Studies, University of East Anglia

REFERENCES

Allais, M. (1953). 'Le Comportment de l'Homme Rationnel Devant le Risque; Critique des Postulats et Axiomes de l'Ecole Americaine', *Econometrica*, Vol. 21, pp. 503-46.

Allais, M. (1979). 'The Foundations of a Positive Theory of Choice Involving Risk and a Criticism of the Postulates and Axioms of the American School', in *Expected Utility Hypotheses and the Allais Paradox*, M. Allais and O. Hagen (eds.), Dordrecht, Reidel. (Paper first published in French in 1953.)

Bell, D. (1982). 'Regret in Decision Making under Uncertainty', *Operations Research*, Vol. 30, pp. 961-81.

Bell, D. (1985). 'Disappointment in Decision Making under Uncertainty', *Operations Research*, Vol. 33, pp. 1-27.

Chew, S. and MacCrimmon, K. (1979). 'Alpha-nu Choice Theory: a Generalization of Expected Utility Theory', Working Paper No. 669, University of British Columbia.

Fishburn, P. (1982). 'Nontransitive Measurable Utility', *Journal of Mathematical Psychology*, Vol. 26, pp. 31-67.

Fishburn, P. (1983). 'Transitive Measurable Utility', *Journal of Economic Theory*, Vol. 31, pp. 293-317.

Fishburn, P. (1984). 'Dominance in SSB Utility Theory', *Journal of Economic Theory*, Vol. 34, pp. 130-48.

Grether, D. and Plott, C. (1979). 'Economic Theory of Choice and the Preference Reversal Phenomenon', *American Economic Review*, Vol. 69, pp. 623-38.

Herstein, I. and Milnor, J. (1953). 'An Axiomatic Approach to Measurable Utility', *Econometrica*, Vol. 21, pp. 291-97.

Hagen, O. (1979). 'Towards a Positive Theory of Preferences under Risk', in *Expected Utility Hypotheses and the Allais Paradox*, M. Allais and O. Hagen (eds.), Dordrecht, Reidel.

Kahneman, D. and Tversky, A. (1979). 'Prospect Theory: An Analysis of Decision under Risk', *Econometrica*, Vol. 47, pp. 263-91.

Lichtenstein, S. and Slovic, P. (1971). 'Reversals of Preference Between Bids and Choices in Gambling Decisions', *Journal of Experimental Psychology*, Vol. 89, pp. 46-55.

Loomes, G. and Sugden, R. (1982). 'Regret Theory: An Alternative Theory of Rational Choice under Uncertainty', *Economic Journal*, Vol. 92, pp. 805-24.

Loomes, G. and Sugden, R. (1983). 'A Rationale for Preference Reversal', *American Economic Review*, Vol. 73, pp. 428-32.

Loomes, G. and Sugden, R. (1985a). 'Disappointment and Dynamic Consistency in Choice under Uncertainty', forthcoming in *Review of Economic Studies*.

Loomes, G. and Sugden, R. (1985b). 'Some Implications of a More General Form of Regret Theory', available from authors.

Machina, M. (1982). ' "Expected Utility" Analysis Without the Independence Axiom', *Econometrica*, Vol. 50, pp. 277-323.

Machina, M. (1983). 'The Economic Theory of Individual Behavior Toward Risk', Technical Report No. 433, Institute for Mathematical Studies in the

24 ROBERT SUGDEN

Social Sciences, Stanford University, California.
Malinvaud, E. (1952). 'Note on von Neumann-Morgenstern's Strong Independence Axiom', *Econometrica*, Vol. 20, p. 679.
Moskowitz, H. (1974). 'Effects of Problem Presentation and Feedback on Rational Behavior in Allais and Morlat Type Problems', *Decision Sciences*, Vol. 5, pp. 225-42.
Neumann, J. von and Morgenstern, O. (1947). *Theory of Games and Economic Behavior*, 2nd edition, Princeton, University Press. 3rd edition 1953.
Samuelson, P. (1952). 'Probability, Utility, and the Independence Axiom', *Econometrica*, Vol. 20, pp. 670-8.
Schoemaker, P. (1982). 'The Expected Utility Model: Its Variants, Purposes, Evidence and Limitations', *Journal of Economic Literature*, Vol. 20, pp. 529-63.
Slovic, P. and Tversky, A. (1974). 'Who Accepts Savage's Axiom?', *Behavioral Science*, Vol. 19, pp. 368-73.

INDIVIDUAL CHOICE UNDER UNCERTAINTY: A REVIEW OF EXPERIMENTAL EVIDENCE, PAST AND PRESENT

Lynda Appleby and Chris Starmer[1]

The purpose of this paper is to review some of the evidence relating to individual behaviour in situations of risk, paying particular attention to the material which relates to new theoretical developments in the field.

The origins of expected utility theory (EUT) can be retraced to Bernoulli (1738) in his explanation of the so-called St Petersberg paradox. Bernoulli proposed that, in situations of risk, individuals behave so as to maximize their 'expected utility'. EUT gained its reputation as the conventional theory of individual choice under uncertainty following its axiomatization by von Neumann and Morgenstern (1947). There are, however, important differences between the two approaches. The Bernoullian concept of utility is based on the notion of a cardinal utility function derived from the utility of consequences experienced under certainty, while the Neumann–Morgenstern notion of utility relates to a cardinal utility function derived from observations of preferences under risk. Furthermore, while Bernoulli's approach is best thought of as a descriptive theory, the behavioural axioms proposed by Neumann and Morgenstern give their theory its normative appeal.

In recent years several new theories of choice under uncertainty have been developed in an attempt to account for observed patterns of behaviour, often experimentally generated, which run contrary to EUT. Perhaps the most well known of these violations, the 'Allais paradox', a special case of the common consequence problem, was reported by Allais as long ago as 1953. This observation, along with other widely reported violations of EUT such as the 'common ratio effect', have attracted considerable attention within the literature. The reason for this is not purely because they conflict with a widely accepted theory. A theory which is never wrong is perhaps little more

[1] Lynda Appleby would like to acknowledge the support of the Economic and Social Research Council for the Centre for Health Economics, University of York.

Chris Starmer would like to acknowledge the support of the Economics Research Centre of the University of East Anglia, and the Economic and Social Research Council Award No. B 00 23 2181 during the period when this paper was being written.

Thanks are also given to G. Loomes and R. Sugden for their advice on earlier drafts.

than a tautology. The problem with these types of violation, from the point of view of an expected utility theorist, is that they represent apparently systematic or predictable, rather than random, violations of the independence principle, the axiom which gives EUT most of its empirical content, and which is regarded by many – for example Savage (1954), Raiffa (1961) and Ellsberg (1961) – as a necessary component of rational choice.

For those convinced by the intuitive reasonableness of the von Neumann–Morgenstern axioms, the persistence of such contradictory behaviour seems paradoxical. But given such faith, it was perhaps an understandable response to elevate EUT to the plane of a normative theory of choice and to view these observed violations as aberrant behaviour which would be eliminated if only people understood the 'irrationality' of their actions. There can be little doubt that EUT has achieved a dominant status in many fields (see for example, Schoemaker (1982), who describes it as the 'major paradigm in decision-making since the Second World War'). The theory is simple and general, generating bold and testable predictions. These features are generally regarded as virtues in a theory, and one would be unlikely to reject a theory of such scope on the basis of a few scattered violations. However, the growing body of reported violations of EUT severely challenge its descriptive reality and predictive ability, and new theoretical developments in the area call for careful assessment of the evidence, particularly when at least some of these theories – for example, Disappointment and Regret – challenge the normative validity of EUT by explaining violations of its axioms in terms of rational optimizing behaviour.

In an earlier paper in this collection Robert Sugden outlined several new approaches to the theory of choice under uncertainty and examined some of the similarities and differences between them. He demonstrated how several commonly observed violations of EUT can be accommodated if indifference curves fan-out in the Machina triangle diagram, and that all of the theories considered are capable of producing fanning-out and hence predicting violations of EUT in a way that is actually observed. That these theories should produce similar predictions is not altogether surprising, since they were designed with the intention of accounting for a body of well-known violations of EUT. However, these theories do not produce identical predictions over all potential risky choice situations. As Sugden shows, not all of these theories lead directly to the implication that indifference curves fan-out, requiring auxiliary assumptions in the case of Regret, Disappointment and Hagen's Three Moment model. While the evidence generated from testing EUT may, to one extent or another, be consistent with the new theories of choice under uncertainty, it is not adequate for testing them. What is required are experiments specifically designed to test novel implications unique to one or a sub-group of these models which will allow discrimination between them.

In subsequent sections of this paper we review some of the most commonly reported violations of EUT and consider whether these cases offer serious cause to reject EUT. We attempt to examine how far the existing evidence is consistent with new theories and point towards some clear gaps in experimental research where there is obvious potential for testing the predictions of some of these new theories. Finally, we refer to some recent publications and research in progress where this work has already begun.

We begin by considering the evidence relating to the Allais paradox and its generalization, the common consequence effect, since it is this class of violation which has stimulated much of the debate between expected utility theorists and those critical of the conventional theory. The majority, though not all, of the reported instances of the common consequence effect can be accommodated within the framework shown below:

$$A: \quad [a, (p + q); c, (1 - p - q)]$$

$$B: \quad [b, (p); 0, (q); c, (1 - p - q)]$$

This offers subjects a choice between two actions A and B, where $0 < a < b$. Choosing A gives a $(p + q)$ chance of receiving a, plus a $(1 - p - q)$ chance of receiving c. On the other hand, choosing B gives b with probability p, c with probability $(1 - p - q)$, and zero with probability q. The common consequence effect is observed when a change in the value of the common consequence c, results in an individual switching preference between A and B. This violates EUT because, according to the independence principle, the preference ordering of A and B should be independent of the value of c, since the probability of receiving c is identical for both A and B. Despite the fact that a number of independent experiments have revealed a tendency for subjects to change from $A > B$ to $B > A$ as c falls (see Moskowitz, 1974; Slovic and Tversky, 1974; Kahneman and Tversky, 1979; MacCrimmon and Larsson, 1979), those committed to EUT do not seem to regard these violations as a significant challenge.

One reason for this is that for those convinced by the normative significance of the axioms of EUT, and in particular the independence axiom, violations of this sort appear to conflict with basic principles of rationality. Nevertheless, it is well known that several decision theorists, such as Savage and Ellsberg, when initially confronted with the Allais paradox, were tempted into violation (see Slovic and Tversky, 1974, p. 368), but after considering their responses concluded that their first reaction was an error. So while they might accept that many people may violate independence when first presented with problems of this sort, it has been argued that the Allais paradox merely fools people into violating sound principles of rationality by presenting them with unrealistic choices involving huge sums of money and very small probabilities beyond the scope of the average individual's normal experience (see for example Morgenstern, 1979).

While it is true that several of the common consequence effects reported in the literature have involved subjects choosing between prospects where the order of magnitude of the outcomes has been millions of dollars (for example Slovic and Tversky or MacCrimmon and Larsson), there is also some evidence of violations where the outcomes are more modest (see the Kahneman and Tversky common consequence effect reproduced in Sugden (1987), where the outcomes are 2,400 and 2,500 Israeli pounds. To put these amounts in perspective, Kahneman and Tversky pointed out that the median monthly income for an Israeli family was around 3,000 pounds.) In addition, MacCrimmon (1968) and Moskowitz (1974) reported a common consequence effect using non-monetary outcomes which seem to us to be quite realistic. Even so, the number of experimentally observed common consequence effects is quite small and also involves a limited range of parameters. For example, in the majority of cases the probability associated with the 'common consequence', $(1 - p - q)$, tends to be very high in relation to (q), which is often around 0.01. Secondly, it is not clear whether the common consequence effect is a general effect which occurs as c varies, or whether it occurs in only a specific range of common consequences, since most of the reported observations are confined to the case where c takes the two values 'a' and '0'. (This latter point is referred to again later in this discussion.) What seems to have added weight to these data is the fact that all the reported violations indicate a systematic bias with respect to EUT, and that a number of subjects will continue to violate in the direction predicted by the fanning-out hypothesis even when attempts are made to explain the logic of the independence principle. (Note: hereafter, prospects are defined only in terms of their non-zero consequences.)

MacCrimmon (1968) presented 38 business executives with hypothetical problems designed to elicit the common consequence effect. After making their choices, subjects were presented with arguments for and against conforming with the axioms. They were asked to provide a critique of each argument and to decide which appeared to be the most logical. Finally, each participant was questioned about his own response. MacCrimmon found that subjects' initial choices often violated independence, and that the majority of subjects, even some who had conformed to the axioms, found Allais-type arguments for violating independence to be 'more logical' than those for conforming. However, during the individual discussion period MacCrimmon found that he was able to convince most subjects who had violated the independence axiom that their initial responses had been mistakes. A later study by Slovic and Tversky (1974), while broadly consistent with MacCrimmon's findings, questioned the neutrality of the final discussion. Their experiment involved two subject groups. After making their initial choices the first group were presented with counter-arguments to whatever choice they had made. They were given time to reflect on their choices and then allowed to change them if they wished. The majority of subjects violated independence with their initial response and very few were persuaded by the counter-arguments with only four out of 29 subjects wishing to change, three of these switching from conforming to violating responses. The second group were presented with the arguments for and against conforming prior to selecting their preferred alternative. Once again the majority of subjects violated independence.

Although the numbers of subjects involved in these experiments was modest (max. = 49), this evidence questions the normative validity of the independence principle, since many people seem inclined to violate independence and be able to justify such action on grounds that seem reasonable to them, even when the logic of the conforming response has been explained to them. It must be pointed out that not everyone is convinced by this type of evidence. Moskowitz (1974), for example, feels that many of his subjects, whether or not they conformed to the axioms, still did not appreciate the arguments that he had given for conforming. However, it can be argued that violations of independence, even in its 'strong' form, as Savage's (1954) 'sure-thing principle', can no longer simply be dismissed as irrational following the development of Disappointment theory, which provides a psychological rationale for such behaviour. What needs further investigation is the range over which the common consequence effect will occur.

Evidence in support of the existence of a common ratio effect is somewhat stronger both in terms of the number of reported instances and the variation in the parameters used. Many of these problems involve choosing between two prospects X and Y, where X gives outcome x with probability p, and Y gives outcome y with probability kp, where $0 < k < 1$; $0 < p \leqslant 1$; and $0 < x < y$. According to EUT, the preference ordering of X and Y should be independent of the value of p (for a simple proof of this see Loomes and Sugden, 1987b). Numerous experiments by Hagen (1979), Kahneman and Tversky (1979), MacCrimmon and Larsson (1979) and Loomes and

Sugden (1987b), have revealed a tendency to switch from $X > Y$ to $Y > X$ as p falls.

A number of these violations fall into the category of the 'certainty effect', a special case of the common ratio effect where p has an initial value of unity. This is observed when subjects choose a certainty in preference to a risky prospect (with a higher expected value), but select the 'more risky' prospect when p falls. In terms of the triangle diagram (Figure 1a), this means, as p falls, switching from a point like X, where the certainty of x is chosen in preference to the prospect Y which offers a high probability of receiving y and a small probability of receiving nothing, to a point such as Y'' (or Y'''), where the prospect offering the highest probability of winning, X'' (or X'''), is rejected in favour of a more risky prospect, Y'' (or Y'''), which offers a lower probability of winning a larger amount. All four of the above experiments produce violations of this sort. This is similar to the majority of common consequence effects where subjects have been observed to switch from choosing A when $c = a$, to B when $c = 0$. This type of effect can be represented as a switch from point A to point B''' in the triangle diagram, Figure 1b. One exception to this is the MacCrimmon and Larsson experiment, which did involve asking subjects to choose between pairs of prospects such as $(A';B')$ and $(A'';B'')$. This did result in reversals from A' to B'' and from A'' to B'''. However, their sample size was small and further investigation of this middle region of the triangle is required.

Observations of the common ratio effect include numerous examples of violations where none of the prospects are certain outcomes. Kahneman and Tversky, and also Hagen, provide evidence of a 'near certainty effect'. In these cases the initial value of p is close to 1 (0.9 and above) and the second value of p is very small (0.01 or

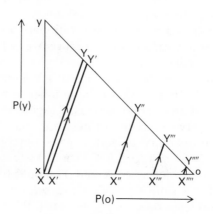

Fig. 1a. The common ratio effect.

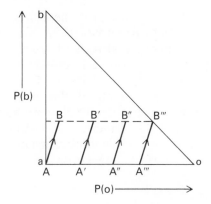

Fig. 1b. The common consequence effect

less). In terms of Figure 1a this type of effect would mean switching, in a similar manner to that described above, but from a point such as X', to Y''''. Taken in isolation, this evidence might perhaps suggest that the common ratio effect relies on one outcome being certain, or very close to certain, and that when we move away from 'certainty' the second probability must be very small in order to induce 'switching'. However, evidence of a more general common ratio effect which does not appear to be dependent upon any kind of certainty effect has been provided by MacCrimmon and Larsson (1979) and Loomes and Sugden (1987b). These two experimental studies revealed that common ratio effects can be produced when p is varied between about 0.75 and 0.2. In fact, Loomes and Sugden found fewer reversals as p falls from 1 to 0.5 than when p falls from 0.5 to 0.167. In terms of Figure 1a this means more switching from X'' to Y''' than from X to Y''. These two experiments also shed light upon the magnitude of the pay-offs required to induce the common ratio effect. MacCrimmon and Larsson varied the outcome x between \$1 and \$1 million in multiples of 10, with $y = 5x$. They found no evidence of a common ratio effect with outcomes of less than \$1,000. This is comparable with the outcomes used by Kahneman and Tversky (3,000–6,000 Israeli pounds) and Hagen (10,000–25 million Norwegian krona (K): £1 being approximately 11.5 K). On the other hand, Loomes and Sugden reported observations of a highly significant common ratio effect with x and y as small as £3 and £4.50 respectively, and notably, in their experiment the participants faced real rather than hypothetical choices.

Evidence of common consequence and common ratio effects does appear to indicate a clear and systematic tendency to violate EUT, in a manner which is consistent with the fanning-out hypothesis.

However, in addition to accounting for these observed phenomena, theories of this class predict further violations of EUT which provide possibilities for direct experimental tests of the hypothesis. The vast majority of the reported common ratio effects have been observed moving from left to right across the bottom of the Machina triangle, as illustrated in Figure 1a, and all of the common consequence effects that can be represented in this framework have similarly been produced in the bottom of the triangle, as in Figure 1b. One implication of the fanning-out hypothesis is that we would expect to be able to produce both of these effects as we move up the triangle as well as when we move across it.

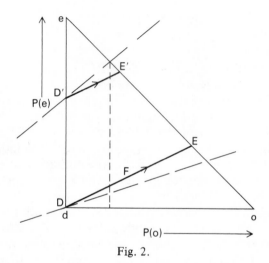

Fig. 2.

Consider Figure 2. If an individual's indifference curves were like those shown as dashed lines, then as we move up the triangle we would expect to observe the common ratio effect ($E > D$ and $D' > E'$) and the common consequence effect ($F > D$ and $D' > E'$). There are no reported instances of either of these two effects occurring for the case where $0 < d < e$. The only experimental evidence of an effect of this type is the negative common ratio effect where $0 > d > e$. This has been reported by Kahneman and Tversky (1979), who produced two such effects, one of which is reproduced in Sugden (1987). MacCrimmon and Larsson (1979) also included several negative common ratio problems for losses in their experiment, but did not detect any significant effect. This effect therefore needs to be replicated and, more generally, what needs to be explored is whether the common ratio effect and the common consequence effect can be observed moving up and across the triangle using both positive and negative outcomes. A project recently begun at the University of East Anglia to test the Machina hypothesis will hopefully shed some light on these issues.

Machina (1983, pp. 69–76) shows how two further violations of the independence axiom, which have been observed experimentally, are also predicted by the fanning-out hypothesis. The first of these, what Machina calls the 'utility evaluation effect', has been found by, among others, Karamarkar (1974), McCord and de Neufville (1984), Cohen and Jaffray (1986) and de Neufville and Delquie (1986). There are a number of experimental methods for recovering an individual's utility function. For a useful summary and critique of the various methods see Farquhar (1984). According to EUT the utility functions generated by these methods should be unique up to a linear transformation. The approach taken by Karamarkar was to choose an appropriate monetary scale, in this case $0 to $100, and to assign an arbitrary utility index to the end points (e.g. $U(0) = 0$, $U(100) = 10$). Constructing a prospect containing these outcomes using an arbitrary probability (p) and then questioning subjects to obtain their certainty equivalent (CE) for the prospect, establishes the utility of the CE since $U(\text{CE}) = p(10) + (1 - p)(0)$. This CE can then be used to generate further points on the utility function so that the entire function can be approximated. Karamarkar found that, contrary to the independence axiom of EUT, the utility function generated was not independent of the value of p used in its assessment. Using progressively higher values for p produced utility functions which lay successively above one another.

Several of the subjects who took part in Karamarkar's experiment commented that providing a CE for a prospect was easiest when the prospect was a 50/50 gamble. On this basis Karamarkar suggested that the function obtained when $p = 0.5$ could perhaps be regarded as the best approximation to the 'true' utility function, with deviations from it being caused by 'imperfect, conservative, subjective processing of probabilities'. While we do not deny that this is a possibility – in fact there is evidence to show that people do not always evaluate probabilities according to conventional probability calculus (Bar-Hillel, 1973) and that people may adopt simplifying heuristics which introduce 'bias' into decision-making (see the review article by Schoemaker (1982), which refers to some of this literature) – there is an alternative explanation for the utility evaluation effect which does not rely on any form of 'imperfection' in the individual's processing of information, and this is closely related to the second of the violations of independence referred to above.

One particular body of research suggests that, relative to the linearity property of EUT, individuals tend to overweight low probabilities relative to high probabilities. Evidence to support this notion, that a scale of subjective probabilities exists which 'distorts' the true objective probabilities in this way, has arisen from experimental applications of the 'Subjective Expected Value' (SEV) model. Both the SEV model and EUT can be accommodated, as restricted forms, in a more general class of 'Subjected Expected Utility' (SEU) models. The SEU theories infer that individuals attempt to maximize $\Sigma \pi(p_i) U(x_i)$, where $\pi(\cdot)$ assigns subjective values to objective probabilities, p_i. SEV models assume that $U(\cdot)$ is linear, whereas EUT purports linearity of $\pi(\cdot)$.

A number of studies, in which estimates of $\pi(\cdot)$ are derived using a linearity assumption for $U(\cdot)$, have produced consistent results of non-linear functions which overweight low relative to high probabilities. (See Preston and Baratta, 1948; Sprowls, 1953; and Nogee and Lieberman, 1960). Although, as Ali (1977) pointed out, a problem with this approach can arise in that, if $U(\cdot)$ is incorrectly assumed to be linear, then non-linearities will enter the estimated function, other experiments by Edwards (1955) and Tversky (1967a, b), in which the SEU model was applied in order to derive joint estimates of $\pi(\cdot)$ and $U(\cdot)$, reached similar conclusions regarding the shape of $\pi(\cdot)$.

Machina's theory has no $\pi(\cdot)$, and hence cannot be said to allow 'underweighting' or 'overweighting' of probabilities, but it can accommodate the sort of behaviour that SEV theorists interpret in this way, since the 'fanning-out' hypothesis does imply a tendency for individuals to exhibit 'oversensitivity to changes in the probability of low probability–outlying events' (Machina, 1983, p. 69).

The existence of a scale of subjectively weighted probabilities, in itself a violation of the independence principle of EUT, could also account for the utility evaluation effect. Figure 3 illustrates the utility evaluation effect where the utility function constructed using $p = 0.75$ lies above that constructed with $p = 0.5$. Consider how this could arise through probability weighting. Having constructed the lower function by the CE method, where $p = 0.5$, we can establish tht £x_1 has a utility of 7.5. Therefore, EUT would predict that if we offered this subject the prospect (£100, 0.75; £0, 0.25), which also has an EU of 7.5 given our initial assumptions ($U(£100) = 10$, $U(0) = 0$), then the subject would choose £x_1 as its CE. The experimental evidence suggests that when $p = 0.75$ there is a tendency for $U(x_1) > 7.5$, and that the individual would choose a CE $x_2 < x_1$). But this is what we would expect if the individual places a proportionately lower weight on $p = 0.75$ relative to $p = 0.5$. While this case is only illustrative since the exact nature of the dependence of the utility function on p would be determined by the functional form of $\pi(\cdot)$, it shows that theories which admit non-linearities in $\pi(\cdot)$ would predict non-uniqueness of the utility function generated

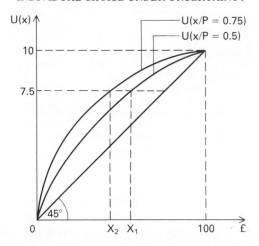

Fig. 3. The utility evaluation effect

by this type of method. Cohen and Jaffray (1985) and de Neufville and Delquie (1986) have both demonstrated how probability weighting appears to produce the utility evaluation effect, and the latter study shows how using a 'lottery equivalent' method can reduce the dependence of the estimated utility function on probability. However, these two studies reach different conclusions about the extent of probability weighting. Cohen and Jaffray's results suggest that $\pi(\cdot)$ is linear until we reach probabilities above 0.9, whereas de Neufville and Delquie's results are consistent with the earlier evidence, which suggests a more general distortion of probabilities. Further research is required to establish the extent of this apparent probability weighting.

Kahneman and Tversky (1979) show that their theory, 'Prospect theory', which is a model of the SEU class incorporating a non-linear $\pi(\cdot)$, can also account for the common ratio and common consequence effects. This means that the fanning-out theories are not the only type of theory capable of explaining the four commonly observed violations of EUT considered so far in this paper. However, Prospect theory does not generate identical predictions to fanning-out, and here we illustrate one situation in which the implications of Prospect theory and Machina's theory diverge, which could provide the basis for experimental tests to discriminate between the two.

Consider the general common consequence problem illustrated in Figure 4. Machina's theory predicts a tendency to switch from $B > A$ to $A > B$ as the common consequence c increases. This

STATES OF THE WORLD	S_1	S_2	S_3
PROB (S_i)	p	q	$1-p-q$
ACTION A	a	a	c
ACTION B	b	o	c

Fig. 4. The generalized common consequence problem in a state-contingent matrix.

follows directly from Machina's Hypothesis II, which implies increasingly risk-averse behaviour as we move from stochastically dominated to stochastically dominating distributions. Prospect theory predicts similar behaviour, but only when c lies in a specific range. We noted earlier that the majority of common consequence effects have been observed when c takes on the two values $c = 0$ and $c = a$. In terms of Prospect theory, when $c = 0$:

$$A \gtrless B \Leftrightarrow \pi(p + q) V(a) \gtrless \pi(p) V(b)$$

or

$$A \gtrless B \Leftrightarrow \pi(p + q) V(a) - \pi(p) V(b) \gtrless 0 \qquad (1)$$

and when $c = a$:

$$A \gtrless B \Leftrightarrow V(a) \gtrless \pi(1 - p - q) V(a) + \pi(p) V(b)$$

or

$$A \gtrless B \Leftrightarrow [1 - \pi(1 - p - q)] V(a) - \pi(p) V(b) \gtrless 0 \qquad (2)$$

In this case the prediction of Prospect theory is the same as Machina, that is a tendency to choose B when $c = 0$ but A when $c = a$. The property which produces this prediction is the 'subcertainty' assumption (Kahneman and Tversky, 1979, p. 281) which implies that for all $0 < p < 1$, $\pi(p) + \pi(1 - p) < 1$. Applying this property to (1) and (2) above;

$$\pi(p + q) + \pi(1 - p - q) < 1$$

or

$$1 - \pi(1 - p - q) > \pi(p + q) \qquad (3)$$

So, from (3), the LHS of (2) is greater than the LHS of (1), allowing $B > A$ in (1) and $A > B$ in (2). Thus, both Machina and Prospect theory predict this 'special case' of the common consequence effect.

More generally, Prospect theory predicts the common consequence effect when $0 < c < a$. In this case, following Kahneman and Tversky's treatment of 'strictly positive prospects' (ibid., p. 276), which implies that if $(p + q) = 1$, and $x > y > 0$, then the utility of the prospect $(x, p; y, q)$

$$= V(y) + \pi(p)[V(x) - V(y)]$$

From this we derive:

$$A \gtreqless B \Leftrightarrow V(c) + \pi(p + q)[V(a) - V(c)]$$
$$\gtreqless \pi(p) V(b) + \pi(1 - p - q) V(c)$$

or

$$A \gtreqless B \Leftrightarrow \pi(p + q) V(a) - \pi(p) V(b)$$
$$\gtreqless V(c) [\pi(1 - p - q) + \pi(p + q) - 1] \quad (4)$$

Subcertainty implies that the RHS of (4) is negative, thus as c increases the RHS falls so there will be a tendency to switch from $B > A$ to $A > B$, so the common consequence effect is predicted for this range of c. Now assume $0 < a < c$ and $c \neq b$. In this case Prospect theory entails;

$$A \gtreqless B \Leftrightarrow V(a) + \pi(1 - p - q)[V(c) - V(a)]$$
$$\gtreqless \pi(p) V(b) + \pi(1 - p - q) V(c)$$

or

$$A \gtreqless B \Leftrightarrow [1 - \pi(1 - p - q)] V(a) \gtreqless \pi(p) V(b) \quad (5)$$

Hence, from (5), when c is greater than a (and not equal to b), the choice between A and B should be independent of c, so that, if Prospect theory is correct, variation of c in this range should not induce any switching between A and B. This could be tested against the predictions of Machina's theory, which suggests that it should be possible to produce the common consequence effect in this region.

The evidence that we have referred to so far has been related to violations of the independence principle, which can be accounted for by a number of different hypotheses. We now briefly review a body of experimental work which has revealed the existence of apparently non-transitive patterns of preference. A distinguishing feature of this evidence is that it not only violates EUT, but also conflicts with the majority of theories capable of accommodating violations of independence. Evidence of non-transitive behaviour has been reported by

May (1954) and Tversky (1969) in situations where subjects have been asked to choose between objects with a number of different characteristics. More recently, economists have become interested in a form of intransitivity which first attracted the attention of psychologists, the so-called 'preference reversal phenomenon'. This effect has been observed in a number of similar experiments where subjects have been asked to choose between two prospects, a '*P*-bet', offering a high probability of winning a small amount, and a '$-bet', offering a small chance of winning a larger amount. Then subjects have been asked to value each of these bets by placing reservation prices on them, r_P and $r_\$$ respectively, which represent the lowest price at which they would be prepared to sell their entitlement to the prospects. Among others, Lindman (1971), Lichtenstein and Slovic (1971, 1973) and Slovic (1975) have all found that a significant number of subjects choose the *P*-bet in the first stage, but then place a greater reservation price on the $-bet.

Grether and Plott (1979) were sceptical about these results. They suggested 13 hypotheses as potential explanations for previous findings, including a wide range of economic, psychological and experimental factors, and replicated earlier experiments controlling for each of these in an attempt to refute the existence of the preference-reversal phenomenon. To their surprise they found that preference-reversals continued to occur, and could not be explained by any of the factors they had suggested. Clearly bemused by their own results they concluded that 'no optimization principles of any sort lie behind even the simplest of human choices' (ibid., p. 623). Pommerehne *et al.* (1982) and Reilly (1982) attempted to overturn their conclusions, using experiments designed to overcome what they believed to be weaknesses in Grether and Plott's methodology, by increasing subjects' motivation to conform with the EUT axioms. However, although the rate of preference-reversals, particularly those observed by Reilly, was lower than that found by Grether and Plott, the phenomenon could not be completely eliminated. A recent study by Berg *et al.* (1983) also seems to confirm the robustness of this phenomenon.

Psychologists, such as Lichtenstein, have argued that the explanation of preference-reversal is to be found in differences in the way that people process information in choice and valuation contexts. In other words, these intransitivities are the result of using two different methods for obtaining preference orderings. However, there is one type of theory which does not rely upon 'information processing' arguments, but explains preference-reversal in terms of the choices made by rational individuals acting on the basis of consistent, but non-transitive, preferences. These are theories based upon regret, where the utility derived from a consequence of one action is influenced by considerations of 'what might have been' had you chosen differently. The basic intuitions behind regret theory were outlined by Sugden (1987) in chapter 1 of this volume, and for a more rigorous development of the implications of regret in relation to the preference-reversal phenomenon the reader is recommended to consult Loomes and Sugden (1983, 1987a).

In a recent experiment, the results of which should be published soon, Loomes and Sugden (1987a) attempted to discriminate between 'information processing' and regret-type explanations for the preference-reversal phenomenon. Their approach was based upon the argument that if regret theory is correct, then preference reversal should be observed not only when subjects are offered a pairwise choice between two prospects and then asked to value them, but also when subjects are given three pairwise choices of the form, '$ vs P', '$ vs C', and 'P vs C', where C is a sum of money for sure. The pure choice analogue to standard preference reversal is then the pairwise cycle: '$P > \$$', '$\$ > C$', and '$C > P$'. Loomes and Sugden designed the questions in such a way that this cycle would be consistent with regret theory, but the opposite cycle would not. They found no significant difference between the responses of the subjects who had made one choice and two valuations, and those who had been asked to make three straight choices. In addition, they found a clear tendency for the number of predicted cycles to exceed the number of unpredicted cycles.

Since regret theory also predicts violations of independence such as the common ratio and common consequence effects, while other theories of the fanning-out class can not account for preference-reversal, it may seem as though the evidence strongly favours the regret-based theories of this class. Unfortunately, such a clear conclusion cannot be drawn. As Sugden (1987) shows, regret theory cannot explain all cases of the common consequence effect. Specifically, regret cannot account for violations of the 'sure-thing principle'. In terms of the generalized common consequence effect, this means that if the choice problem was presented in the form of the state contingent matrix shown in Figure 4, where the common consequence 'c' occurs in a given state of the world, then regret theory would not predict the switch of preference from $A > B$ to $B > A$ as c falls. However, the common consequence effect has been observed using this type of presentation (see, for example, Moskowitz, 1974).

Similarly, the predictions of regret theory in the case of the common ratio effect depend critically on the presentation of the problem. Consider Kahneman and Tversky's common ratio problem which is also reported in Sugden (1987). They presented this as two pairwise choices of the form:

Question 1. Choose between: $X = (3{,}000, 1.00)$ and
$Y = (4{,}000, 0.80)$
Question 2. Choose between: $X' = (3{,}000, 0.25)$ and
$Y' = (4{,}000, 0.20)$

While theories of the fanning-out class generally imply increasingly risk-prone behaviour as p falls, predicting the tendency — which is actually observed by Kahneman and Tversky — to choose X in question 1 and Y' in question 2, the crucial factor affecting preferences in regret theory is the comparison between the outcomes of each action in different states of the world. The above presentation does not, therefore, provide us with the information necessary to generate predictions from regret theory.

If instead we reproduce this problem in state-contingent matrices, where the columns of each table represent states of the world, with the probability that each state will occur shown in the first row, we can introduce a new parameter (ω) which measures the degree of overlap between the states of the world in which action X' gives 3,000 and action Y' gives 4,000. (More formally, ω can be defined as the probability that X' gives 3,000 conditional on Y' giving 4,000.) It then becomes clear that question 2 can be represented in any number of ways for ω in the range $0 \leqslant \omega \leqslant 1$. Figures 5a and 5b illustrate the two extreme cases. For any theory other than regret there is no real difference between the choices offered in Figures 5a and 5b, but the 'degree of overlap', ω, is critical in regret theory: from the point of view of regret, the choice between $X'a$ and $Y'a$ is essentially different from that between $X'b$ and $Y'b$. For example, $X'a$ gives a 0.20 chance of receiving 3,000 when you might have had 4,000 had you chosen differently (a regret experience), plus a 0.05 chance of receiving 3,000 when you might have got nothing (a rejoicing experience), whereas action $X'b$ gives a 0.25 chance of receiving 3,000 when you might have got nothing, plus a 0.20 chance of getting nothing when you might have received 4,000. When $\omega = 1$, as in Figure 5a, regret theory predicts $X \gtrless Y \Leftrightarrow X'a \gtrless Y'a$, but in the case of Figure 5b, where $\omega = 0$, regret theory predicts a tendency towards the common ratio effect (i.e. $X > Y$ then $Y'b > X'b$). The intuition behind the latter case is to suggest that those individuals who choose X in question 1 may be repelled by $X'b$, since choosing this option may result in the 'greatest regret', that of getting nothing when you might have received 4,000 had you chosen differently. More generally, regret theory predicts a tendency towards the common ratio effect as ω falls. (For a proof of this see Loomes and Sugden, 1987b).

QUESTION 1.

	0.25	0.75
X	3000	3000
Y	0	4000

QUESTION 2.

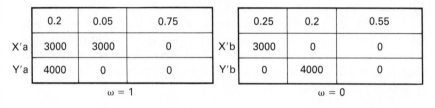

X'a	0.2	0.05	0.75
X'a	3000	3000	0
Y'a	4000	0	0

$\omega = 1$

Fig. 5a.

X'b	0.25	0.2	0.55
X'b	3000	0	0
Y'b	0	4000	0

$\omega = 0$

Fig. 5b.

Fig. 5. The common ratio problem in state-contingent matrices.

What this means is that, potentially, there are two separate factors at work in the common ratio effect; changes in probability p, and changes in the degree of overlap ω. While all common ratio problems involve changes in probability, in many of the cases where the common ratio effect has been experimentally observed it is not possible to determine how the state-contingent matrices should be specified, and hence whether any of this behaviour can be attributed to a regret effect. Loomes and Sugden (1987b) conducted an experiment designed to assess the relative importance of these two variables. They presented subjects with pairwise choices laid out clearly in state-contingent matrices, and designed to elicit the common ratio effect. One sub-group of their subjects were given problems where the matrices were constructed with $\omega = 1$ to control for regret. This produced a highly significant common ratio effect and, although regret cannot account for the violations when $\omega = 1$, these observations need not necessarily be regarded as violations of regret, since they can be explained by disappointment theory, which is perhaps more of a complement to regret than a competitor. A second group of subjects were given similar problems, identical except for the layout of the matrix which, in this case, was constructed so that $\omega = 0$ in the expectation that a regret effect would add to the number of subjects committing the common ratio effect. While there was some evidence of a significant regret effect at work, it was quite modest.

Loomes and Sugden suggested that the relatively small contribution of regret could be due to the fact that so many violations of EUT were being produced even when controlling for regret. However, they found that, in one case, fewer reversals were produced in the case where the regret effect should have been operating ($\omega = 0$). More recent work by Loomes (1986) found a somewhat weaker disappointment effect but a stronger and more consistent regret effect, which perhaps suggests that the one example of behaviour counter to regret in the earlier experiment was something of an exception. Although the support for regret and disappointment effects is mixed, work in this area is still at a fairly early stage. It is nevertheless significant that in both of the above experiments EUT could only account for between 30 and 40 per cent of observed choices, while, taken together, disappointment and regret theory account for 80–90 per cent of observations.

CONCLUSIONS

There is quite a large body of experimental evidence which casts doubt upon the validity of EUT as a descriptive and normative theory of choice under uncertainty, together with a growing number of new theories which attempt to explain these observed violations. While no single theory so far developed appears able to account for all of these data, several of the new approaches appear promising. What we have stressed is the need for experimental work to investigate novel implications of these theories which will allow us to assess their predictive ability and discriminate between them. Some of this work has already begun, but there is still much to be done in this expanding field. Finally, a word or two of caution. First, in our enthusiasm to design theories capable of explaining all forms of observed behaviour, we must be careful that those theories do not become so complex as to be mere tautological representations of all retrospective evidence; and second, there may be considerable benefits to be had from more multidisciplinary research to combine some of the work done by psychologists on the limitations of human information processing and cognitive processes with the more 'restrictive' mathematical modelling perpsective of economists.

Centre for Health Economics, University of York (L.A.)
Economics Research Centre, University of East Anglia (C.S.)

REFERENCES

Ali, M. (1977). 'Probability and Utility Estimates for Racetrack Bettors', *Journal of Political Economy*, Vol. 85, pp. 803-15.

Allais, M. (1953). 'Le Comportement de l'Homme Rationnel Devant le Risque; Critique des Postulats et Axiomes de l'Ecole Americaine', *Econometrica*, Vol. 21, pp. 503-46.

Allais, M. and Hagen, O. (eds.) (1979). *Expected Utility Hypotheses and the Allais Paradox*, Holland, D. Reidel.

Bar-Hillel, M. (1973). 'On the Subjective Probability of Compound Events', *Organisational Behaviour and Human Performance*, Vol. 9, pp. 396-406.

Berg, J. E. *et al.* (1983). 'Preference Reversal and Arbitrage', in *Research in Experimental Economics*, Smith, V. L. (ed.), Vol. 3, pp. 31-72, Greenwich, Connecticut, JAI Press.

Bernoulli, D. (1738). 'Specimen Theoriad Novae de Mensura Sortis', *Commentarii Academiae Scientiarum Imperiales Petrapolitane*, Vol. 5, pp. 175-92. (Translated by L. Somer (1954), *Econometrica*, Vol. 22, pp. 23-36.)

Cohen, M. and Jaffray, J. Y. (1986). 'Preponderance of the Certainty Effect Over Probability Distortion in Decision Making Under Risk', draft manuscript, University of Paris.

de Neufville, R. and Delquie, P. (1986). 'Exploration of the Influence of Certainty and Probability "Effects" on the Measurement of Utility', Manuscript, MIT.

Edwards, W. (1955). 'The Prediction of Decisions Among Bets', *Journal of Experimental Psychology*, Vol. 50, pp. 201-14.

Ellsberg, D. (1961). 'Risk, Ambiguity and the Savage Axioms', *Quarterly Journal of Economics*, Vol. 75, pp. 643-69

Farquhar, P. H. (1984). 'Utility Assessment Methods', *Management Science*, Vol. 30, pp. 1283-300.

Grether, D. and Plott, C. (1979). 'Economic Theory of Choice and the Preference Reversal Phenomenon', *American Economic Review*, Vol. 69, pp. 623-38.

Hagen, O. (1979). 'Towards a Positive Theory of Preferences Under Risk', pp. 277-302 in Allais and Hagen (1979).

Kahneman, D. and Tversky, A. (1979). 'Prospect Theory: An Analysis of Decision Under Risk', *Econometrica*, Vol. 47, pp. 263-91.

Karmarker, U. (1974). 'The Effect of Probabilities on the Subjective Evaluation of Lotteries', Working Paper No. 689-74, Sloan School of Business, MIT.

Lichtenstein, S. and Slovic, P. (1971). 'Reversals of Preferences Between Bids and Choices in Gambling Decisions', *Journal of Experimental Psychology*, Vol. 89, pp. 46-55.

Lichtenstein, S. and Slovic, P. (1973). 'Response-Induced Reversals of Preference in Gambling: An Extended Replication in Las Vegas', *Journal of Experimental Psychology*, Vol. 101, pp. 16-20.

Lindman, H. (1971). 'Inconsistent Preferences Among Gambles', *Journal of Experimental Psychology*, Vol. 89, pp. 390-7.

Loomes, G. (1986). 'Further Evidence of the Impact of Regret and Disappointment in Choice Under Uncertainty', University of York I.R.I.S.S. Discussion Paper 119.

Loomes, G. and Sugden, R. (1983). 'A Rationale for Preference Reversal', *American Economic Review*, Vol. 73, pp. 428-32.

Loomes, G. and Sugden, R. (1987a). 'Preference Reversal: Information Processing Effect or Rational Non-Transitive Choice?', mimeo, available from authors.

Loomes, G. and Sugden, R. (1987b). 'Testing for Regret and Disappointment in Choice Under Uncertainty', *Economic Journal RES/AUTE Conference Supplement*, in press.

MacCrimmon, K. (1965). 'An Experimental Study of the Decision Making Behaviour of Business Executives', unpublished dissertation, University of California, Los Angeles.

MacCrimmon, K. (1968). 'Descriptive and Normative Implications of the Decision Theory Postulates', in *Risk and Uncertainty*, Borch, K. and Mossin, J. (eds.), New York, Macmillan, pp. 3-23.

MacCrimmon, K. and Larsson, S. (1979). 'Utility Theory: Axioms Versus Paradoxes', pp. 333-409 in Allais and Hagen (1979).

Machina, M. (1983). 'The Economic Theory of Individual Behaviour Toward Risk', Technical Report No. 433, Institute for Mathematical Studies in the Social Sciences, Stanford University, California.

May, K. (1954). 'Intransitivity, Utility and the Aggregation of Preference Patterns', *Econometrica*, Vol. 22, pp. 1-13.

McCord, M. and de Neufville, R. (1984). 'Utility Dependence on Probability: An Empirical Demonstration', *Journal of Large Scale Systems*, Vol. 6, pp. 91-103.

Morgenstern, O. (1979). 'Some Reflections on Utility', pp. 175-83 in Allais and Hagen (1979).

Moskowitz, H. (1974). 'Effects of Problem Presentation and Feedback on Rational Behaviour in Allais and Morlat-Type Problems', *Decision Sciences*, Vol. 5, pp. 225-42.

Mosteller, F. and Nogee, P. (1951). 'An Experimental Measurement of Utility', *Journal of Political Economy*, Vol. 59, pp. 371-404.

Nogee, P. and Lieberman, B. (1960). 'The Auction Value of Certain Risky Situations', *Journal of Psychology*, Vol. 49, pp. 167-79.

Pommerehne, W., Schneider, F. and Zweifel, P. (1982). 'Economic Theory of Choice and the Preference Phenomenon: A Re-examination', *American Economic Review*, Vol. 72, pp. 569-74.

Preston, M. and Baratta, P. (1948). 'An Experimental Study of the Auction Value of an Uncertain Outcome', *American Journal of Psychology*, Vol. 61, pp. 183-93.

Raiffa, H. (1961). 'Risk, Ambiguity and the Savage Axioms', *Quarterly Journal of Economics*, Vol. 75, pp. 690-4.

Reilly, R. (1982). 'Preference Reversal: Further Evidence and Some Suggested Modifications of Experimental Design', *American Economic Review*, Vol. 72, pp. 576-84.

Savage, L. (1954). *The Foundations of Statistics*, New York, Wiley.

Schoemaker, P. J. H. (1982). 'The Expected Utility Model: Its Variants, Purposes, Evidence and Limitations', *Journal of Economic Literature*, Vol. 20, pp. 529-63.

Slovic, P. (1975). 'Choice Between Equally Valued Alternatives', *Journal of Experimental Psychology: Human Perception and Performance*, Vol. 1, pp. 280-7.

Slovic, P. and Tversky, A. (1974). 'Who Accepts Savage's Axiom?', *Behavioural Science*, Vol. 19, pp. 368-73.

Sprowls, R. (1953). 'Psychological-Mathematical Probability in Relationships of Lottery Gambles', *American Journal of Psychology*, Vol. 66, pp. 126-30.

Sugden, R. (1987). 'New Developments in the Theory of Choice Under Uncertainty', in this collection.

Tversky, A. (1967a). 'Utility Theory and Additivity Analysis of Risky Choices', *Journal of Experimental Psychology*, Vol. 75, pp. 27-36.

Tversky, A. (1967b). 'Additivity, Utility and Subjective Probability', *Journal of Mathematical Psychology*, Vol. 4, pp. 175-201.

Tversky, A. (1969). 'Intransitivity of Preferences', *Psychological Review*, Vol. 76, pp. 31-48.

von Neumann, J. and Morgenstern, O. (1947). *Theory of Games and Economic Behaviour*, 2nd edn., Princeton, Princeton University Press.

THE THEORY OF PRINCIPAL AND AGENT
PART I

Ray Rees

1. INTRODUCTION

A large and interesting class of problems in economics involves delegated choice: one individual has the responsibility for taking decisions
supposedly in the interests of one or more others, in return for some
kind of payment. Examples are a manager running a firm on behalf
of its shareholders, an employee working for an employer, an
accountant handling the tax affairs of a client, an estate agent selling
someone's house, an investment advisor administering a trust fund
or share portfolio, a public policy maker, and so on. It turns out that
when this situation is modelled, its formal structure is applicable to
an even wider class of problems, where no formal delegation relationship is explicitly involved. For example, a person taking out fire,
theft or health insurance will take a decision on the level of some
activity which would reduce the risk of the event insured against and
this will affect the probable income of the insurer; a firm handling
dangerous chemicals will take decisions which affect the likelihood
and extent of damage which would be caused to others by an accident.
The theory of principal and agent is intended to apply to any situation
with the following structure: one individual, called the agent and
denoted A, must choose some action a from some given set of
actions $\{a\}$. The particular outcome x which results from this choice
depends also on which element from some given set of states of the
world, $\{\theta\}$, actually prevails at the relevant time, so that uncertainty
is intrinsic to the situation. The outcome x generates utility to a
second individual, the principal, denoted P. A contract is to be defined
under which P makes a payment y to A. A's utility depends both on
this payment y and the value of the action, a. The main purpose of
principal-agent theory is to characterize the optimal forms of such
contracts under various assumptions about the information P and A
possess or can acquire and thereby, hopefully, to explain the characteristics of such contracts which are actually observed. It should be
stressed that the term 'contract' is to be interpreted very broadly.
It may refer to a formal document, such as an insurance policy or
sharecropping agreement, or to an implicit contract, such as may
characterize an employment relationship, or to some penalty–reward
system which may not formally be a contract at all – for example,

46

the rules under which liability for damages following escape of dangerous chemicals is assessed. As usual in economics, the formal structure suggested by a particular instance of a problem is capable of much wider application.

This paper provides a survey of the literature on principal-agent theory in the following sense. I shall set out the model of the problem which has been formulated in the literature and give an exposition of the main results so far derived. This is the subject of Part 1. In Part 2 I go on to examine the main areas of application of the theory. Naturally, in developing the exposition I will refer to the papers which have developed the analysis and results. However, I make no attempt to discuss or evaluate individual papers explicitly – this is not a survey of the 'who said what and when (and were they right?)' kind. The main aim of the paper is to give a clear account of the theory and some existing or potential applications, and, hopefully, to show to economists not already familiar with them that they involve some interesting and relevant economic ideas.

PART 1:   THEORY

1.   *The Formal Model*

We begin by setting out the model which will be used throughout the rest of the paper. The principal, P, has a Neumann–Morgenstern (N–M) utility function $u(x-y)$, which is not directly dependent on the state of the world, θ, and which is bounded and continuously differentiable to any required order. In particular, $u' > 0$ and $u'' \leqslant 0$, so we rule out risk-attracted behavior. Likewise the agent, A, has a N–M utility function $v(y, a)$ with $v_y > 0$, $v_{yy} \leqslant 0$, $v_a < 0$, $v_{aa} > 0$, so A, also, can only either be risk-neutral ($v_{yy} = 0$) or risk-averse ($v_{yy} < 0$). The assumption that a yields disutility to A is adopted because in most applications a is interpreted as effort or expenditure incurred by A in acting on behalf of P. Note that P is indifferent to A's choice of a as such, and cares only about the value of the outcome net of the portion of it he must pay to A. This is therefore a potent source of conflict of interest between P and A.[1] If, as we assume, A will always act in his own best interests, then in designing the contract it must be recognized that the disutility he receives from

---

[1] The two papers by Ross (1973, 1974), which initiated study of the principal-agent problem, in fact assume that a does not enter into A's utility function. A conflict of interest then arises if the two utility functions are essentially different, i.e. if there do *not* exist $\alpha > 0$, β such that $v \equiv \alpha u + \beta$ (recall that N–M utility functions are unique up to a positive linear transformation). If a is excluded from v, however, the model is then one purely of risk-sharing, and does not encompass the problem of incentives and moral hazard, which would generally be regarded as a central issue in the principal-agent relationship. The following sections should make this point clear.

a may cause him not to act in P's best interests. Naturally we will have a lot more to say about this problem in what follows.

Without serious loss of generality, we can take the set of states of the world $\{\theta\}$ to be given by the closed unit interval $[0, 1]$. A substantive assumption is that both P and A have identical probability beliefs concerning the state of the world, represented by the probability density function $f(\theta)$. This is a significant restriction, because it might be thought that one aspect of the principal-agent relationship would be that A would possess better information on the likely occurrence of states of the world, as well as on the definition of the states themselves, than P. At some points in what follows the consequences of assuming different probability beliefs will be suggested, but the literature is entirely based on the assumption of identical probability beliefs and a full generalization is not available.

Given A's choice of a, which is made *before* the state of the world is known, the value of the outcome x will vary with θ, and so we can write $x = x(a, \theta)$. We assume $x(\cdot, \cdot)$ is continuously differentiable to any required order, with $x_a \geqslant 0$, $x_{aa} \leqslant 0$, and, for convenience, $x_\theta > 0$, so that higher values of θ represent in some sense more favorable states. We can think of x_a as the marginal product of a, and we are assuming this is always positive but nonincreasing.

With this notation, the basic principal-agent problem can be stated as follows. P is to choose a payment schedule, which in its most general form specifies a payment y to A, which could depend on x, θ, a, and some other variable,[2] z, i.e. $y = y(x, \theta, a, z)$. The variable z could be thought of as something which gives (usually imperfect) information either about a, or about θ, and which is costlessly available. A central assumption in principal-agent theory, which distinguishes it from the literature on incentive compatibility (for which see Hammond (1979) and the companion papers in that symposium) is that the payment schedule can depend only upon variables which *both* parties can observe. It is assumed that A knows a (as well as $u(\cdot)$) and can observe both x and θ. Hence different possibilities arise only in respect of the information available to P. It is always assumed that P knows $x(a, \theta)$ (as well as $v(\cdot, \cdot)$) and can always observe x. It follows that if he can observe one of a and θ he can deduce the other, *ex post*, from $x(a, \theta)$. We therefore have two cases of interest:

(i) P can observe a (or θ) and therefore θ (or a). In that case he does not need z, since further (imperfect) information is redundant.[3]

---

[2] Needless to say, in a fully general treatment any or all of x, a and z could be vectors rather than scalars. Nothing essential is lost by restricting the exposition to the simpler case considered here.

[3] Harris and Raviv (1978) provide rigorous proofs of this and some other assertions which will be taken for granted here. Harris and Raviv also show that the results given in this paper for the case in which a is chosen before the state of the world is known extend quite readily to the case where a is chosen after θ is known.

Also, the payment schedule can be taken to depend on θ alone and P chooses this payment schedule and a value of a for A in such a way as to maximize his own expected utility, subject to the constraint that A receive at least some minimum expected utility, $\bar{v}^0$, referred to as his *reservation utility*.[4] As is shown in the next two sections, in this case a first-best optimum risk-sharing contract is possible, with the moral hazard or incentive problem being solved by what is known as a *forcing contract*. This result extends to the case in which a is observable only with some random error, provided a certain boundedness condition is met.

(ii) P can observe neither a nor θ. In this case we have a true moral hazard problem. P must recognize that given some fee schedule, A will choose a to maximize his own expected utility, and this will in general imply a value of a other than that for which the fee schedule is optimal. The lack of observability of a (and θ) means that P cannot correct this directly, and so a constraint, which we can call the *incentive constraint*, must be added to the reservation utility constraint in P's optimization problem.[5] In other words, P must take account of the fact that his choice of a payment schedule will determine a value of a *via* A's maximization procedure and thus affect the final equilibrium. In general, this leads to a departure from the optimal risk-sharing solution: there is a tradeoff between the gains from sharing risk and the need to control A's choice of a – the provision of incentive. It can also be shown that when a variable z exists which gives information about a, however 'noisy', and which is contingent on θ, it is, except when A is risk-neutral, optimal to incorporate it into the contract and make y contingent on it, although this result would presumably be modified if z were costly to acquire.

In the following five sections we go on to analyse these cases. The analysis draws heavily on Holmström (1979) and Shavell (1979), with reliance on Harris and Raviv (1978) for rigorous proofs of what is here simply asserted. The principal-agent problem proper is essentially case (ii), but it will be useful to consider case (i) first as a point of departure.

---

[4] This reservation utility is never discussed at any length in the literature. It is usually taken as 'market determined' and left at that. Yet it turns out to be important because at the solution to most models A receives only $\bar{v}^0$, with P appropriating all the gains from trade (indeed, the only paper to consider the issue of whether, in equilibrium, $v > \bar{v}^0$, explicitly, is Grossman and Hart (1983), in Proposition 3). Clearly what is required is some theory of the market interaction between principals and agents, a suggestion for further research made at the very outset, by Ross (1973), and so far not taken up.

[5] This additional constraint then creates a second-best problem relative to the problem in case (i). In fact the structure is quite analogous to the types of problems first considered in the theory of the second-best – see, for example, Lipsey and Lancaster (1956), and Davis and Whinston (1965).

2. Optimal Risk Sharing

Since the central problem of principal-agent theory is to find a fee schedule which optimally trades off the benefits of risk-sharing with the costs of providing an incentive to the agent, it is useful to begin by considering the question of risk-sharing in isolation. This can be done by taking the general model just set out and fixing the value of the agent's action arbitrarily, at $a = a^0$. We then assume that a and/or θ can be costlessly observed so that y can be taken to depend only on θ. By a risk sharing optimum is meant a payment $y^*(\theta)$ from P to A which is Pareto efficient, i.e. which maximizes P's expected utility for some given minimum level of A's utility $\bar{v}^0$. Thus, we seek a solution to the problem:[6]

$$\max_{y(\theta)} \int_0^1 u(x(a^0, \theta) - y(\theta)) f(\theta)\, d\theta \text{ s.t.} \int_0^1 v(a^0, y(\theta)) f(\theta)\, d\theta \geqslant \bar{v}^0 \quad (R)$$

The solution[7] $y^*(\theta)$, which specifies a payment from P to A at each θ, can be characterized by the following condition[8]

$$-u'(x - y^*) + \lambda v_y = 0, \quad \forall \theta \in [0, 1] \tag{1}$$

where λ can be interpreted as a conventional Lagrange multiplier which is not, it should be noted, a function of θ.

Since, from (1), we have that $\lambda = u'/v_y$, the ratio of marginal utilities of income of P and A at each θ, we conclude that P's non-satiation in income implies $\lambda > 0$. It follows that the constraint in (R) must be satisfied as an equality $-A$ receives only his reservation utility $\bar{v}^0$.

If we take two states $\theta_1 \neq \theta_2$, then (1) implies (with obvious notation)

$$\frac{u'(\theta_1)}{v_y(\theta_1)} = \frac{u'(\theta_2)}{v_y(\theta_2)} \Rightarrow \frac{u'(\theta_1)}{u'(\theta_2)} = \frac{v_y(\theta_1)}{v_y(\theta_2)} \tag{2}$$

Thus, an implication of optimal risk-sharing is that P and A's marginal rates of substitution of income between any two states are equal. The thoroughly conventional nature of this result is brought out if we represent the situation as in Figure 1. This is an Edgeworth–Bowley box, with horizontal length given by $x(a^0, \theta_1)$ and vertical length

---

[6] Strictly we should also impose upon this problem the condition that

$$y(\theta) \in [y^0, x(a^0, \theta)], \forall \theta$$

where $y^0 \gtrless 0$ is some lower income bound for A, but for simplicity we assume an interior solution: in each state both P and A receive a positive share of the outcome x.

[7] This is found by forming the function $\{u + \lambda(v - v^0)\} f(\theta)$ and finding the maximum of this w.r.t. y at each θ; i.e. we carry out a pointwise maximization.

[8] This solution appears first to have been developed by Borch (1962).

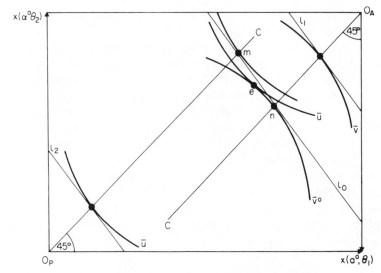

Fig. 1. Optimal risk-sharing

given by $x(a^0, \theta_2)$, incomes in states θ_1 and θ_2, respectively. P's indifference curves, which show loci of constant expected utility are drawn with reference to origin O_P, and A's with reference to origin O_A. The 45° lines from each origin are certainty lines; along $O_P C$ for example, P enjoys complete income certainty. The slopes of the straight lines[9] l_0, l_1, l_2 are the probability ratios $f(\theta_1)/f(\theta_2)$, and, given the assumption of identical probability beliefs, are the same for P and A. The indifference curve $\bar{v}^0$ corresponds to A's reservation utility, and so one equilibrium consistent with condition (1) is exemplified by point e. Clearly this is a standard type of condition for Pareto efficiency in consumption allocations, where the state-contingent incomes $y(\theta)$ and $x(\theta) - y(\theta)$ are thought of as ordinary commodities.

Two further results which turn out to be of interest in principal-agent theory can be illustrated in the figure. Suppose P is risk-neutral. Then his indifference curves are like the lines l_0, l_1, l_2 in the figure.[10]

---

[9] It is no accident that the convex indifference curves are tangent to these lines along the certainty lines $O_P C$ and $O_A C$. For example, since *expected utility* is constant along an indifference curve, we must have

$$\frac{dy\,(\theta_2)}{dy\,(\theta_1)} = \frac{-f(\theta_1)\,v_y(\theta_1)}{f(\theta_2)\,v_y(\theta_2)}$$

But at $y(\theta_1) = y(\theta_2)$, $v_y(\theta_1) = v_y(\theta_2)$, and so marginal rate of substitution of state-contingent incomes is equal to the probability ratio at such a point.

[10] Thus, in footnote 9, set $v_y(\theta_1) = v_y(\theta_2)$ for all y, since risk-neutrality implies that A's marginal utility of income is independent of income. Then $dy_2/dy_1 = -f(\theta_1)/f(\theta_2)$ for all y. Then the same would obviously hold for P's marginal rate of substitution.

Again, it follows from the assumption of identical probability beliefs that the only point at which tangency with A's reservation indifference curve $\bar{v}^0$ can take place is along his certainty line $O_A C$, at n. Thus, optimal risk-sharing with P risk-neutral and A risk-averse implies that P 'fully insures' A by giving him a payment which is independent of θ, i.e. a *certain* income, and P bears all the risk. The converse occurs if A is risk-neutral and P risk-averse — the equilibrium would be at m in the figure, with P receiving a guaranteed income and A bearing all the risk. With both risk-neutral, any point along the line l_0 is an equilibrium.

These remarks can be generalized if we enquire into the possible forms of the payments schedules which are implicitly defined by condition (1). Insight into these can be gained by differentiating the condition w.r.t. θ, recalling that $\lambda = u'/v_y$ is constant across θ. We then obtain

$$-u''\left(\frac{\partial x}{\partial \theta} - \frac{\mathrm{d}y^*}{\mathrm{d}\theta}\right) + \lambda v_{yy} \frac{\mathrm{d}y^*}{\mathrm{d}\theta} = 0 \qquad (3)$$

We can now introduce the Pratt–Arrow index of absolute risk aversion, defined as:

$$r_P \equiv \frac{-u''}{u'}, \quad r_A \equiv \frac{-v_{yy}}{v_y}$$

Then, substituting for λ in (3) and rearranging gives:

$$\frac{\mathrm{d}y^*}{\mathrm{d}\theta} = \frac{r_P}{r_P + r_A} \frac{\partial x}{\partial \theta} \qquad (4)$$

Given risk aversion, r_P, $r_A > 0$, and so (4) implies that if, as θ increases, x increases (as was earlier assumed), then so does y, but at a slower rate. A sufficient condition for a *linear* payments schedule, i.e. a schedule of the form $y = \alpha x + \beta$, is clearly that both A and P have constant absolute risk-aversion, since in that case $r_P/(r_P + r_A)$ is constant, and integrating (4) over θ would give:

$$y^*(\theta) = \alpha x(a^0, \theta) + \beta, \quad \alpha = \frac{r_P}{r_P + r_A} \qquad (5)$$

where β is a constant of integration. Moreover, if $r_P = 0$, implying that P is risk-neutral, we see immediately that we must have

$$y^*(\theta) = \beta \qquad (6)$$

implying that P bears all the risk as already illustrated in Figure 1. If A is risk-neutral, $r_A = 0$ and we must have a payment schedule of the form:

$$y^*(\theta) = x(a^0, \theta) - \gamma \tag{7}$$

i.e. A makes a fixed payment γ to P and takes the residual income.

Although the simplicity of each of these special cases is attractive, in general constant risk aversion, let alone zero risk aversion, would be regarded as rather special. If, as would more usually be assumed, r_P and r_A are both decreasing in income, the shape of $y(\theta)$ will depend on the relative changes in risk aversion as well as on the shape of $x(a^0, \theta)$ and so $y(\theta)$ could be nonlinear, convex or concave, or neither.[11] No doubt a taxonomy of cases is possible, but this would take us far from our present purpose. The case of pure risk-sharing is a preliminary step in examination of the principal-agent model, so let us return to this by considering the implications of allowing a to vary.[12]

3. The Incentive Problem

We now show that in the present case, with a observable, a 'first-best' Pareto optimum with respect to both risk-sharing and A's choice of a is available. Thus, P can solve the problem

$$\max_{a, y(\theta)} \int_0^1 u(x(a, \theta) - y(\theta)) f(\theta) \, d\theta \text{ s.t.} \int_0^1 v(a, y(\theta)) f(\theta) \, d\theta \geqslant \bar{v}^0 \quad (FB)$$

with a as well as y now variable. Note that since a is to be chosen before the state of the world is known, it will not depend on θ. A first-best Pareto optimum will then be an optimal action a^* for A and an associated optimal payment schedule $y^*(\theta)$. The contract between P and A would then specify this schedule in exchange for A choosing a^*. As we shall see, A does have an incentive to cheat on the contract and, given that he will receive $y^*(\theta)$, choose some $\hat{a} \neq a^*$. However, if P can costlessly observe a then the contract can contain a 'forcing clause': if, ex post, $\hat{a} < a^*$ then some $\hat{y}(\theta) < y^*(\theta)$ will be paid, and of course $\hat{y}(\theta)$ can be made sufficiently unattractive

---

[11] Thus, differentiating (4) w.r.t. θ would show that even if $d^2x/d\theta^2$ is signed, and both utility functions have diminishing risk aversion, we cannot in general sign $d^2y^*/d\theta^2$ – everything depends on the relative rates at which risk aversion of A and P diminish.

[12] The effect of divergent probability beliefs of P and A can be briefly indicated. In that case (1) becomes

$$-u'f(\theta) + \lambda v_y g(\theta) = 0 \tag{1'}$$

where $g(\theta) \neq f(\theta)$ is A's probability density on θ. (4) then becomes

$$\frac{dy^*}{d\theta} = \left(\frac{r_P}{r_P + r_A}\right) \frac{\partial x}{\partial \theta} + \left(\frac{1}{r_P + r_A}\right) \left\{ \frac{g'}{g} - \frac{f'}{f} \right\} \tag{4'}$$

Thus the way in which the optimal payment y^* varies with x or θ now depends also on the probability beliefs of P and A, and constant absolute risk aversion is no longer sufficient for linearity of the payments schedule, and risk-neutrality of either A or P no longer gives the simple 'full insurance' results previously described.

as to force A to choose a^* (recall that P knows $v(y,a)$). Let us therefore examine the first-best solution corresponding to the absence of the incentive problem.

The solution to FB can be characterized by the conditions:

$$-u' + \lambda v_y = 0 \tag{8}$$

$$E[u'x_a + \lambda v_a] = 0 \tag{9}$$

where the expectations operator E has replaced the integral notation. Again, the Lagrange multiplier $\lambda > 0$, given $u' > 0$. Thus A receives only $\bar{v}^0$. Note that, since a is chosen optimally, condition (8) is identical to (1), and we have optimal risk-sharing just as before: *given* choice of a, P and A share the risk associated with the resulting distribution of x in a Pareto-efficient way. The new element is condition (9), which relates to the optimal choice of a and has a straightforward interpretation. In any one state of the world, $u'x_a$ can be interpreted as the marginal value product of a measured in terms of P's utility or 'u-utils', i.e.

$$\frac{du}{da} = \frac{\partial u}{\partial x}\frac{\partial x}{\partial a}$$

Then, λv_a can be interpreted as the marginal cost of a in 'u-utils': at the optimum, $\lambda = u'/v_y$ gives the number of 'u-utils' P has to give up to yield A one 'v-util'; while v_a gives the number of 'v-utils' A requires to be paid to supply the marginal bit of a (recall $v_a < 0$). Thus $(u'x_a + \lambda v_a)$ is net marginal value product of a in 'u-utils'.[13] Now if a were state-contingent P would choose a so as to set this net marginal value product at zero (marginal value product equals marginal cost) in each state. But because a must be chosen before the state of the world is known, the marginal value product and marginal cost are equalized in expected value terms — on average across all states.

Since our earlier analysis of the form of the risk-sharing contract was conducted for arbitrary a, it applies equally now for a at the optimal value of a^*. The important point is that observability of a implies that Pareto-efficient risk-sharing is still possible. The two special cases of P risk-neutral and A risk-neutral are again of interest. Thus, suppose P is risk-neutral so that u' is a constant. Then from the earlier analysis we know that y^* is a constant and so, since a is inde-

---

[13] Thus, the dimension of λ is

$$\frac{u\text{-utils}/\$}{v\text{-utils}/\$} = \frac{u\text{-utils}}{v\text{-utils}}$$

and the dimension of λv_a is

$$\frac{u\text{-utils}}{v\text{-utils}} \cdot \frac{v\text{-utils}}{\text{units of } a} = \frac{u\text{-utils}}{\text{units of } a}$$

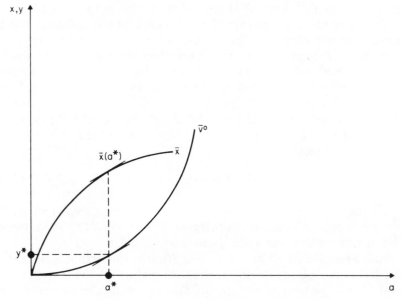

Fig. 2. Optimal a with P risk-neutral

pendent of θ, we must have that in each state $v(y^*, a^*) = \bar{v}^0$. On standard assumptions, we can draw this contour of A's utility function as $\bar{v}^0$ in Figure 2, treating y as certain. If we treat u' as a constant in (9), substitute for λ, and note that both v_a and v_y are independent of θ, we have:

$$E[x_a] = \frac{-v_a}{v_y} \qquad (10)$$

or, at the optimum the expected marginal product of a is equated to A's unique marginal rate of substitution between a and income. Then, define the function:

$$\bar{x}(a) = \int_0^1 x(a, \theta) f(\theta) \, d\theta \qquad (11)$$

which gives the expected value across θ of x at each a. This is graphed as the curve $\bar{x}$ in Figure 2. Then the optimum for a risk-neutral P is given by a^* in the figure, since at this point the slope of $\bar{x}(a)$ is equal to the slope v_a/v_y of $\bar{v}^0$. This has a straightforward interpretation. To induce A to choose any given a, P will offer him a fixed payment (efficient risk-sharing) which must lie on $\bar{v}^0$ ($\lambda > 0$, so A receives only his reservation utility). Hence, $\bar{v}^0$ is a type of 'total cost curve' to P.[14] Since P is risk neutral, the output distribution $x(a, \theta)$ can be valued at its expected value, and so the vertical distance between the two curves in Figure 2 can be thought of as P's 'expected net income'. P then seeks to maximize this, implying that he wants A to choose a^*, and pays him y^* in exchange. P's income distribution, $x(a^*, \theta) - y^*$, will then be given from the distribution $x(a^*, \theta)$ of which $\bar{x}^*$ is the expected value.

In the case where A is risk-neutral, P retains a constant payment, γ, and so again u' is constant. But v_y is also constant (risk-neutrality), and so (9) becomes:

$$E[x_a] = -E\left[\frac{v_a}{v_y}\right] \tag{12}$$

In this case, the optimal a equates the expected marginal product with the expected value of A's marginal rate of substitution between a and income, which, for $a = a^*$, varies with $x(a^*, \theta) - \gamma$.

Thus, when P can observe a or θ costlessly, the first-best is attainable. If he can observe neither, then the nature of the incentive or moral hazard problem is as follows. Since θ cannot be observed the payment must be expressed as conditional on x. If P naively seeks to implement the solution derived in this section, he could find $x = x(a^*, \theta)$, and offer A the payment schedule $y^*[x(a^*, \theta)]$, that is, he rewards A upon the occurrence of an observed x on the assumption that $a = a^*$ and that the observed x is derived from the distribution $x(a^*, \theta)$. If A is individually rational, he will then solve the problem:

$$\max_a \int_0^1 v(y^*[x(a, \theta)], a) f(\theta) \, d\theta \tag{AR}$$

that is, he will choose an a in the light of the income distribution which will result under the payment schedule $y^*(x)$. But there is no guarantee in general that the solution to (AR), which we can denote by $\hat{a}$, is the same as a^*, the solution to (FB). For example, if P is risk-neutral $y^*(x) = \beta$. But substituting into v in (AR) will result[15] in $\hat{a} = 0$: why should A incur any disutility if he will be paid anyhow? More generally, the solution to (AR) must satisfy the condition:

$$E\left[v_y\left(\frac{dy^*}{dx} x_a + \frac{v_a}{v_y}\right)\right] = 0 \tag{13}$$

---

[14] Grossman and Hart (1983) use the idea of the cost of inducing A to choose some a extensively to develop a wide set of interesting results for a special case of the principal-agent problem, in which A's utility function takes the form $v(y, a) \equiv G(a) + K(a) V(y)$, encompassing both additive ($K(a) \equiv 1$) and multiplicative ($G(a) \equiv 0$) separability, and where the action a affects the probabilities of occurrence of a fixed, finite set of outcomes rather than the values of the outcomes themselves.

[15] In this case strictly the nonnegativity condition $a \geqslant 0$ would have to be added to AR, otherwise $v_a < 0$ implies $\hat{a} \to \infty$.

This can be compared to the condition determining a^* which, from (8) and (9) is

$$E\left[u'\left(x_a + \frac{v_a}{v_y}\right)\right] = 0 \qquad (14)$$

In income terms, the marginal product of a to A is $(dy^*/dx)x_a$, since the effect on his own income of a change in x is determined *via* the payment schedule, while to P the marginal product of a is x_a, given y. Since, from (4) $dy^*/dx < 1$ at a^*, the two differ in their valuation of the marginal product of a quite apart from the differences in their marginal utilities of income.

Intuitively, the problem is that since P's choice of a is not optimal for A given the associated payment schedule $y^*(x)$, it will be possible for A to make himself better off by choosing $a \neq a^*$ if he can do this unobserved and unpenalized. This is the moral hazard problem. Before examining how P must deal with this, we consider two cases in which the incentive problem does not arise. The first is that in which A is risk-neutral. Here the first-best solution is available essentially because when P gives A the first-best payment schedule. A's optimal choice of a is the first-best level of a, so the incentive constraint is in effect not binding. The second case is where, although a cannot be observed perfectly, it can be observed with a random error *which is independent of θ*. In this case, by means of a forcing contract, the first best is again available.

A is Risk-Neutral

Harris and Raviv (1978) and Shavell (1979) show that if A is risk neutral, so that v_y is a constant, then P can achieve a first-best allocation and no incentive problem arises. This can be expressed in the form of the proposition that if A is risk neutral, a contract which specifies y contingent *only* on x is at least as good as one which makes y contingent on a and θ as well as x. Thus, information about a or θ has no value, or, to put this another way, it does not matter if a and θ cannot be observed. Here we will give a simple account of the proposition which brings out its essential point.

Recall that first-best risk-sharing when A is risk-neutral requires that P retain a fixed payment γ and A receive the residual uncertain income $x(a, \theta) - \gamma$. The condition for first-best optimal choice of a, from (12), is

$$E[x_a] = -\frac{E[v_a]}{v_y}$$

If now, even though a is not observable, P offers A the *same* payment schedule (i.e. asks for the same fixed payment γ) then A will

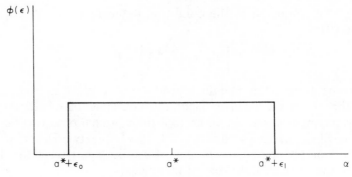

Fig. 3. Observable $\alpha = a + \epsilon$

choose a to solve

$$\max_{a} \int_{0}^{1} v(x(a, \theta) - \gamma, a) f(\theta) \, d\theta \qquad (ARN)$$

which, with v_y constant, yields precisely condition (12). Thus, in this case, A's choice of a does *not* differ from P's given the payment schedule. A will of course accept the fee schedule $x(a, \theta) - \gamma$, because, since γ is derived from the solution to the first-best problem, it satisfies the reservation utility constraint. Essentially then, the incentive constraint described previously is non-binding at P's optimum.

4. *Imperfectly Observable a*

A relaxation of the assumption of nonobservable a, which turns out to have strong implications, was suggested by Harris and Raviv (1976, 1978).[16] Suppose that P can observe a random variable $\alpha = a + \epsilon$, where ϵ has zero mean and probability $\phi(\epsilon) > 0$ on some interval $[\epsilon_0, \epsilon_1]$ and zero elsewhere. Thus there is a kind of measurement error in P's observation of a. The key point is that ϵ is independent of θ, the state of the world. Then it is easy to show that P can adopt a forcing contract to achieve the first-best solution, and so a moral hazard problem does not really arise. Suppose for example that ϵ is uniformly distributed over $[\epsilon_0, \epsilon_1]$, as illustrated in Figure 3, where a^* is again P's first-best value of a. It is of course assumed that P knows the function $\phi(\epsilon)$. Then P need simply threaten an arbitrarily low y[17] if he observes some $\alpha < a^* + \epsilon_0$, since this occurs

---

[16] See also the comments by Shavell (1978), fn. 4, and Holmström (1978), p. 75.

[17] For example, a 'Stalinist' solution might have A taken out and shot.

if and only if $a < a^*$. Since A will not choose $a > a^*$, for a given payment schedule, he will then choose a^*.

If $\phi(\epsilon)$ was *not* positive only on an interval, i.e. if it were positive everywhere on the real line (for example, if ϕ is the normal distribution), then P is involved in a problem of hypothesis testing. At its simplest, this would involve choosing some critical value, α^*, such that an observation $\alpha < \alpha^*$ would be taken to indicate $a < a^*$ even though there is some positive probability that $a = a^*$. Hence P would have to weigh up the losses from 'type 1' and 'type 2' errors – respectively, the errors of falsely rejecting $a = a^*$ and of falsely accepting that – in choosing α^*. This problem does not appear to have received explicit attention in the literature, possibly because in outline it looks less interesting than the case in which P observes not a simple distorted value, but rather a variable z which depends upon *both* a and θ. The implication of such a possibility of observation will be considered in Section 6, below. First, we consider the solution to the mixed risk-sharing and incentive problem.

5. *Solutions to the Principal-Agent Problem*

We now assume that P can observe only the outcome x and has no information whatever about a and θ. Then his problem is taken to be that of choosing a payment schedule $y^*(x)$ which maximizes his expected utility, taking into account the constraint that A must receive at least his reservation utility and will, given any $y(x)$, choose an a which maximizes his own expected utility.

A formal approach to this problem would be to take the problem *FB* and append to it condition (13) as a constraint, implying that P's choice of $y(x)$ will now take account of its effect on A's choice of a *via* A's maximization condition. This indeed was the approach adopted by Harris and Raviv (1976), Ross (1973), and Spence and Zeckhauser (1971). It turns out, however, that this problem is not well-behaved. If $y(x)$ is not restricted to some finite interval at each x, an optimal solution to the problem may well not exist, as shown by Mirrlees (1975). If $y(x)$ *is* restricted to a finite interval, as is quite reasonable, the derivative $y'(x)$ which appears in condition (13) may not in fact exist at all points. Since the approach to solution of the problem, based on the calculus of variations, takes $y'(x)$ as a control variable in solving the problem, this is a serious weakness.

An alternative approach, suggested by Mirrlees (1974, 1975), and developed further by Holmström (1978) gets around this difficulty by eliminating θ from the problem and regarding x itself as the basic random variable with respect to which expected values are taken. Thus, given some a, there is an x for each θ with associated probability density $f(\theta)$. Then the function $x(a, \theta)$ and the density func-

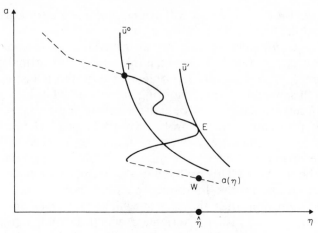

Fig. 4. Non-uniqueness of a for given η

tion $f(\theta)$ jointly determine a probability distribution for x. An increase in a is taken to shift this distribution rightward, with the proviso, required on technical grounds, that the upper and lower bounds of its distribution, which will be at $x_1 \equiv x(a, 1)$ and $x_0 \equiv x(a, 0)$ respectively, are invariant to changes in a. This means that however much a the agent chooses, the outcome x is unchanged in the most favorable state $\theta = 1$, and the least favorable state $\theta = 0$.

It turns out, however, that this approach does not guarantee the uniqueness of a solution to condition (13), i.e. there may be multiple solutions to A's problem of maximizing his expected utility subject to a *given* payment schedule $y(x)$, and this may in turn imply that the conditions for a solution to the principal-agent problem derived under the Mirrlees–Holmström procedure do not in fact characterize an optimum. This is neatly illustrated[18] by a diagram in Grossman and Hart (1983), and reproduced here as Figure 4. In the figure, η refers to a payment schedule (*not* a value of y) ranked in (continuous) order of P's preference from left to right, and a is again A's action. The possibility of multiple choice of a for given payment schedule η is reflected in the shape of the curve $a(\eta)$, which illustrates A's choice of a for each η. However, given any η, A will choose only an a on the dotted portion of the curve because he prefers less a to more and so these points dominate the others. P's indifference curves are as shown (though a is not a direct argument of u it enters indirectly *via* x). Then, the Mirrlees–Holmström procedure characterizes P's

---

[18] From a suggestion by Andreu Mas-Colell. The recognition of the non-uniqueness problem itself is attributed to an unpublished paper, Mirrlees (1975).

optimum as being at point E in the figure, since it yields the highest utility of all the points which satisfy A's first-order condition (13), but T is in fact the true optimum, since it is the best point for P out of the points which he can actually induce A to choose – setting $\hat{\eta}$ would induce point W, not E. The existence of this possibility is a pity[19] since, as Holmström shows, the procedure he adopts leads to a relatively simple characterization of an optimal solution to the principal-agent problem.

It would seem from this discussion that only two courses are open. One could guarantee a well-behaved problem by making some more-or-less drastic simplification of the structure.[20] Alternatively, one could assume the uniqueness problem does not exist and just enjoy the niceness of the results that follow. In a certain sense the problem is purely a theoretical one: if P knows $v(y, a)$ and $x(a, \theta)$, then he knows the relationship between A's choice of a and any payment schedule that might be chosen, and so, in principle at least, could always find a global optimum. For example, in Figure 4, if P knows the curve $a(\eta)$, then why should *he* be fooled into choosing point E? However, given our analytical concerns the problem is a substantive one: we wish to characterize an optimal solution using standard procedures and have to take seriously the risk that they do not work properly for all cases.

Here we provide an exposition of the Holmström–Mirrlees approach, since, taken across the literature, this seems to combine the most general form of problem-structure with the simplest statement of the results, one which gives a clear insight into the effects of introducing the incentive constraint. Thus:

(i) $v(y, a) \equiv v_1(y) - v_2(a)$, the additive separability assumption.

(ii) Take x as the random variable, whose distribution is derived

---

[19] The non-uniqueness problem is not hard to establish. To guarantee a unique global solution to the problem

$$\max J(a) \equiv \int_0^1 v(y\,[x(a, \theta)], a)\, f(\theta)\, d\theta$$

we require J to be strictly concave in a for all a but:

$$J''(a) = \int_0^1 \left\{ y'x_a \left[v_{yy} y'x_a + 2v_{ya} + \frac{v_{aa}}{y'x_a} \right] + v_y x_a^2 y'' + v_y y'x_{aa} \right\} f(\theta)\, d\theta$$

which cannot be signed in general because the sign of y'' is not known. Certainly multiple local optima cannot be ruled out and Mirrlees' example shows that they can plausibly exist.

[20] Thus Grossman and Hart take a special form of the v-function, assume P is risk-neutral (although most of their results generalize), take a finite set of outcomes $\{x_1, \ldots, x_n\}$ independent of a, and make the associated probabilities $\{f_1, \ldots, f_n\}$ functions of a. Holmström assumes the v-function is additively separable in y and a and takes a fixed interval of x-values over which the probability distribution changes with a, though, as already noted, this is still not sufficient to guarantee uniqueness.

from $x(a, \theta)$ and $f(\theta)$, and is written $\phi(x, a)$. It remains the case that the payment schedule is expressed in terms of the observable variable, x. However, x itself is now invariant to a, since it is in essence the state variable.

(iii) An important property of ϕ is: $\phi(x, a) \equiv 0$ for $x \notin [x_0, x_1]$, for all a, and $\phi(x, a) > 0$ for $x \in [x_0, x_1]$.

Figure 5 illustrates the assumed type of behavior of ϕ as a changes. For higher a the whole distribution shifts to the right, but with unchanged support, $[x_0, x_1]$. Note that, for given x, it is assumed:

(iv) The derivatives ϕ_a, ϕ_{aa} are well defined, with $\phi_a \lessgtr 0$, as the figure illustrates. Thus, increased a makes low values of x less, and high values of x more probable.

(v) The distribution resulting from a higher value of a is always preferred by P to one resulting from a lower value of a. Thus increasing a leads to 'better' distributions of x.

The incentive constraint now is the first-order condition for solution of the problem of maximizing A's expected utility w.r.t. a, i.e.

$$\max_a \int_{x_0}^{x_1} v_1[\hat{y}(x)]\, \phi(x, a)\, \mathrm{d}x - v_2(a) \qquad (A)$$

yielding:[21]

$$\int_{x_0}^{x_1} v_1[\hat{y}(x)]\, \phi_a(x, a)\, \mathrm{d}x - v_2'(a) = 0 \qquad (15)$$

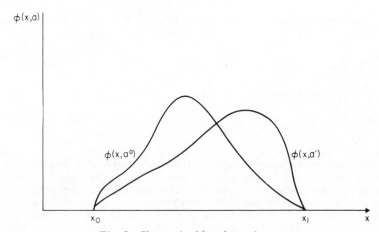

Fig. 5. Change in $\phi(x, a)$ as a increases

where $\hat{y}(x)$ is any given payment schedule. Given (15), P now has the problem of finding a function $y(x)$ to solve

$$\max_{y(x),\,a} \int_{x_0}^{x_1} u(x - y(x))\, \phi(x,a)\, \mathrm{d}x$$

$$\text{s.t.} \int_{x_0}^{x_1} v_1[y(x)]\, \phi(x,a)\, \mathrm{d}x - v_2(a) \geqslant \bar{v}^0$$

$$(PA)$$

$$v_2'(a) = \int_{x_0}^{x_1} v_1[y(x)]\, \phi_a(x,a)\, \mathrm{d}x$$

where the first constraint is again A's reservation utility and the second is the incentive constraint from (15). It should be recalled that x is *not* a variable in this optimization — it plays the same role as did θ in the earlier problem. Then, associating multipliers λ and μ (not dependent on x) with the respective constraints we have the conditions:[22]

$$\{-u' + \lambda v_1'\}\, \phi(x,a) + \mu v_1' \phi_a(x,a) = 0 \qquad (16)$$

$$\int_{x_0}^{x_1} u\phi_a\, \mathrm{d}x + \lambda\left[\int_{x_0}^{x_1} v_1\phi_a\, \mathrm{d}x - v_2'\right] + \mu\left\{\int_{x_0}^{x_1} v_1\phi_{aa}\, \mathrm{d}x - v_2'' = 0\right\} \quad (17)$$

First note that in (17), the middle term in square brackets is zero from the incentive constraint. The conditions can then be written:

$$\frac{u'}{v_1'} = \lambda + \mu\phi_a/\phi \qquad (18)$$

$$E[u\phi_a] = -\mu E[\mathrm{d}^2 v/\mathrm{d}a^2] \qquad (19)$$

where

$$E[\mathrm{d}^2 v/\mathrm{d}a^2] \equiv \int_{x_0}^{x_1} v_1\phi_{aa}\, \mathrm{d}x - v_2''$$

is a notation designed to bring out the fact that the incentive constraint is of the form $E[\mathrm{d}v/\mathrm{d}a] = 0$, and the third term in (17) is then simply the derivative of this w.r.t. a. It can be shown (see Holm-

[21] The usefulness of the separability condition on v can be seen in the simplicity of condition (15).

[22] Strictly we should take account of the constraint that $y(x)$ lies in some closed interval at each x, e.g. $0 \leqslant y \leqslant x$. For simplicity, I assume here that the solution is always at an interior point of such an interval. The conditions are obtained by differentiating through by y for each x, and differentiating through by a for all x (since a is chosen before x is known, y after).

ström, p. 90), that $\mu > 0$, so the incentive condition represents a binding constraint[23] on P. (18) then shows that risk-sharing will not be Pareto-efficient (compare condition (1)) and is distorted by the need to take account of the incentive effects on A, i.e. the effect of the choice of y, given x, on A's choice of a and hence the effect on the probability of getting x, ϕ_a. The simplicity of the earlier results on the form of the risk-sharing contract is also lost: this now cannot be completely determined by the attitudes to risk, but will also depend in general on how ϕ_a and ϕ vary with x, i.e. on the underlying functions $f(\theta)$ and $x(a, \theta)$.[24]

However, Holmström is able to establish some interesting results on the precise way in which the payment schedule will change as a result of the incentive constraint, and these can be described quite simply if we redefine the problem slightly. Interpret λ now *not* as the multiplier associated with the reservation utility constraint, but simply as a *fixed weight* given to A's expected utility[25] in forming the maximand of the problem:

$$\max_{y(x),\, a} \int_{x_0}^{x_1} u\phi \, dx + \lambda \int_{x_0}^{x_1} \{v_1 - v_2\} \, \phi \, dx \text{ s.t.} \int_{x_0}^{x_1} \frac{dv}{da} \phi \, dx = 0 \quad (PA')$$

The solution to this problem is evidently identical in form to conditions (18) and (19), but we have the added advantage that λ is now a

---

[23] It is easy to verify for Holmström's model that, as we saw earlier, if P solves his first-best problem then the incentive constraint will not be satisfied in general. Thus, in the present case we would have

$$\max_{y(x),\, a} \int_{x_0}^{x_1} u(x - y(x)) \, \phi(x, a) \, dx \text{ s.t.} \int_{x_0}^{x_1} v_1 [y(x)] \, \phi(x, a) \, dx - v_2(a) \geq \bar{v}^0$$

yielding

$$u'/v_1' = \lambda \quad \text{and} \quad E[u\phi_a] + \lambda \{E[v_1\phi_a] - v_2'\} = 0$$

where the second condition clearly differs from the incentive constraint. However, $\mu > 0$ is a rather stronger result than $\mu \neq 0$, and in his proof of this Holmström assumes the second-order condition for problem (A) is satisfied, something which may not be true in general. Also note that where A is risk neutral, in effect $\mu = 0$ because the incentive constraint is not binding.

[24] Thus, differentiating through (18) gives:

$$\frac{dy^*}{dx} = \frac{r_P}{(r_P + r_A)} \frac{u'}{v_1'} + \frac{\mu}{r_A + r_P} \left(\frac{\phi_{ax}}{\phi} - \frac{\phi_a \, \phi_x}{\phi^2} \right)$$

So, for $\mu > 0$, $r_P = 0$ does not imply $dy^*/dx = 0$ unless restrictions are placed on ϕ. This expression may perhaps explain why Grossman and Hart found it not possible to assign even such simple properties as monotonicity to $y(x)$.

[25] In other words, we now simply seek a Pareto optimum relative to the incentive constraint, where λ determines the utility distribution in the final allocation. This latter may, but need not, coincide with $\bar{v}^0$ for A. This problem could have the interpretation that P and A bargain efficiently over the contract, and P does not necessarily get all the gains from trade.

constant (and is certainly non-zero – it is not clear from Holmström's analysis that $\lambda \neq 0$ in general, since having to meet the incentive constraint could lead to A receiving more than $\bar{v}^0$). Then consider condition (18), and note that, because of diminishing marginal utility, $u'(x - y)/v_1'(y)$ is increasing in y for *given* x. Now suppose, for given x, we have the *first-best* $y^*(x)$ such that:

$$\frac{u'(x - y^*(x))}{v_1'(y^*(x))} = \lambda \qquad (20)$$

There are two sets of values of x of interest: first, $X^+ = \{x \mid \phi_a(x,a) > 0\}$ and secondly, $X^- = \{x \mid \phi_a(x, a) < 0\}$ (refer back to Figure 5). Then if we add to (20) the term $\mu \phi_a/\phi$, with λ constant, to obtain (18), we observe, since $\mu > 0$, that u'/v_1' must increase when $\phi_a > 0$, and decrease when $\phi_a < 0$. That is, $y(x) > y^*(x)$ when $x \in X^+$, and $y(x) < y^*$ when $x \in X^-$. Thus the incentive effect requires deviation from optimal risk-sharing by increasing A's payment in states when increased a increases their probability, and by reducing A's share in states when increased a reduces their probability. One implication of this is that a risk-neutral P would not now make a fixed payment to A.

The second-best solution is *strictly* worse for both P and A than the first-best, implying that there are efficiency gains to be had if only a could be observed[26] by P. This then leads to the question: suppose some variable z can be acquired costlessly by P, which gives some kind of information about a. Should it then be incorporated into the contract, in the sense that payment to A should be contingent on observed z, so that y would differ, for *given* x, if z differed? As the next section shows, the answer is yes, in general, even though z may give very imperfect information about a.

6. The Use of Imperfect Information About a

Suppose now that although a and θ cannot be observed directly, there is some variable z which provides information about a in the following specific sense. The value of z depends on a and θ, i.e. we can write $z(a, \theta)$, so that a change in a shifts the entire distribution of z. Then, since we have $x(a, \theta)$, there will, for some given a, be a joint probability distribution of x and z. P is assumed to be able to observe z costlessly, and also to know the joint probability density function, which can be written $\phi(x, z, a)$. Then, the question is,

---

[26] Note that A would *also* benefit from a move to the first-best. This might suggest the thought: then why does A not agree to provide P with the information on his choice of a? The answer is of course that we then have a problem of incentive compatibility: if the contract is made conditional on A's *report* of a then A has an incentive to manipulate this information to his own advantage.

given some outcome for x, will it pay P to use the outcome value of z in determining the payment he makes to A?

On the face of it, it is not immediately obvious that information of this kind necessarily would be incorporated into a contract by making y contingent on both x and z. As Harris and Raviv argue, although the increased information about probable values of a is a benefit, there is also a cost in that this information is uncertain, and so if P and A are risk-averse this may make the incorporation of z into the contract unattractive. However, as Harris and Raviv, Shavell and Holmström show, it is *always* optimal to incorporate such information into the contract when a and θ are not observable (except, as we have already indicated, where A is risk-neutral), so that the benefit of extra information outweighs whatever cost the extra uncertainty might impose (although the assumption that z can be observed costlessly is important here).

For a proof of this proposition the reader is referred to Shavell (1979, appendix, p. 69). Here we adopt the simpler and more transparent approach of Holmström, who incorporates z into P's optimization problem in a straightforward way and then shows how condition (18) is affected.

The problem can now be taken as that of defining a payment schedule $y(x, z)$ where, formally, z, like x, is treated as a state variable. The function $\phi(x, z, a)$ gives the joint probability of x and z given a, and P's problem now becomes

$$\max_{y(x,z),a} \int_{x_0}^{x_1} \int_{z_0}^{z_1} u(x - y(x, z)) \, \phi(x, z, a) \, \mathrm{d}z \, \mathrm{d}x$$

$$\text{s.t.} \int_{x_0}^{x_1} \int_{z_0}^{z_1} v_1(y) \, \phi(x, z, a) \, \mathrm{d}z \, \mathrm{d}x - v(a) \geqslant \bar{v}^0$$

$$\int_{x_0}^{x_1} \int_{z_0}^{z_1} v_1(y) \, \phi_a(x.z.a) \, \mathrm{d}z \, \mathrm{d}x - v'(a) = 0 \qquad (PAz)$$

which differs from the previous formulation (PA) only in that expectations must be taken with respect to the joint distribution of the random variables x and z. Since we maximize w.r.t. y at each pair of values (x, z) we obtain as the counterpart to (18):

$$\frac{u'}{v_1'} = \lambda + \mu \, \frac{\phi_a(x, z, a)}{\phi(x, z, a)} \qquad (21)$$

Thus, if ϕ_a/ϕ varies with z, the payment P will make to A on observation of x will now be modified in the light of the observation of z. For example, if ϕ_a varies inversely with z, the payment P makes to A for a given x will be lower when z is incorporated into the contract than when it is not. The essential reason for incorporating z into the contract is not that it provides additional information about the likely value of a – after all, given the payment schedule, P knows exactly what that will be – but rather because it provides a more discriminating way of giving A an incentive to increase his value of a. Or, equivalently, it reduces the cost to P of providing A with the right kind of incentive. This can be put intuitively in the following way. If the contract depends on x alone, then, given the distribution $\phi(x, a)$ a high value of x could be observed, and a correspondingly high payment made to A, with given probability, even though a is low. Similarly, a low value of x could be observed and a low payment made even when A chooses a high a. Each of these possibilities is undesirable from the point of view of providing an incentive to A to choose high a. If now some variable z is observable, whose value, let us assume, also increases with a and θ, it becomes less likely that high values of *both* x and z would be observed when a is in fact low, and also less likely that low values of *both* x and z would be observed when a is in fact high. Thus, incorporating z into the contract reduces the chance of wrongly rewarding low a and wrongly penalizing high a. This improves the incentive properties of the contract.[27]

7. Conclusions to Part 1

In this part of the paper we have set out what may be regarded as the 'basic' principal-agent model and have explained the main results on contracts which have been derived from this. Where a is either directly observable or observable up to a bonded random error, a first-best risk-sharing contract is feasible, which will involve a clause penalizing A for choosing an a below the optimal level. In this case if A is risk-neutral P retains a fixed sum and A bears all the risk; if P is risk-neutral A receives a fixed sum and P bears all the risk. Indeed, if A is risk-neutral then the first-best is available to P even when he

---

[27] For example, suppose A can choose a from the set $\{1, 2, 3\}$, and the following distributions of x and z are then possible:

$a =$	1	2	3
$x = 0$	0.8	0.5	0.2
$x = 1$	0.2	0.5	0.8
$z = 0$	0.9	0.5	0.1
$z = 1$	0.1	0.5	0.9

where x can be only either 0 or 1 and likewise for z. Then under a contract based on x alone, A could be rewarded for a 'high' effort level, even when he sets $a = 1$, with a probability of 0.2, but this could only happen with a probability of 0.02 if z is incorporated into the contract. Likewise A could be penalized for a low value of x with a probability of 0.2 even if he had set $a = 3$, while this probability falls to 0.02 if z is incorporated. Thus, use of the information on z allows better design of the contract.

cannot observe a, since A, in acting in his own interests, will choose the first-best value of a provided P offers him the first-best fixed payment. The incentive problem proper then arises when A is risk averse and neither a nor θ is observable. In that case there is a genuine second-best problem. The optimal contract now must take account of the need to influence A's choice of a – the incentive requirement – and so will have to provide for a different payment schedule than that which optimally shares risk. For example, a risk-neutral P would not now pay A a fixed sum. In general, the incentive requirement calls for a higher payment to A at relatively high values of x and a lower payment at relatively low values of x, as compared to optimal risk-sharing, in order to induce A to increase a from the below-optimal level which his distaste for a would otherwise lead him to choose. Finally, if there is costlessly available information on some variable z whose distribution of values depends on a, the optimal second-best contract will always incorporate this to make the payment to A contingent on both x and z, essentially because it reduces the chances of wrongly rewarding A for low a, and wrongly penalizing him for high a, and thus improves the incentive properties of the contract.

There have been a number of interesting extensions to the 'basic' model in the recent journal literature, and there are also some possible extensions, not yet made, which could be discussed. However, it would seem most useful to consider these at the conclusion of this paper, after we have examined some applications of the basic model. This is the subject of Part 2.

REFERENCES

Borch, K. (1962). 'Equilibrium in a Reinsurance Market', *Econometrica*, Vol. 30, No. 3, pp. 424-44.
Davis, O. A. and Whinston, A. B. (1962). 'Welfare Economics and the Theory of the Second Best', *Review of Economic Studies*.
Grossman, S. J. and Hart, O. D. (1983). 'An Analysis of the Principal–Agent Problem', *Econometrica*, Vol. 51, No. 1, pp. 7-45.
Hammond, P. (1979). 'Straightforward Individual Incentive Compatibility in Large Economies', *Review of Economic Studies*, Vol. 46, pp. 263-82.
Harris, M. and Raviv, A. (1976). 'Optimal Incentive Contracts with Imperfect Information', Carnegie Mellon University, mimeo.
Harris, M. and Raviv, A. (1979). 'Optimal Incentive Contracts with Imperfect Information', *Journal of Economic Theory*, Vol. 20, pp. 231-59.
Holmström, B. (1979). 'Moral Hazard and Observability', *Bell Journal of Economics*, Vol. 10, pp. 74-91.
Lipsey, R. G. and Lancaster, K. (1956/7). 'The General Theory of the Second Best', *Review of Economic Studies*, pp. 11-32.

Mirrlees, J. (1974). 'Notes on Welfare Economics, Information and Uncertainty', in Balch, McFadden and Wu (eds.), *Essays in Economic Behavior Under Uncertainty*, Amsterdam, North Holland Publishing Co.

Mirrlees, J. A. (1975). 'The Theory of Moral Hazard and Unobservable Behaviour – Part I', Nuffield College, Oxford, mimeo.

Ross, S. (1973). 'The Economic Theory of Agency: The Principal's Problem', *American Economic Review*, Vol. 63, pp. 134-9.

Ross, S. (1974). 'On the Economic Theory of Agency and the Principle of Similarity', in Balch, McFadden and Wu (eds.), *Essays in Economic Behavior Under Uncertainty*, Amsterdam, North Holland Publishing Co.

Shavell, S. (1979). 'Risk-sharing and Incentives in the Principal-Agent Relationship', *Bell Journal of Economics*, Vol. 10, pp. 55-73.

Spence, M. and Zeckhauser, R. (1971). 'Insurance, Information and Individual Action', *American Economic Review*, Vol. 61, pp. 380-7.

THE THEORY OF PRINCIPAL AND AGENT
PART 2

Ray Rees

1. INTRODUCTION

In Part 1 of this paper (published in the previous issue of this journal) I set out a model of the principal–agent relationship and examined the main results on the optimal forms of contract under varying assumptions about the nature of the informational asymmetries that were present. In this second part I go on to examine first some models which can be viewed as applications of the basic structure considered so far. This structure is concerned essentially with the type of incentive problem known, in the literature in insurance markets, as *moral hazard*. A second type of incentive problem, that of *adverse selection*, also tends to be present in principal–agent relationships, and so section 5 of this paper considers how the model can be revised to handle this. The paper concludes with a brief discussion of some further theoretical generalizations currently appearing in the literature, and of possible directions for further work.

2. SOCIAL INSURANCE FOR RISKY PRODUCTION

One of the earliest analyses of the principal–agent problem was carried out by James Mirrlees (1974). Although not presented as such – it was posed as a problem in welfare economics under uncertainty – its structure conforms very closely to the model set out in Part 1 of this paper, and Mirrlees' model was clearly very influential in Holmström's (1978) study of the problem. Suppose we have a large number of producer/consumers who are identical in respect both of their utility and production functions. Production is subject to random shocks which are identically and independently distributed (i.i.d.) across producers. Thus at any point in time some producers will have high output and consumption, others low output and consumption – in the absence of government intervention each producer consumes his own output in this one-good economy. Each producer therefore takes the role of the agent, while the principal is a planner

70

who seeks to redistribute output across producers given the realization of any one set of outputs actually produced. In the notation of Part 1 of this paper a is a producer's input level, y the consumption he receives from the planner, x is his output level, and $\phi(x, a)$ gives the probability density of x for each a. Precisely the same assumptions on ϕ and on each producer's utility function $v_1(y) - v_2(a)$ are made as in section 5 of Part 1. The principal's optimization problem is, however, specified a little differently because of the interpretation of the problem. The planner seeks to maximize a social welfare function which is identical with the expected utility of each producer in line with an individualistic specification of the social welfare function. In addition, the condition that A must receive some minimum utility is replaced by one requiring 'budget balance' – the redistribution policy must satisfy the condition that aggregate consumption equal aggregate production.

The assumption of identical individuals and i.i.d. shocks allows the problem to be formulated quite simply in terms of the utility and production of just one individual – we can proceed *as if* there were just one agent.[1] Thus the *first-best* problem is:

$$\max_{y, a} \int_{x_0}^{x_1} v_1(y) \, \phi(x, a) \, \mathrm{d}x - v_2(a) \qquad (MFB)$$

$$\text{s.t.} \int_{x_0}^{x_1} x\phi(x, a) \, \mathrm{d}x - \int_{x_0}^{x_1} y\phi(x, a) \, \mathrm{d}x \leqslant 0$$

where the constraint requires average consumption not to exceed average production.[2] The consumption given to each producer, y, of course depends on observed output x. The solution to this problem requires:

$$v'(y^*(x)) = \lambda$$

where λ is the multiplier associated with the constraint. Thus at the optimal input level a^* each producer's marginal utility of income must be the same across all x. Since we assume producer risk aversion, $v_1'' < 0$ and so the condition requires a constant y^* for all x. The constraint then implies that this must equal the mean output at a^*. Thus in the first best solution, optimal social insurance implies that a producer who does better than average should hand over the excess of his output over the mean, and one who does worse will

[1] Thus although there are in principle many agents this is not in any real sense a 'multi-agent model'. For discussion of recent work on these, see section 6 below.

[2] Strictly, the constraint should specify that for *each* realization of x, total consumption of all producers cannot exceed total production. However, presentation and analysis of the problem are much simplified by supposing that the number of producers is sufficiently large and production shocks sufficiently small to allow averaging over realizations of x.

have his consumption made up to the mean. We have perfect risk-pooling.

The incentive problem is then obvious: since each producer is guaranteed the mean consumption whatever his output and a yields disutility he has an incentive to reduce a and plead bad luck. Thus we have to introduce an incentive constraint in the form of the producer's first-order condition for an expected utility maximum with respect to a, for given y, i.e. we must attach to the problem the constraint

$$\int_{x_0}^{x_1} v_1 \phi_a \, dx - v_2' = 0$$

Re-solving the planner's problem with this added constraint we obtain, as the counterpart to condition (18) of section 5 in Part 1:

$$\frac{\lambda}{v_1'} = 1 + \mu \frac{\phi_a}{\phi} \tag{1}$$

where μ is the multiplier associated with the incentive constraint. It can be shown that on the assumptions of this model both λ and μ are positive. Using precisely the argument applied to equation (20) of Part 1, we can show that as x increases, the left-hand side of (1) must increase, requiring v_1' to fall and, given $v_1'' < 0$, y must then increase. Thus the first-best redistribution policy has to be modified to provide an appropriate incentive, by giving a producer low consumption when his output is low, and increasing it when his output is high: low outputs are penalized and high outputs rewarded.

Figure 1 brings out the nature of the optimal redistribution policy. In (a) of the figure, $v_1'(\bar{x})$ shows the first-best marginal utility and moving anti-clockwise around the figure shows the resulting consumption value $\bar{y}$. Under the second-best solution, $h(x)$ shows the kind of relationship between realized output and marginal utility implied by (1), and with the marginal utility function as shown in (b) this maps into the payoff function $y^*(x)$ in (d). The precise form of the function $h(x)$ depends on λ, μ, and, in particular on the behaviour of the ratio ϕ_a/ϕ as x increases, given that a is set at its optimal value $\hat{a}$, i.e. $h(x)$ depends on the distribution $\phi(x, \hat{a})$.

As Mirrlees shows, the applicability of this approach (described in Part 1 of this paper as the Mirrlees–Holmström procedure) does depend quite vitally on the form of $\phi(x, a)$. Thus recall that a property of ϕ is that increasing a reduces the probability of low values of x and increases that of higher values, so that ϕ_a is negative for some x and positive at others. But condition (1) requires that ϕ_a must not become 'too' negative, since the left-hand side is always positive. Mirrlees shows that in a quite reasonable example of a log-

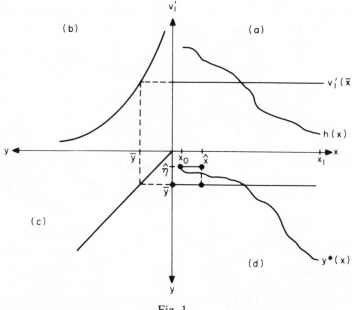

Fig. 1.

normal output distribution, ϕ_a/ϕ tends to $-\infty$ as x goes to zero, implying that (1) can only hold if $\mu = 0$, i.e. it prescribes the first-best policy which we know cannot be optimal. Mirrlees then shows that in such a case the planner should adopt the following policy, illustrated in Figure 1. Choose a low value of x, say $\hat{\chi}$, and a corre-spondingly low value of y, say $\hat{\eta}$. Then any producer experiencing output $x \leqslant \hat{\chi}$ will receive $\hat{\eta}$. The choice of $\hat{\chi}$ and $\hat{\eta}$ is made to give a suitably small proportion of producers who will be heavily penalized in this way. The remaining producers will receive the first-best con-sumption y^*. Thus the optimal $y(x)$ function is the discontinuous one:

$$y(x) = \hat{\eta} \qquad x \in (x_0, \hat{\chi}]$$
$$y(x) = \bar{x}(a^*) \quad x \in (\hat{\chi}, x_1]$$

Then by this policy *all* producers can be induced to choose the first-best effort level a^*: the threat of a sufficiently low consumption, although it will be imposed upon any one producer with small probability, is enough to induce socially optimal behaviour by everyone.

The problem with this kind of policy, which could perhaps be called a 'policy of savage reprisal', is its ethical unacceptability. If the policy is effective, everyone supplies the socially optimal a^*, no-one shirks, and yet those to whom fate deals the unkindest blows are the ones punished by low consumption. It would seem more reasonable to adopt the converse policy: select some x, say $\tilde{\chi}$, and an income $\tilde{\eta}$, such that:

$$y(x) = \bar{x}(a^*) \quad x \in [x_0, \tilde{\chi}]$$

$$y(x) = \tilde{\eta} \quad x \in (\tilde{\chi}, x_1]$$

Thus the incentive to set a^* comes about by rewarding highly the most fortunate, with everyone else consuming the average. Though undoubtedly inegalitarian *ex post*, its *ex ante* equality may make it socially more acceptable. Indeed it may not be very different from the way in which redistribution mechanisms in reality actually work — for the very rich taxation tends to be an optional sacrifice.

3. MORAL HAZARD IN AN INSURANCE MARKET

The analysis of the economics of insurance markets was the specific context in which many of the features of principal–agent problems were first explored. There is quite a large literature on the subject[3] but here we shall focus on a relatively simple model developed by Shavell (1979).

It is often the case that an individual can take some kind of action or incur some expenditure which will affect either the probability of incurring some loss or the size of the loss which can occur. In assessing the premium to charge for insurance against the loss, the insurer will have to assume some value for this action. However, if the individual takes out *full coverage* insurance, under which he will be paid the full amount of the loss in the event it occurs, he loses incentive to take (costly) action to reduce its size or probability. This is the phenomenon known as *moral hazard*. But this of course is simply a name for what we have identified as the incentive problem central to principal–agent relationships when a is not observable. We can identify a as the action the insured takes to safeguard against loss. Examples would be: expenditure on fire prevention or burglar alarms in the case of house insurance; taking exercise and stopping smoking in the case of health or life insurance; and driving carefully and spending money on vehicle maintenance in the case of motor insurance. We would then define x as the individual's wealth contingent on the occurrence of events which cause loss, and $\phi(x, a)$ as the probability distribution of these events given a, with y as the payment the insurer (the 'principal') may make to the insured (the 'agent').

[3] For example see: Arrow (1971, 1963), Ehrlich and Becker (1972), Helpman and Laffont (1975), Spence and Zeckhauser (1970), Stiglitz (1974), Townsend (1976) and Zeckhauser (1970).

In fact, in order to concentrate on aspects of the situation specific to insurance markets further simplifications of the structure can be made. Assume that there are only two possible states of the world. In one a fixed loss L will be incurred and in the other there is no loss. If $\bar{x}$ is A's wealth before the loss then his wealth distribution is $(\bar{x}, \bar{x} - L)$ if he does not insure. Thus $\phi(x, a)$ takes on only two values for any a, so let us define $\phi(a)$ as the probability of *not* incurring a loss and $1 - \phi(a)$ as that of doing so, with $\phi'(a) > 0, a \geqslant 0$. Then y takes on only two values: $y = 0$ with probability $\phi(a)$ and $y \in [0, L]$ with probability $1 - \phi(a)$. This definition of y on the interval $[0, L]$ is made because an important aspect of insurance contracts is the *degree of coverage* they give. The response to the moral hazard problem has been to give less than full coverage, i.e. to set $y < L$, thus leaving the insured to carry some of the risk. This is intended to provide the insured with an incentive to take action to reduce the chance of loss. An insurance contract is then a pair of values (p, y), where $p \geqslant 0$ is the insurance premium, paid whether or not loss occurs, and $y \in [0, L]$ is the payment the insurer makes to the insured. We then want to characterize an optimal insurance contract, paying particular attention to the degree of coverage it implies.

A's wealth will be:

$$x_1 \equiv \bar{x} - p - a \text{ with probability } \phi(a)$$

$$x_2 \equiv \bar{x} - p - a - L + y \text{ with probability } 1 - \phi(a)$$

Note that a further simplification is made by treating a as an expenditure subtracted from wealth, so that A's utility function is now simply $v(x_j)$, $j = 1, 2$. We also simplify the treatment of P's utility. Suppose that the insurer is faced with a large number of identical individuals with i.i.d. risks, and moreover that the insurance market is perfectly competitive with, in particular, no entry barriers. Then in equilibrium insurance contracts must be characterized by the condition that they imply zero expected profit, i.e. we can replace P's utility function by the simple break-even constraint

$$p = (1 - \phi(a)) y \tag{2}$$

so that this 'actuarially fair' premium, for a given payment y, must be charged.

The nature of the incentive problem can be easily seen[4] from the definitions of the x_j and p. If $y = L$, then $x_1 = x_2$, and so A will

---

[4] It is straightforward to show that in the case where no incentive problem exists, i.e. a is observable, the first-best involves full coverage with $y = L$. P solves the problem:

$$\max_{y,a} \phi(a) v(x_1) + (1 - \phi(a)) v(x_2) \text{ s.t. } p = [1 - \phi(a)] y \text{ and } 0 \leqslant y \leqslant L$$

Given the optimal action a^*, after simplification the optimal condition for $y < L$ becomes

$$v'(x_2) = v'(x_1)$$

which cannot be satisfied with $y < L$ since then $x_2 < x_1$ and $v'' < 0$ implies $v'(x_2) > v'(x_1)$. The condition can only be satisfied with $y = L$ and $x_1 = x_2$, i.e. full coverage.

maximize his expected utility by setting $a = 0$; he is quite indifferent to the effect of that on $\phi(a)$. If p in (2) is set on the assumption $a > 0$, therefore, and given $\phi' > 0$, the insurer must lose. If $y < L$, on the other hand, $x_2 < x_1$ and so the probability of loss will matter to A. The incentive constraint as usual results from the maximization of A's expected utility given the terms of the contract, i.e. we solve:

$$\max_{a \geqslant 0} \bar{v} = \phi(a) \, v(x_1) + (1 - \phi(a)) \, v(x_2)$$

yielding

$$\frac{\partial \bar{v}}{\partial a} = [v(x_1) - v(x_2)] \, \phi' - \{\phi v'(x_1) + (1 - \phi) \, v'(x_2)\} \leqslant 0$$

$$a \geqslant 0 \quad a \frac{\partial \bar{v}}{\partial a} = 0 \quad (3)$$

At $x_1 = x_2$ the first term vanishes while $v' > 0$ always, and so with full coverage $\partial v / \partial a < 0$ and $a = 0$ is optimal, as we just saw. With partial coverage $x_1 > x_2$ and so $v(x_1) > v(x_2)$. The first term in (3) can then be interpreted as the marginal expected benefit to A of a small increase in a, while the second term is interpreted as the marginal expected cost (both in terms of utility). Optimal $a > 0$ then equates these.

Let us now assume that $\bar{v}$ is strictly concave in a, so that (3) yields, for each (p, y), a unique solution for a. We can then regard   as a function $a(p, y)$, with $a = 0$ if $y = L$. The principal's problem is then to choose a contract (p, y) which maximizes A's expected utility subject to the break-even constraint (2). It is convenient to eliminate this break-even constraint by solving from:

$$p = (1 - \phi[a(p, y)]) \, y$$

for p as a function of y, $p(y)$, implying in turn the function $\alpha(y) = a(p(y), y)$. Substituting into A's utility function for p and a then gives the single variable maximization problem:

$$\max_{y} \phi(\alpha(y)) \, v(x_1(y)) + (1 - \phi(\alpha(y))) \, v(x_2(y)) \text{ s.t. } 0 \leqslant y \leqslant L \quad (MH)$$

It is worth noting that the problem we have just defined is an inversion of the usual kind of principal–agent problem, in which we maximize P's utility subject to a given utility level for A. Here, P will be indifferent among all contracts which break even, while from that set we find the one which maximizes A's utility. This can again be given an explanation in terms of competitive markets. If P did *not* offer a contract which maximized A's utility then another seller of insurance could always find entry profitable by offering A a preferred contract.

Note also that we do not rule out the possibility that the optimal solution to the *second-best* problem *MH* may involve full coverage. Provided the insurer takes account of the fact that $a = 0$ in that case, so that he sets a premium $p^0 = (1 - \phi(0)) L$, he is quite indifferent to the degree of coverage – all break-even contracts are for him equally good. As we shall see, it may then happen that for A the contract with (p^0, L), under which he sets $a = 0$, may then be optimal. The requirement imposed by the second best problem is only that the optimal values p^*, y^* and a^* be mutually consistent, given A's maximizing behaviour.

The Kuhn–Tucker condition for problem *MH* is:

$$\phi'\alpha'(v(x_1) - v(x_2)) + \phi v'(x_1) x_1' + (1 - \phi) v'(x_2) x_2' \begin{cases} \leqslant 0 \text{ if } y^* = 0 \\ = 0 \text{ if } 0 < y^* < L \\ \geqslant 0 \text{ if } y^* = L \end{cases}$$

$$\text{(4)}$$

We can then define the necessary condition for full coverage to be second-best optimal in the following way. If $y^* = L$ then $x_1 = x_2$ and so the condition becomes:

$$v(x_1) [\phi x_1' + (1 - \phi) x_2'] \geqslant 0 \tag{5}$$

Since $v'(x_1) > 0$ it can be divided out; then differentiating through the definitions of x_1 and x_2 gives, after some simplification, the condition

$$\phi x_1' + (1 - \phi) x_2' = (y^* \phi'(a^*) - 1) \frac{da}{dy} \geqslant 0 \tag{6}$$

It can be shown that $da/dy < 0$, i.e. reducing coverage increases the preventative activity, and so (6) yields, with $y^* = L$ and $a^* = 0$:

$$L\phi'(0) \leqslant 1 \tag{7}$$

Now since $p^0 = (1 - \phi(0)) L$ with y fixed at L, $dp/da = -L\phi'$, and so the left-hand side of (7) represents the marginal benefit, in terms of reduced premium, which would flow from increasing a at the full coverage point. The marginal cost of doing this is of course 1. Thus full coverage is second-best optimal only if the marginal reduction in the fair premium brought about by a small increase in a is less than the marginal cost of a, at the point (p^0, L), with $a = 0$.

A similar argument can be used to show that coverage will never be zero. From (4) we see that $y^* = 0$ is impossible if at that point the expression is positive. With $p = y = 0$ we again have $x_1 = x_2$, the first term in (4) vanishes and the sign of the second depends only on x_1' and x_2'. Differentiating through the definitions and setting

$y^* = 0$ shows that these derivatives are both positive (given $\alpha' < 0$), as required. Intuitively, a small reduction in a at $y = 0$ involves, to the first order, no increase in premium but saves the marginal cost of a.

Finally, condition (6) suggests an interpretation of an interior optimum with $0 < y^* < L$. At the induced value a^* the rate at which premium would fall with increasing a is just equal to the marginal cost of a. This solution will tend to occur where the loss L is very large and the action a is very effective in reducing the probability of loss, since in such a case the condition for full coverage in (7) is unlikely to be satisfied – at zero preventative activity the marginal benefit from premium reduction will exceed the marginal cost of the activity.

In this section we have concentrated on the moral hazard type of incentive problem, by assuming that all buyers of insurance were identical, and that the essential problem was that the insurer could not observe the value of a and so enforce a particular probability of loss $1 - \phi(a)$. A further incentive problem arises when buyers are of different types, i.e. they have different functions $\phi(a)$, and the insurer does not know the precise type to whom he is selling insurance. This is the problem of *adverse selection* and section 5 below considers the general formulation for problems of this kind.

Note finally that the result discussed in Part 1 of this paper, on the value of imperfect information about a, is directly applicable here. If it is possible to acquire information in the form of some random variable z whose distribution depends on a, then the incentive properties of the contract are always improved if y is made conditional on it. If z represents the value of a plus some random measurement error which is bounded below, it will then be possible to enforce a first-best optimal contract provided a large enough penalty can be imposed upon A for an observed z which could not possibly be consistent with the optimal a.

4. FURTHER APPLICATIONS

Space constraints rule out detailed consideration of other applications of the 'basic model', but clearly many are possible. For example we could consider the case of the owner of a firm who delegates decision-taking responsibility to a manager. The counterpart of x would then be profit, which depends on the manager's effort level a and the state of the world θ. The owner's utility depends on profit net of his payment to the manager, and, with the manager's effort unobservable, the problem is to provide the manager with appropriate incentives as well as to share risk. The optimal contract will then specify the manager's payment contingent on profit. If the manager is risk-neutral he can be asked to make a fixed payment to the owner and retain all remaining profit, but if he and the owner are risk averse then both will receive incomes which vary with profits, with the manager receiving larger payments when profits are high and conversely. A type of incentive scheme which is quite common in practice is the *linear* payoff function $y(x) = \alpha + \beta x$, where α would be a 'basic salary' and β a fixed profit share. However, there is nothing in the model to suggest that the second-best optimal payment function is linear, and so clearly real-world incentive mechanisms have to depart from strict optimality to be practicable.

In formal terms a straightforward extension of this model would be to the case in which the firm is a public firm owned by the state and again operated by a manager.[5] The outcome x would then be some measure of social welfare, and a bonus system for the manager could be constructed which maximizes expected social welfare subject to the incentive constraints. An interesting question is why in reality managers of public firms are not offered this type of contract. They are usually paid fixed salaries and such attempts to solve the incentive problem as are made tend to take the form of constraints, intervention in decision-taking and detailed monitoring. In this case principal–agent theory may form the basis for a critique of the institutional structure. On the other hand, the problem of observability of the outcome – 'social welfare' – or of its specification in a way which could be made the basis for an incentive contract, may constitute an insuperable obstacle, and so the actual control mechanisms should be regarded perhaps as the only feasible *type* of mechanism, though possibly capable of improvement.

A classic application of principal–agent theory has been to the case of sharecropping (see in particular Stiglitz (1974)). The principal is the landowner, the agent is the tenant, x is the value of the crop, y is the tenant's share and a is his effort. The theory then provides immediate conclusions concerning the optimal forms of cropsharing contract under the various possible cases defined on whether or not the landowner can observe the state of the world and the tenant's effort, and on the risk-aversion or risk-neutrality of each party.

Finally, we can consider application of the model to the case of stochastic externalities. The agent can be thought of as a firm, x would be the social cost caused by pollution, y would be a fine or pollution charge levied on the firm, a would be the level of some costly pollution-reducing activity, and the principal could be thought of as a 'social planner'. Pollution may be caused by chance as well as by the firm's 'negligence' or expenditure on a. Where a can be ob-

[5] Thus Navajas (1984) considers this model at some length.

served – negligence can be assessed up to a bounded random error – the first-best levels of pollution and preventative activity are attainable by means of a forcing contract. If the planner is risk-neutral while the firm is risk-averse, this should involve a fixed payment by the firm – a 'pollution licence fee'. Where negligence cannot be assessed – a is non-observable – then a penalty schedule based on pollution damage alone must be constructed, which at high pollution levels penalizes the firm more heavily than in the first best, and at low pollution levels does so less heavily. The model thus provides a useful framework within which to consider the debate concerning the precise ways of controlling stochastic externalities.

5. ADVERSE SELECTION MODELS IN PRINCIPAL-AGENT THEORY

So far in this paper I have concentrated on the situation in which the agent has to take an action which is unobservable by the principal – the moral hazard problem. However, there is a second type of informational asymmetry which can also characterize principal-agent relationships. This is where the agent possesses some information prior to choosing an action which, if known by the principal, would influence the choice of action he would like the agent to make. The agent is then required to pass some message to the principal which depends on the 'private information' he has. Since the chosen effort, outcome and payoff to the agent may all depend on the message he transmits, the agent may have an incentive to misrepresent his information. Examples would be where in an insurance market an individual who is a bad risk may seek to represent himself as a good risk, or in a labour market an individual with low productivity may represent himself as having high productivity. The design of the contract will then have to take account of this problem of 'adverse selection'. In this section we consider, in the simplest possible context, the main characteristics of the optimal form of contract in such a case.

The simplest way to adapt the model of Part 1 to this problem is to assume that A knows the state of the world variable, θ, before taking his decision. In addition we suppose that the message he must transmit is a value of θ – we consider only *direct* transmission mechanisms. Following some message $\hat{\theta}$ he will be instructed to take some action $a(\hat{\theta})$ and receive a payoff $y(\hat{\theta})$. In choosing these functions P must take into account the incentive A may have to report a false θ. To simplify the problem further, suppose θ may take one of only two possible values, θ_1 or θ_2, with $\theta_1 < \theta_2$, and also that P is risk-neutral.

The first step in solving the problem is to note that attention may be confined to those contracts which induce A to reveal the true value of θ. This *revelation principle* (Myerson (1979)) follows from the fact that if, under some contract, it is optimal for A to give a false value of θ then another contract can always be defined which induces A to tell the truth and which makes no-one worse off. Thus suppose that when θ_1 is true A finds it optimal to report θ_2, and obtain utility v_2, while when θ_2 is true it is better to report θ_1 and receive v_1. P can then define a new contract by giving A v_2 if he reports θ_1, and v_1 if he reports θ_2. It must then be optimal for A to tell the truth, if it previously was optimal for him to lie, and he is no worse off under the new contract, while P also cannot be worse off than under the previous contract. Thus, any contract which induces A to lie can be replaced by one which induces truth without making anyone worse off, and so attention can be restricted to the class of contracts which induce truth-telling.

The principal's problem can then be represented as:

$$\max_{y_j, a_j} E[x(a_j, \theta_j) - y_j] \text{ s.t. } v_1(y_j) - v_2(a_j) \geqslant v^0$$

$$v_1(y_j) - v_2(a_j) \geqslant v_1(y_i) - v_2(a_i)$$

$$\text{when} \quad \theta = \theta_j \quad i, j = 1, 2 \quad i \neq j \quad (AS)$$

where $y_j = y(\theta_j), a_j = a(\theta_j)$.

The first constraint in the problem ensures A receives his reservation utility for *each* value of θ_j, which assumes that he can reject the contract after he has learned θ (if he does not know θ at the time the contract is concluded). The second constraint imposes the requirement that at the optimal solution (y_j^*, a_j^*), $j = 1, 2$, A must be no worse off when reporting the true θ than when lying.

The nature of the optimal solution to this problem can be most clearly brought out if we use $x_j = x(a_j, \theta_j)$ to derive the function $\alpha(x_j, \theta_j) = a_j$, then substitute for a_j in A's utility function to express it as:

$$v_1(y_j) - v_2(\alpha(x_j, \theta_j)) \equiv v(y_j) - w(x_j, \theta_j)$$

We then consider solutions in the (x_j, y_j)-space, which are of course equivalent to those which would be found in the (a_j, y_j)-space. The main properties of the optimal solution are illustrated in Figure 2 and can be stated as follows:

$$v(y_2^*) - w(x_2, \theta_2) > v(y_1^*) - w(x_1^*, \theta_1) = v^0 \tag{i}$$

The optimal contract gives A his reservation utility in the case where $\theta = \theta_1$, but yields him more than this if $\theta = \theta_2$. To see this, consider A's indifference curves denoted θ_1^0 and θ_2^0 in Figure 2. These repre-

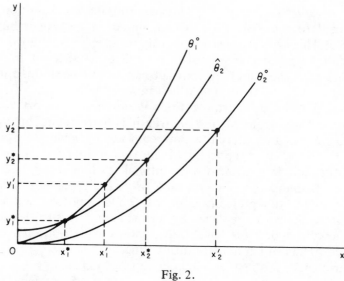

Fig. 2.

sent A's reservation utility – along them A's utility is v^0. θ_2^0 is flatter than θ_1^0 because, by assumption, for *given* x, a falls as θ rises (θ_2 is a 'more productive' state than θ_1) and so less y is needed to yield v^0 in θ_2 than in θ_1. For any x, the higher is y the lower is P's utility and so P would prefer to hold A to his reservation utility if possible. This cannot be done for *both* states, however, but only for θ_1 (the less productive state). Thus suppose P offered the contract (x_1', y_1') if A reports θ_1 and (x_2', y_2') if A reports θ_2. Then clearly A will always report θ_1 since (x_1', y_1') is in the strictly better set of θ_2^0 and (x_2', y_2') is in the strictly worse set of θ_1^0. In other words A would report θ_1 if θ_2 were true because the reduction in a implied by x_1' more than compensates for the fall in income to y_1'.

$$v(y_1^*) - w(x_1^*, \theta_2) = v(y_2^*) - w(x_2^*, \theta_2) \qquad \text{(ii)}$$

The optimal points lie on the indifference curve $\hat{\theta}_2$ which passes through (x_1^*, y_1^*), the optimal solution for θ_1. In that case A is indifferent between reporting θ_1 or θ_2 when θ_2 is true, and so, it is assumed, he will tell the truth. He will certainly report θ_1 if that is true since (x_2^*, y_2^*) is below θ_1^0. Thus given (x_1^*, y_1^*), $\hat{\theta}_2$ is the lowest of A's indifference curves consistent with A's reporting θ_2 when it is true and so (x_2^*, y_2^*) must be on it.

$$(x_1^*, y_1^*) \ll (x_1', y_1') = \text{argmax } x - y \text{ s.t. } v(y_1) - w(x_1, \theta_1) \geqslant v^0$$

$$(x_2^*, y_2^*) = \text{argmax } x - y \text{ s.t. } v(y_2) - w(x_2, \theta_2) \geqslant \hat{v}$$

$$\text{(iii)}$$

where $\hat{v}$ is the value of A's utility along $\hat{\theta}_2$. Thus, suppose P knew that the true state was θ_1. Then he would solve the problem:

$$\max x_1 - y_1 \text{ s.t. } v(y_1) - w(x_1, \theta_1) \geqslant v^0$$

which would have as its solution (x_1', y_1'), since at that point

$$\left.\frac{dy}{dx}\right|_{v^0} \equiv \frac{dw}{dx_1}(x_1', \theta_1) \left/ v_1'(y_1') = 1\right.$$

which is the necessary condition for solution of this problem. (x_1', y_1') could therefore be called the first-best solution if θ_1 is true. Then the optimal *second-best* solution involves lower values of A's payoff, effort, and output than this first best. If θ_2 is true, on the other hand, and given that A must receive the utility $\hat{v} > v^0$ ($\hat{v}$ corresponds to $\hat{\theta}_2$) (x_2^*, y_2^*) can be chosen to solve the problem:

$$\max x_2 - y_2 \text{ s.t. } v(y_2) - w(x_2, \theta_2) \geqslant \hat{v}$$

because *any* point on $\hat{\theta}_2$ is good enough to induce A to report θ_2 and so P can choose the point which is best for himself. Thus we have

$$\left.\frac{dy}{dx}\right|_{\hat{v}} \equiv \frac{dw}{dx_2}(x_2^*, \theta_2) \left/ v_1'(y_2^*) = 1\right.$$

Thus (x_2^*, y_2^*) is first-best relative to $\hat{v}$, but is different from (x_2', y_2'), the first-best in θ_2 relative to v^0. This is because of the assumption that the marginal utility of income v_1' diminishes with income so that at each x successively higher indifference curves have greater slopes. If v_1' were constant then $(x_2^*, y_2^*) = (x_2', y_2')$ and so in θ_2 the solution is first-best relative to all utility levels.

To see why (x_1^*, y_1^*) is less than the first-best pair of values, we can use the following argument. At (x_1', y_1'), the slope of θ_1^0 is 1, and so a small reduction in x_1 can be accompanied by an *equal* reduction in y_1 leaving both A and P no worse off *if* θ_1 is true. On the other hand, this would allow (x_2^*, y_2^*) to be on a lower indifference curve than $\hat{\theta}_2$, i.e. one passing through the new point on θ_1^0, and so P will have a higher utility if θ_2 is true. But in that case P will have a higher *expected* utility by making such a change, and so (x_1', y_1') cannot be an optimal solution to the problem AS. The same argument shows that (x_1^*, y_1^*) cannot be to the right of (x_1', y_1') so it must be to the left.

$$(x_1^*, y_1^*) \ll (x_2^*, y_2^*) \tag{iv}$$

Optimally, A's income, effort and output will be higher in θ_2 than in θ_1. This follows from the implicit assumption that $\hat{\theta}_2$ is everywhere flatter than θ_1^0. If $\hat{\theta}_2$ were steeper than θ_1^0 over some range then this inequality could be revised.

This highly simplified discussion of the problem has served to bring out the main characteristics of the optimal contract in the adverse selection problem. Under the contract the agent's income and effort increase with θ. At the lowest value of θ the agent is held at his reservation utility, but at a higher value he does better than this. Thus, as compared with the situation in which the principal knows which θ is true, the agent does better and the principal worse, while effort and output are lower for all θ. The gains to the agent arising out of the information asymmetry could perhaps be interpreted as the rents he can command from the monopoly of his private information.

As an application and illustration of this model we can consider the 'new Soviet incentive model' introduced into the Soviet economy in the 1970s, and given a succinct exposition in Weitzman (1976). Under the previous system of central planning, enterprises were given a planned output target and then were paid a bonus if actual output exceeded this target. Given that the output target would be based on information on productive potential supplied by the enterprise, it would be in the interests of the enterprise to under-report its productive potential, thus obtaining a bonus without having to exert extra effort. Because of inherent uncertainties in production planning, the excess of actual over planned production could be attributed to chance and extra effort rather than the misrepresentation of productive potential. Thus we have an incentive problem of the type considered in this section.

The solution to the problem embodied in the new Soviet incentive model is as follows. In the preliminary stage of the planning process the planner proposes a tentative production target, say $\bar{x}$, and an associated bonus $\bar{y}$ if that target is met. In the second stage the enterprise responds with its own proposed production target $\hat{x}$ and the *planned* bonus $\hat{y}$ it will receive is then given by the relation

$$\hat{y} = \bar{y} + \beta(\hat{x} - \bar{x}), \beta > 0 \qquad (8)$$

where β is a parameter set by the planners. This of course simply defines the planned bonus as a linear function of the enterprise's own proposed target. In the final *implementation* phase of the planning process, the actual bonus y paid to the enterprise is determined according to the function:

$$y = \begin{cases} \hat{y} + \alpha(x - \hat{x}) & x \geq \hat{x} \\ \hat{y} - \gamma(\hat{x} - x) & x < \hat{x} \end{cases} \qquad (9)$$

where x is actual output. An important feature of the planning process is that the parameters must satisfy the condition:

$$0 < \alpha < \beta < \gamma \qquad (10)$$

The question we consider is the extent to which this type of incentive scheme will solve the incentive problem and lead the enterprise to propose its true productive potential.

We can apply the model set out earlier by supposing there are only two levels of potential output, $\hat{x}_1$ and $\hat{x}_2$, with $x_j = \hat{x}_j + \epsilon, j = 1, 2$ as actual output. ϵ is a random variable with zero mean and finite variance. Weitzman argues that provided the parameters α and γ are appropriately chosen, this scheme *can* solve the incentive problem. Thus consider Figure 3.[6] The dashed line has the slope β, and the lines kinked at $\hat{x}_1$ and $\hat{x}_2$ have left-hand slopes of γ and right-hand slopes of α. Then suppose $\hat{x}_2$ is the true productive potential of the enterprise. If the enterprise under-reports by proposing $\hat{x}_1$, then its actual bonus will lie somewhere along the line kinked at $\hat{x}_1$. If in fact it knew for sure that x will equal $\hat{x}_2$, i.e. the enterprise is not subject to production uncertainty, then, Weitzman argues, it would never report $\hat{x}_1$ because it will do worse than if it reported $\hat{x}_2$. Similarly if $\hat{x}_1$ is true then the enterprise does best by truthfully reporting that. If on the other hand the enterprise also does not know ϵ *ex ante*, it is possible that it might do better by reporting $\hat{x}_1$ when $\hat{x}_2$ is true, since for some $\epsilon_1 > 0$, $\epsilon_2 < 0$, $\hat{x}_1 + \epsilon_1 > \hat{x}_2 + \epsilon_2$. However, given the probability density on ϵ, Weitzman shows that α and γ can always be chosen in such a way as to make this unattractive to the enterprise.

Weitzman is, however, incorrect in arguing that determination of α and γ according to his analysis is alone sufficient to solve the incentive compatibility problem. For simplicity, let us assume that the enterprise is not subject to production uncertainty, so that if it specifies an output $\hat{x}_j$ it can achieve that with certainty. Then the analysis of Figure 2 tells us exactly what the incentive scheme in Figure 3 should look like: we should have, for $j = 1, 2$, $(\hat{x}_j, \hat{y}_j)$ in Figure 3 exactly equal to (x_j^*, y_j^*) in Figure 2, implying a value of β of $(y_2^* - y_1^*)/(x_2^* - x_1^*)$ – though the incentive scheme must not allow intermediate values of x to be chosen because, at this value of β, such (x, y) pairs would lie in the better set of $\hat{\theta}_2$ in Figure 2 and so x_2^* would never be proposed when θ_2 is true.

To see what can go wrong, suppose:

(a) $\beta < (y_2^* - y_1^*)/(x_2^* - x_1^*)$, i.e. $\hat{y}_2 < \hat{y}_2^*$. Then $\hat{x}_2$ will not be proposed when θ_2 is true – the increase in income does not compensate the enterprise for the increase in effort required to produce x_2^* when θ_2 is true.

(b) $\beta > (y_2^* - y_1^*)/(x_2^* - x_1^*)$, i.e. $\hat{y}_2 > y_2^*$. Then if $(\hat{y}_2, \hat{x}_2)$ is in the better set of θ_1^0 in Figure 2, $\hat{x}_1$ will not be proposed although θ_1 is true: the extra income given to the more productive enterprise is

[6] My colleague John Bennett has used this diagram in his teaching for several years and I am grateful for his permission to use it here.

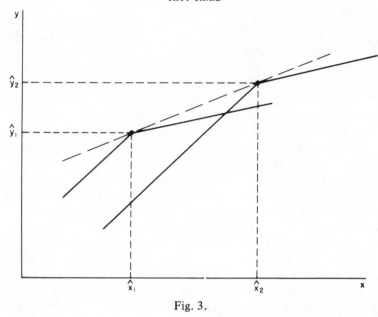

Fig. 3.

more than enough to compensate for the extra effort the less productive enterprise has to put in to appear more productive. Alternatively, if $(\hat{y}_2, \hat{x}_2)$ is in the worse set of θ_1^0, the enterprise will truthfully propose $\hat{x}_j$ when θ_j is true, $j = 1,\ 2$, but the planner is paying too high a price for the truthful revelation of θ_2.

These comments are not intended to detract from the ingenuity of the Soviet incentive scheme. Rather, they are meant to supplement Weitzman's analysis by showing that if the value of β used in the planning process correctly reflects the income–effort preferences of the manager, then indeed the scheme does induce truthful revelation of productive capacity. But calculation of the relation between α, β and γ in the way suggested by Weitzman does not in itself solve the problem.[7]

6. FURTHER THEORETICAL DEVELOPMENTS

The most obvious generalization to the principal–agent models considered so far in this paper is to vary the assumption that a single principal faces a single agent. The case of several principals and one agent (which has not been considered in the literature) seems potentially much the less interesting generalization, even if quite relevant

---

[7] Thus Weitzman suggests (p. 254) that 'if the enterprise knows for sure how much [x] can be produced it will always get the maximum bonus by setting [$\hat{x}$] equal to that value'. We have shown here that this need not be true if the 'wrong' β is set.

in reality: consider for example a firm with several shareholders. The essential problem here would seem to be one of reconciling the conflicts of interest among principals, which would seem to be essentially the problem of constructing a group utility function, after which we have essentially the same problem as before. The problem of 'aggregating' welfare functions has of course been much studied and there seems little of interest specifically to the principal–agent problem.

On the other hand the problem of a single principal with several agents holds out interesting possibilities and has been studied in a number of recent papers.[8] The basic idea is that, as before, each agent will choose an action in the light of the incentive scheme proposed by the principal, and the output of each agent is a function of this action and a random variable. The question is then whether the principal can use information on the output or performance of one agent in the incentive contract of another. A strong form of such an incentive contract is a *tournament*, in which agents are ranked according to their output and rewarded on the basis of their position in the rank order. An interesting question then concerns the conditions under which the principal does better using a tournament than he does under a system of individual second-best optimal incentive contracts.

A problem common to all models is that of specifying the way in which agents choose their actions given their strategic interdependence: the principal–agent model now contains a subgame to be played out among agents. The usual assumption is that the chosen actions constitute a Nash equilibrium of this subgame: under the incentive contract each agent chooses his optimal action treating all others' actions as given. The possibility of collusive behaviour among agents is quite unexplored.

The essential result in this class of models is that where the random variables in agents' output functions are independently distributed then, as we already saw in sections 2 and 3, the individual incentive contracts are also independent[9] and are superior to a tournament; if the random variables are perfectly correlated, i.e. they constitute a 'common shock', then the principal can, if he can threaten a large enough punishment, achieve the first best (see Mookherjee (1984), p. 440). The intuition underlying this result is clear. If the random variables of two agents are perfectly correlated

---

[8] See Demski and Sappington (1984), Green and Stokey (1983), Holmström (1982), Lazear and Rosen (1981), Mookherjee (1984), and Nalebuff and Stiglitz (1983).

[9] In the sense that payment to agent j is independent of output of agent k. Independence of the distributions of the agents' random variables is necessary, as well as sufficient, for Independence of the incentive contracts. For a proof see Mookherjee (1984), p. 438. Intuitively, to make agent i's payment contingent on k's output in this case simply adds pure uncertainty to i's contract with no gain in incentive.

then the one with lower output must have supplied less effort. Therefore, if the agents do not collude, shirking is detectable and, provided a heavy enough punishment can be threatened, it can always be deterred. Finally, since independence of random variables is necessary for independence of contracts, i's contract will depend on j's output when their random variables are correlated, though the first-best will not be achievable when this correlation is less than perfect. Here, another agent's output is playing a role somewhat similar to the random variable z discussed in section 6 of Part 1 of this paper. For example, if the random shocks are strongly positively correlated for two agents, then it is unlikely that the output of one would be very low and that of the other very high when the former is *not* shirking, and so making payments contingent on both outputs improves the incentive properties of the contract.

Even with the generalization to more than one agent, the principal-agent models considered in this paper are still very restrictive in the view they take of the strategic aspects of the situation. The principal is usually seen as a kind of Stackelberg leader: he chooses the contract to maximize his utility given the reaction function of the agent as defined by his maximization condition. As already mentioned, if there are several agents they adopt the zero conjectural variation behaviour which characterizes Cournot–Nash equilibrium. Moreover, each decision-taker is assumed to know the utility function(s) of the other(s) as well as having the same probability density on the random variable(s). Finally, the cases of moral hazard and adverse selection were modelled as distinct types of principal–agent problem, but clearly both types of situation could occur simultaneously – an agent may possess private information, which he reports to the principal, he then must take an action which is not observable by the principal in the face of residual random shocks also not observable by the principal.

A full generalization has been suggested by Roger Myerson (1983), in the form of a model of a *Bayesian game* with incomplete information, as defined by Harsanyi (1967–8), and further developed by Mertens and Zamir (1982). This model takes the following form. Suppose there are n players, indexed $i \in \{1, \ldots, n\}$, with D_i the set of possible actions or decisions for player i. Each player may be of one of a number of possible 'types', t_i, and T_i is the set of all possible types i could be. A type t_i is a complete description of i's information and beliefs about anything relevant to the game, which is not also fully known to other players, i.e. it describes a possible state of i's private information. Each player also possesses a probability distribution on the set of possible types of each other player, where this distribution may also depend on his own type. Finally, each player has a utility function which specifies a utility for each possible set of actions of all players, and each possible set of types of all players, including himself. A Bayesian game of incomplete information is then a specification of each player's decision set, type set, probability distributions on others' type sets (he of course knows his own type), and utility function. Then the various principal–agent models we have been considering are (very) special cases of such a game. It would appear then that provided one is prepared to accept the strong rationality postulates underlying this kind of game, it does provide a framework within which to consider more general principal–agent problems.[10]

7. CONCLUSIONS

In this paper I have sought to provide an expository survey of the main models of principal–agent theory, and of some of their applications. This has been far from an exhaustive survey of the literature and no attempt has been made to evaluate individual contributions. My hope is that economists not already familiar with this body of theory will see in it an interesting set of ideas which could be applied in their own work.

University College Cardiff

REFERENCES

Arrow, K. J. (1963). 'Uncertainty and the Welfare Economics of Medical Care', *American Economic Review*, Vol. 53, pp. 941–73.
Arrow, K. J. (1971). 'Insurance, Risk and Resource Allocation', in *Essays in the Theory of Risk-Bearing*, Chicago, Markham.
Demski, J. S. and Sappington, D. (1984). 'Optimal Incentive Contracts with Multiple Agents, *Journal of Economic Theory*, Vol. 33, pp. 152–71.
Ehrlich, I. and Becker, G. S. (1972). 'Market Insurance, Self-Insurance and Self-Protection', *Journal of Political Economy*, Vol. LXXX, pp. 623–48.
Green, J. and Stokey, N. (1983). 'A Comparison of Tournaments and Contracts', *Journal of Political Economy*, Vol. 91, pp. 349–64.
Groves, T. (1982). 'On Theories of Incentive Compatible Choice with Compensation', ch. 1 in Hildenbrand (ed.), *Advances in Economic Theory*, Cambridge, Cambridge University Press.
Harris, M. and Townsend, R. M. (1981). 'Resource Allocation under Asymmetric Information', *Econometrica*, Vol. 49, pp. 231–59.

[10] But see Groves (1982) for a somewhat critical view of this kind of generalization.

Harsanyi, J. C. (1967-8). 'Games with Incomplete Information Played by Bayesian Players', *Management Science*, Vol. 14, pp. 159-89, 320-34, 486-502.

Helpman, E. and Laffont, J-J. (1975). 'On Moral Hazard in General Equilibrium Theory', *Journal of Economic Theory*, Vol. 10, pp. 8-23.

Holmström, B. (1982). 'Moral Hazard in Teams', *Bell Journal of Economics*, Vol. 13, pp. 324-40.

Lazear, E. P. and Rosen, S. (1981). 'Rank-Order Tournaments as Optimum Labour Contracts', *Journal of Political Economy*, Vol. 89, pp. 841-64.

Mertens, J-F. and Zamir, S. (1982). 'Formalization of Harsanyi's Notions of "Type" and "Consistency" in Games with Incomplete Information', CORE discussion paper, Université Catholique de Louvain.

Mirrlees, J. (1974). 'Notes on Welfare Economics, Information and Uncertainty', in Balch, McFadden and Wu (eds.), *Essays in Economic Behaviour Under Uncertainty*, Amsterdam, North-Holland.

Mookherjee, D. (1984). 'Optimal Incentive Schemes with Many Agents', *Review of Economic Studies*, Vol. LI, pp. 433-46.

Myerson, R. (1979). 'Incentive Compatibility and the Bargaining Problem', *Econometrica*, Vol. 47, pp. 61-3.

Myerson, R. (1983). 'Bayesian Equilibrium and Incentive – Compatibility: an Introduction', Center for Mathematical Studies in Economics and Management Science, Northwestern University, Discussion Paper 548.

Nalebuff, B. and Stiglitz, J. (1983). 'Prices and Incentives: Towards a General Theory of Compensation and Competition', *Bell Journal of Economics*, Vol. 14, pp. 21-43.

Navajas, F. (1984). 'Principal-Agent Theory and Public Enterprise', D.Phil. dissertation, Oxford University.

Pauly, M. V. (1974). 'Overinsurance and Public Provision of Insurance', *Quarterly Journal of Economics*, Vol. LXXXVII, pp. 44-62.

Shavell, S. (1979). 'On Moral Hazard and Insurance', *The Quarterly Journal of Economics*, pp. 541-62.

Spence, A. M. and Zeckhauser, R. (1971). 'Insurance Information and Individual Action', *American Economic Review*, Vol. LXI, pp. 380-7.

Stiglitz, J. (1974). 'Risk Sharing and Incentives in Sharecropping', *Review of Economic Studies*, pp. 219-55.

Townsend, R. (1976). 'Optimal Contracts and Competitive Markets with Costly State Verification', Carnegie-Mellon University, mimeo, 1976.

Weitzman, M. (1976). 'The New Soviet Incentive Model', *Bell Journal of Economics*, Vol. 7, pp. 251-7.

Zeckhauser, R. (1970). 'Medical Insurance: A Case Study of the Trade-off Between Risk-Spreading and Appropriate Incentives', *Journal of Economic Theory*, Vol. 2, pp. 10-26.

THEORIES OF INDIVIDUAL SEARCH BEHAVIOUR

C. J. McKenna

1. INTRODUCTION

Search behaviour is a natural and very common response to uncertainty. It is both a method of improving on the information available and of expanding the number of alternatives from which to choose. Search enables us to test our impressions against actual possibilities and thereby leads us to make more satisfactory choices.

'Search' in this broad sense is used to describe behaviour in many areas including the biological sciences and psychology. In economics the study of search problems intensified, naturally enough, while the 'economics of information' was developing its formal structure in the early 1960s [Stigler (1961, 1962)]. The further irrepressible growth in uncertainty economics since the early 1970s [Hey (1979)] has been composed in part of a rapid growth in the study and applications of search theory, most notably in the context of labour market problems.

This survey presents the principal findings of this large research effort. Attention focusses on the individual search behaviour and for the most part the exposition is presented without particular context except where discussion of specific results warrants illustration. To the extent that we do make use of concrete examples these will relate usually to one of the two main areas of application – consumer search and job search. The former is given particular attention in Section 6.

Three important areas which do not concern us directly are the responses of market participants to the search behaviour of others, properties of market or economy-wide equilibrium when search takes place and the econometric issues arising from search behaviour. What remains however is a large literature of almost bewildering variety. Our approach is not historical nor is there space here to go through all the derivations of each model. The approach is to outline the analytical framework of the major models and to simply state the results. The details of the derivations are contained in the references.

91

2. OPTIMAL SEARCH DECISIONS

We are concerned exclusively with 'optimal' search rules. That is, we restrict attention to those search procedures which maximize an objective function given constraints imposed on behaviour by the searcher's environment and circumstances. We do not therefore study behavioural rules or *ad hoc* rules [Hey (1982)].

We start with a quite general specification of an optimal search procedure although most developments in the literature make use of one or other of two important special cases. Indeed the historical development of search theory has made the completely general specification a relative newcomer to the literature. The search process operates as follows. An individual is interested in an economic variable on which (indirect) utility ultimately depends. This variable, which may be a product price, a wage rate, an insurance quote and so on, is randomly distributed in the market and the location of any particular value is unknown *a priori* – hence the inducement to search. Time is divided into 'periods' (defined generally in terms of economic criteria rather than in calendar time) and in each period, t, the individual chooses to inspect or sample the distribution n_t times. Search takes place for any number of periods during the searcher's lifetime and stops when a sufficiently attractive value of the variable is discovered – the set of 'acceptable' values is denoted by $\mathscr{A}_t$, where the t subscript allows for the possibility that the acceptance set is time-dependent. Thus search ends at the first discovery of a value in $\mathscr{A}_t$. The searcher's problem is to choose a sequence of ordered pairs, $\{(n_t, \mathscr{A}_t)\}_0^T$ (where T is the searcher's horizon) given that each inspection is costly. A search process along these lines has been shown to be optimal by Morgan and Manning (1985). In this section I assume that the probability distribution $f(\cdot)$ of the random variable of interest, X, is known to the searcher, time-invariant and has the associated distribution function $F(x)$ defined over all $x \in R^+$ where x is a realization of X. The case where $f(\cdot)$ is itself of uncertain form and where observations made on x in each period serve to provide information on the 'true' form of the distributions is considered below under the heading of 'adaptive' search. Since, in this section, the distribution is invariant to observed values of x the model is referred to as a 'static' search model.[1]

Denote by $V_t(\hat{x}_t)$ the maximum utility when t periods remain, and the best value of x available is $\hat{x}_t$. We are to imagine that a period of search has just been completed and as a result, the best available offer is $\hat{x}_t$. Hence the individual is at a decision point as to accept $\hat{x}_t$

---

[1] The terminology is taken from Kohn and Shavell (1974).

(thus terminating search[2]) or to continue searching. In the model of this section $\hat{x}_t$ is a value of x observed in period t only. That is, the best available value is not one discovered in a period prior to t — the individual searches without being able to *recall* previously discovered values. The case of searching *with recall* is discussed in the section on 'the recall problem'.

Having completed the current period's sampling and obtained, say n_t observations of which $\hat{x}_t$ is the maximum, the searcher's problem is either to accept $\hat{x}_t$ in which case the utility obtained is $U_t(\hat{x}_t)$ or to continue searching with expected return $S_{t-1}(n_{t-1})$. As a preliminary we first establish the condition for the searcher's optimal choice of within-period sample n_t. This is obtained from the maximization of the return to searching once more, $S_t(n_t)$ given by:

$$S_t(n_t) = \bar{u} - c(n_t) + \beta \int_0^\infty V_t(Y)\phi(Y|n_t)\, dY \qquad (1)$$

This requires some explanation. By choosing a sample of n_t for period t, the searcher obtains a 'fall-back' utility $\bar{u}$ but incurs the total search cost $c(n_t)$ (measured in utility units).[3] The present value of the *expected* utility obtained from the sample maximum is given by the final term in (1). Firstly, the discount factor, $\beta \equiv (1 + r)^{-1}$, where r is an interest rate or discount rate. Secondly, Y is the random variable 'sample maximum' and has a density conditioned by the sample size given by $\phi(Y|n_t)$. Thus $\hat{x}_t$ is a realization of the random variable Y drawn from $\phi(Y|n_t)$. The distributions $\phi(\cdot|n)$ and $f(\cdot)$ are easily shown to be associated by:

$$\phi(y|n) = nF(y)^{n-1}f(y) \qquad (2)$$

Using (1) and (2) the choice of n_t in any period t is the nearest integer n_t satisfying:

---

[2] The literature contains several examples in which the acceptance of a value x_t does not terminate the search process. Results along these lines for the model under discussion here may be found in Benhabib and Bull (1983). Other examples, largely in the job search literature in which 'on-the-job' search is permitted, are Burdett (1978, 1979) and Hey and McKenna (1979).

[3] It is inconsequential for this model whether search takes place for x-values or for associated utility values since utility (as will be seen) is monotonic in x which, combined with $f(x)$ can be used to induce a distribution of utility values. Furthermore the assumption that utility is separable in reward and cost is a considerable simplification. The search problem when utility depends on net wealth so that search costs are included as an argument of the utility function is rather more involved. An example of a model in the job search literature along these lines is Hall et al. (1979). See also Whipple (1973).

$$c'(n_t^*) = \beta \int_0^\infty V_t(Y)\{F^{n_t^* -1}(Y)f(Y)[n_t^* \ln F(Y) + 1]\}\, dY \qquad (3)$$

The left hand side of (3) is the marginal cost of the sample n_t while the right hand side represents the present value of the expected marginal gain of sampling n_t.[4] Assuming that the sample size associated with the next period's search has been chosen optimally according to (3) we may write $V_t(\hat{x}_t)$ defined earlier as the maximum utility when t periods remain and the best value of x available is $\hat{x}_t$ as,

$$V_t(\hat{x}_t) = \max\{ U_t(\hat{x}_t), S_{t-1}(n_{t-1}^*) \} \qquad (4)$$

It remains now to determine the set of acceptable values for period t, $\mathscr{A}_t$.

Our preoccupation with sample maxima thus far has resulted from the assumption that a higher value of the variable of interest increases utility and hence higher values are strictly preferred to lower values, or:

$$U_t'(\hat{x}_t) > 0$$

and

$$V_t'(\hat{x}_t) > 0$$

Consider a particular value of $\hat{x}_t$, say $\hat{x}_t^*$ which equates the two terms on the right hand side of (4). The existence and uniqueness of $\hat{x}_t^*$ may be guaranteed by some quite reasonable restriction such as $U_t(0) < S_{t-1}(n_{t-1}^*)$ which combined with $U_t'(x_t) > 0$ and the fact that $S_{t-1}(n_{t-1}^*)$ is independent of $\hat{x}_t$ gives a single $\hat{x}_t^*$ satisfying;

$$U_t(\hat{x}_t^*) = S_{t-1}(n_{t-1}^*) \qquad (5)$$

Hence, $\hat{x}_t^*$ makes the searcher indifferent between accepting exactly $\hat{x}_t^*$ and searching once more. The situation is illustrated in Figure 1. Hence given such a value $\hat{x}_t^*$ we know, using (4) and the properties of U_t and $S_{t-1}(\cdot)$ that

$$V_t(\hat{x}_t) = \begin{cases} S_{t-1}(n_{t-1}^*) & \hat{x}_t < \hat{x}_t^* \\ U_t(\hat{x}_t) & \hat{x}_t \geqslant \hat{x}_t^* \end{cases} \qquad (6)$$

Thus the searcher maximizes $V_t(\hat{x}_t)$ by continuing search if $\hat{x}_t < \hat{x}_t^*$ and accepting $\hat{x}_t$ (thus discontinuing search) if $\hat{x}_t \geqslant \hat{x}_t^*$. It is apparent therefore that in this model the set $\mathscr{A}_t$ takes the relatively simple form,

$$\mathscr{A}_t = \{ \hat{x}_t \,|\, \hat{x}_t \geqslant \hat{x}_t^* \} \qquad (7)$$

---

[4] It is easily shown that $E[Y|n]$ is increasing in n.

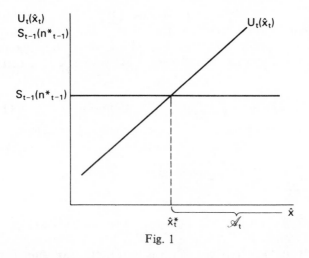

Fig. 1

and the searcher's inter-period search rule is

$$\text{Accept } \hat{x}_t \text{ and terminate search if } \hat{x}_t \in \mathscr{A}_t$$
$$\text{Reject } \hat{x}_t \text{ and search again if } \hat{x}_t \notin \mathscr{A}_t \tag{8}$$

where $\mathscr{A}_t$ is given by (7) and $\hat{x}_t^*$ is the solution to (5).

A further useful result is apparent once we substitute $U_t(\hat{x}_t^*)$ for $S_{t-1}(n_{t-1}^*)$ in (6) and take the one-period forward expectation,

$$\int_0^\infty V_{t-1}(Y)\phi(Y|n_{t-1}^*)\,\mathrm{d}Y = U_{t-1}(\hat{x}_{t-1}^*)\,\Phi\,(\hat{x}_{t-1}^*|n_{t-1}^*)$$

$$+ \int_{\hat{x}_{t-1}^*}^\infty U_{t-1}(Y)\phi(Y|n_{t-1}^*)\,\mathrm{d}Y \tag{9}$$

so that, using the one-period forward version of (1),

$$U_t(\hat{x}_t^*) = \bar{u} - c(n_{t-1}^*) + \beta U_{t-1}(\hat{x}_{t-1}^*)\,\Phi\,(\hat{x}_{t-1}^*|n_{t-1}^*)$$

$$+ \beta \int_{\hat{x}_{t-1}^*}^\infty U_{t-1}(Y)\phi(Y|n_{t-1})\,\mathrm{d}Y \tag{10}$$

Equation (10) is a very common form of result in search theory, and we may gain additional insight into its interpretation in the context of an important special case. Before doing so, there are some results available for the model as it stands. These are summarized without proof.

1. As $T \to \infty \, n_t^* = n_{t-1}^*$ all t [Morgan (1983)]. As the time horizon facing the individual becomes indefinitely large the intensity of intra-period sampling is constant. Proofs of the following results are available for the case where $c(n) = kn$ where k is a constant and $T < \infty$,

2. (i) $S_t(n_t^*) > S_{t+1}(n_{t+1}^*)$ Benhabib and Bull (1983)

    (ii)[5] $n_{t+1}^* < n_t^*$ Gal *et al.* (1981)

    (iii) $\dfrac{\mathrm{d}n_t^*}{\mathrm{d}\bar{u}} \geqslant 0, \ \dfrac{\mathrm{d}n_t^*}{\mathrm{d}k} \leqslant 0$

3. $\hat{x}_{t+1}^* > x_t^*$ Gal *et al.* (1981)[6]

The return to search is a decreasing function of time (2(i)) which leads to searchers increasing the likelihood of terminating search by extending the sample size (2(ii)). The intra-period intensity of search is a non-decreasing function of fall-back utility and a non-increasing function of search costs (2(iii)). The last result is of particular importance since it states that the intra-period intensity of search decreases with the unit search cost – an intuitively plausible result. Finally, with the finite horizon the set of acceptable values expands with continued search, thus making the termination of search more likely. The literature has tended to refer to the solution $\hat{x}_t^*$ to (5) as a 'reservation value' (corresponding to 'reservation price' in the context of consumer search and 'reservation wage' in the context of simple job search models) hence $U_t(\hat{x}_t^*)$ is the searcher's reservation utility at a time t periods before T.

It is apparent that there are two dimensions to search activity in this model involving both within-period search and search extending over time. The literature has treated these two dimensions as alternatives and in economics it was the choice of sample size which was developed first as the search method [Stigler (1961, 1962)] – known now as the Fixed Sample Size (FSS) procedure. The FSS analysis effectively rules out the possibility of being 'dissatisfied' with *all* observations in a single sample and hence ignores the decision to take further samples. In the context of the more general model the FSS is a one-period model and its solution is similar to the problem max $S(n)$, where $S(n)$ would be given by (1) (with $\beta = 1$). The sample

---

[5] See Morgan and Manning (1985) for a full discussion of this property.

[6] A further result is also available for those with a knowledge of the stochastic dominance literature. Namely, if a distribution $F_2(\cdot)$ stochastically dominates $F_1(\cdot)$ (in the first degree) then the acceptance set under $F_2(\cdot)$ is smaller, and hence $\hat{x}_t^*$ higher than under $F_1(\cdot)$ for all t [Gal *et al.* (1981)].

size $n > 0$ effects of parameter changes as in 2(iii) above apply to this single period FSS model.

With one or two exceptions [Wilde (1977)] most of the search literature has developed along the intertemporal dimension and these models are known as Sequential Search models. The sequential search procedure, therefore, is to terminate search by accepting a value but otherwise continue searching offers sequentially (using one at a time). The simplest sequential search model is probably the following and is derived from the main model of this section by setting $n = 1$, $c(n) = k$, $Y = X$, $\hat{x}_t = x_t$, $\phi(Y|n_t) = f(X)$, $\beta = 1$, $\bar{u} = 0$ and $t \rightarrow \infty$ (implying $x_t = x$ all t).[7] Using obvious notation we have,

$$V(x) = \max\{U(x), S\} \tag{11}$$

$$S = -k + \int_0^\infty V(X)f(X)\, dX \tag{12}$$

The equivalent of (5) is now

$$U(x^*) = S \tag{13}$$

and that of (6) is[8]

$$V(x) = \begin{cases} S & x < \tilde{x}^* \quad \text{(continue)} \\ U(x) & x \geqslant x^* \quad \text{(stop)} \end{cases} \tag{14}$$

giving,

$$U(x^*) = -k + U(X^*)F(x^*) + \int_{x^*}^\infty U(X)f(X)\, dX \tag{15}$$

as the equivalent of (10). Solving (15) gives

$$k = \int_{x^*}^\infty [U(X) - U(x^*)]f(X)\, dX \tag{16}$$

or equivalently

$$U(x^*) = \frac{-k + \int_{x^*}^\infty U(X)f(X)\, dX}{[1 - F(x^*)]} \tag{17}$$

---

[7] See for example Lippman and McCall (1976).
[8] A simple proof that the stopping rule takes the form suggested here may be found in Hey (1979a).

$$= \frac{-k}{[1 - F(x^*)]} + E[U(X)|x \geqslant x^*] \qquad (18)$$

The first term in the right hand side of (18) is the expected total search cost being the product of the unit (per period) search cost and the expected duration[9] of search $[1 - F(x^*)]^{-1}$. It is easily shown that $dx^*/dk < 0$. The finite horizon $(T < \infty)$ version of this simple model is often used and instead of (15) we have,

$$U_t(x_t^*) = -k + \beta U_{t-1}(x_{t-1}^*)F(x_{t-1}^*) + \beta \int_{x_{t-1}^*}^{\infty} U_{t-1}(X)f(X)\, dX \qquad (19)$$

and the result in 3. above goes through as before.

The literature making use of the simple sequential search model in both the finite and infinite horizon versions is large. A comprehensive survey of the job search aspects is contained in McKenna (1985). Some developments in the area of consumer search are summarized in Section 6 below. However before considering some of the more important extensions of the model it is worth considering the search procedures suggested in this section so far.

It has been established that the general model outlined at the beginning of this section is superior both to the Fixed Sample Size rule and the sequential rule taken singly [Morgan and Manning (1985)]. The intuitive reason for this is that by relaxing the constraint that only one observation be collected within a period we improve upon the sequential search procedure while taking repeat samples (if necessary) relaxes the constraint of the simple FSS strategy. A pure FSS rule in which exactly the predetermined number of observations (no more, no less) must be made regardless of how desirable early observations may be is dominated by a sequential rule unless there are economies of scale from sampling more than one observation.[10] In the general model of this section there are within period economies because if only one observation is made at a time a whole period must elapse before the next observation is made and time-wasting may be avoided if multiple observations are made within the period. Clearly the time structure-essentially determined by the period of discount rather than by calendar time – plays a

---

[9] In the empirical job search literature $[1 - F(x^*)]$, the probability of leaving unemployment in this simple case is known as the hazard rate.

[10] This has been shown for some time [Wilde (1977)]. See also some experiments and other suggestions for 'mixed' strategies in Gastwirth (1976).

In addition to single or multiple observations within a period there is the further possibility of *at most* one offer or quote being obtained. Lippman and McCall (1978) discuss this case. Also the choice of search *intensity* may be approached in other ways, for example as an exercise in the allocation of time [Seater (1977)].

crucial role. The optimality of the pure form of FSS or of the sequential rule alone therefore results from the imposition of constraints which may or may not be regarded as reasonable, depending on the particular context.[11]

One further type of constraint suggested earlier is that of the availability of past search discoveries. In the models of this section only the current period (maximum) offer is available for selection. We now explore other possibilities along lines of *recall* of past observations.

3. THE RECALL PROBLEM

Under conditions of *full recall* the quantity $\hat{x}_t$ is the maximum (as at period t from the horizon) of *all* samples taken up to and including that in the current period. The complication is that with this value carried over with continued search the return to search now depends on the available maximum. Bearing in mind the new interpretation of $\hat{x}_t$ we have, in place of (4)

$$V_t(\hat{x}_t) = \max\{U_t(\hat{x}_t), S^r_{t-1}(\hat{x}_t, n^{r*}_{t-1})\} \tag{20}$$

where

$$S^r_{t-1}(\hat{x}_t, n^{r*}_{t-1}) = \bar{u} - c(n^{r*}_{t-1}) + V_{t-1}(\hat{x}_t)\Phi(\hat{x}_t \mid n^{r*}_{t-1})$$

$$+ \int_{x_t}^{\infty} V_{t-1}(Y)\phi(Y \mid n^{r*}_{t-1}) \, dY \tag{21}$$

which reflects the fact that if the result of period $(t-1)$s search $\hat{x}_{t-1} < \hat{x}_t$ (with probability $\Phi(\hat{x}_t)$) then the utility is $V_{t-1}(\hat{x}_t)$ while if $x_{t-1} \geq x_t$ the new expected maximum utility (multiplied by $Pr[Y \geq \hat{x}_t \mid n^{r*}_{t-1}]$) is the final term in (21). Firm propositions about the behaviour of the sequence $\{n^{r*}_t, \mathscr{A}_t\}$ are difficult to establish for the general case with full recall. The reason that the form and behaviour

[11] There are of course many other types of restrictions imposed on behaviour in these models which may also be regarded as unreasonable. The most important are those regarding the informational environment and alternative models have been put forward suggesting procedures involving more or less prior information on market opportunities. Some models of the latter class are suggested below in Section 5. Of the former group Salop (1973) has suggested that search is not an entirely random selection procedure but that the more favourable opportunities are located first in a *systematic* way and their availability discovered. Weitzman (1979) has suggested a procedure in which not one but several identifiable distributions of X may characterize a market (or set of markets) in which case the most favourable distributions are sampled first. Thus whilst each *distribution* is approached systematically, search within each distribution is random.

of $\mathscr{A}_t$ is more difficult to establish is that a large sample maximum not only serves to give a higher utility from terminating search but also increases the return to continued search. However adopting the convention that $S_T \equiv 0$ the method of backward induction may be used to solve for the sequence $\{n_t, \mathscr{A}_t\}$ with the following results.

1. The reservation utility is constant with full recall [Gal *et al.* (1981)].

2. (i) If search is preferred in $t-1$ then $n_{t-1}^{r*} = n_t^{r*}$ (the sample size is a nondecreasing function of time). [Morgan (1983)].

    (ii) As the search horizon approaches the sample size chosen with full recall is no greater than that with no recall, i.e. $n_{T-1}^{r*} \leqslant n_{T-1}^{*}$. [Morgan (1983)].

Interestingly the stronger result associated with 2(ii) that $n_t^{r*} = n_t^{*}$ all $t \in [0, T-1]$ has not been proven [Morgan (1983)].

It has been recognized that the assumptions of no recall and of full recall are extremes and attempts have been made to model the intermediate case of *partial recall*. Analyses along these lines are prompted by the considerations of the searcher operating not in isolation but in competition with other searchers. This leads to the idea that during the time elapsed since an observation was first made the offer may (or may not) have been removed from the market.

Gal *et al.* (1981) have studied the case in which the current period observations have a probability q of being available for selection and all previous period's observations are lost. Effectively the searcher is sampling not from the distribution $F(X)$ but from the distribution $G(Z)$ where

$$Z = \begin{cases} X \text{ with probability } q \\ 0 \text{ with probability } (1-q) \end{cases}$$

and the analysis of the general model proceeds with the additional parameter q.[12]

In the context of a purely sequential model Karni and Schwartz (1977) specify partial recall to mean that an offer observed τ periods ago is available in the current period with probability $p(\tau)$ which is known to the searcher. Using a special case, it is found that the reservation utility under partial recall is bounded above by the reservation utility under perfect recall and is bounded below by that under no recall.

At about the same time, Landsberger and Peled (1977) adopted the notion that at any time t at which the maximum observed

---

[12] The comparative-statics on q are in effect the stochastic dominance results referred to in footnote 6.

offer so far is $\hat{x}_t$, the value $\hat{x}_t$ *alone* is available with probability q — a constant independent of time elapsed and on the size of $\hat{x}_t$. No other past offer is available except the maximum of all previous offers, and with that probability q. This is an uncomfortable assumption since we would expect higher offers to be more likely to disappear from the market.

These attempts, despite their obvious shortcomings have yet to be improved upon. Most desirable would be a formulation in which the probability that a previous offer is available depends both on its magnitude and on the time elapsed since inspection.

4. RESIDUAL UNCERTAINTY

In the model developed so far the discovery of a particular value x enables the searcher to calculate (among other things) exactly the utility to be derived by the acceptance of x. The concept of residual uncertainty is motivated by the realization that not all utility-generating variables are observable as part of the random selection process. Indeed some important, generally 'qualitative', properties of goods, services, jobs and people are not readily observable and may only be discovered by 'experience'. In this sense 'experience' implies that a choice is made prior to the full revelation of all the attributes of interest to the searcher. Hence at the decision point, on x, there is residual uncertainty about other attributes associated with x but not directly observable. If x is accepted the hidden attribute, say z, will become apparent sooner or later as the total utility experienced exceeds or falls short of that initially expected to be generated by x. There may be a subsequent decision point this time on the total utility offered by the (x, z) combination and plans may be revised [Hey and McKenna (1981), McKenna (1979, 1980), Wilde (1979)]. This possibility was first explored by Borjas and Goldberg (1978). The consequences of this for the model developed earlier may be seen by observing that the initially observed x may well provide information about z and hence of the final utility to be experienced.

We follow the literature by assuming that having drawn x from the (marginal) distribution $F(X)$ the searcher forms the conditional distribution of Z, say $G(Z|x)$. It is clear now that the acceptability of any particular x-value depends on how it is (stochastically) associated with Z since, intuitively if high x is also associated with high z (and utility is increasing in both) then higher xs are preferred to lower values. If x and z are inversely related the position is less clear cut and depends on the degree of (the negative) association between x

and z and on their relative weighting in the utility function. A sample case, using the purely sequential rule will help in the illustration.

Suppose that x and z carry equal weight in the utility function and write the expected utility from accepting an x as

$$\bar{U}(x) = \int_0^\infty U(x + Z)g(Z|x)\,\mathrm{d}Z \qquad (22)$$

then (11) and (12) become

$$V(x) = \max\{\bar{U}(x), S\} \qquad (23)$$

$$S = -k + \int_0^\infty V(X)f(X)\,\mathrm{d}X \qquad (24)$$

Before we investigate the form of $\bar{U}(x)$ in (22) we attempt to establish the reservation value rule as in (13).

Clearly, as before S is independent of x, however, $\bar{U}(x)$ need not be monotonic in x and hence the solution to

$$\bar{U}(x^*) = S \qquad (25)$$

need not be unique. The position is illustrated in Figure 2 and outlined in full in McKenna (1979). The most we may say in general is that

$$\left.\begin{array}{l} x \in \mathscr{A} \text{ and search stops if } \bar{U}(x) \geqslant S \\ x \notin \mathscr{A} \text{ and search continues if } \bar{U}(x) < S \end{array}\right\} \qquad (26)$$

Evidently, in view of Figure 2 the set $\mathscr{A}$ need not be connected. The monotonicity of $\bar{U}(x + z)$ may be illustrated in a simple case. Suppose that the expected utility to accepting an x value is simply

$$\bar{U}(x) = x + \int_0^\infty Zg(Z|x)\,\mathrm{d}Z \qquad (27)$$

Integration by parts gives

$$\bar{U}(x) = x + \int_0^\infty [1 - G(Z|x)]\,\mathrm{d}Z \qquad (28)$$

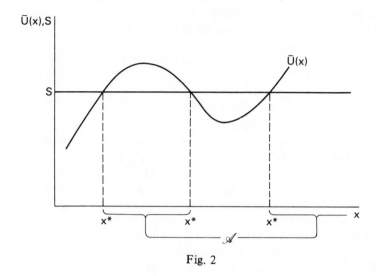

Fig. 2

so that $\bar{U}'(x) > 0$ all x only if

$$1 - \int_0^\infty \frac{\partial G(Z|x)}{\partial x}\, dZ > 0 \qquad (29)$$

and this is certain to be the case if

$$- \int_0^\infty (\partial G/\partial x)\, dZ > 0$$

— for example if larger x induces stochastically dominant distributions of $G(Z|\cdot)$ — or more crudely, if higher xs are associated with (stochastically) larger Zs. However it is apparent from these conditions (and others) that $\bar{U}(x)$ need not be monotonic increasing in x.

Finally, it is of interest to note that the form of $\bar{U}(x)$ used in (27) permits no consequences to follow from the realization of z — the searcher merely accepts passively that (perhaps) the promise of high utility on the basis of the x-value did not materialize. For many cheap consumer-goods this is surely an adequate representation. For expensive goods and jobs most people would react and even in the case of cheap goods an unhappy experience may result in no repeat purchases. Further explorations along these lines — in which action is taken on the realized z-value in the form of a second-stage decision point — are available in Cressy (1983), Hey and McKenna (1981),

McKenna (1980), Wilde (1979), and Wilde and Schwartz (1979). An example is outlined in Section 6 below.

5. ADAPTIVE SEARCH

Adaptive search takes place when the form of the distribution of X is itself uncertain and must therefore be estimated. The most reasonable presumption is that search activity not only serves as a utility-generating process but also as a means of confirming (or otherwise) the searcher's prior beliefs about the true distribution of Xs. In other words in addition to their potential role in providing utility (as in the 'static' case) observations may provide *information* on the entire distribution of offers. There are many ways in which this information may be integrated formally into old estimates of the distributions to arrive at a new estimate. For example, Bayes' Theorem is motivated by considerations of this type, and as long as the prior distribution falls within a given class, standard results provide rules for the updating of estimates [Degroot (1970)].

Optimal rules for 'adaptive' models are available under certain circumstances [Morgan (1985)] although these rules do not always take the 'reservation utility' form. To see why, suppose that, in the spirit of the purely sequential search model without recall, that the 'reservation value' is $\hat{x}_t$, then we know that, in the static case *any* offer greater than $\hat{x}_t$, will be accepted and search will terminate. Now consider the 'adaptive' case and suppose that given the state of information about the current estimate of $F(X)$, say $F_t(X)$, $\hat{x}_t$ is indeed a value which makes the searcher indifferent between searching and accepting $\hat{x}_t$. The search in t generates a value, say x_t which has the property that $x_t > \hat{x}_t$ *and* that $F_t(X)$ – the current estimate of the 'true' distribution $F(X)$ is unaffected by x_t. In this case it is clear that (as long as utility is increasing in x) the $x_t > \hat{x}_t$ will be accepted. However, suppose that an $x_t > \hat{x}_t$ is observed which is so large as to warrant a revision of $F_t(x)$ such that the distribution is thought now to be much more favourable than previously. In this case the search opportunities appear to be more favourable and continued search prefered as shown by the rejection of x_t. Thus the predetermined 'reservation value' $\hat{x}_t$ is in fact *not* a reservation value since an $x > \hat{x}_t$ may be rejected.

A fuller discussion of this problem is contained in Axell (1974), Rothschild (1974), and Rosenfield and Shapiro (1981). By and large the additional complexity of adaptive models has not been justified by the additional insights they offer. Consequently, there are few models of this type.

6. AN APPLICATION – SEARCH AND THE CONSUMER

It is useful to summarize some of the general results with a specific example aimed at bringing out some of the economic results obtained from search theory. I have chosen one of the most popular areas of application – that of search in a consumer goods market.

We start by following most of the literature in assuming that the search for the lowest price of a single commodity is an activity which is independent of other consumer activities both in the goods market and elsewhere. This excludes from consideration the allocation of time and income-generating process and also consumption of other goods. Later we look at the search problem in the context of a more conventional theory of consumer choice, however the problem of the allocation of time between work and leisure is not discussed – interested readers are referred to Seater (1977) and Siven (1974).

In the simplest case of pure sequential search without recall, let $V_t(\hat{p}_t)$ be the maximum utility when t periods remain and the current price observed is $\hat{p}_t$. Suppose at most one unit of the good is desired and that the good is of uniform quality. The utility from purchasing the good at price $\hat{p}_t$ is $U_t(\hat{p}_t) > 0$, with $U_t'(\hat{p}_t) < 0$, and the return to continued search is S_{t-1}, which is independent of $\hat{p}_t$. We have,

$$V_t(\hat{p}_t) = \max\{U_t(\hat{p}_t), S_{t-1}\} \tag{30}$$

so that $V_t'(\hat{p}_t) \leqslant 0$. The searcher then obviously chooses a 'reservation price' $\hat{p}_t^*$ such that search continues if $\hat{p}_t > \hat{p}_t^*$ and search stops if $\hat{p}_t \leqslant \hat{p}_t^*$, in which case one unit of the good is consumed. It is an easy matter to show (following our earlier analysis) that an increase in search cost raises the reservation price.

In an obvious extension along residual uncertainty lines we may characterize any good by the pair (p, q) where p is price as before and q some measure of quality. A model along these lines though with an infinite search horizon, is developed in Hey and McKenna (1981). As our discussion of Section 4 suggests the reservation price rule will be maintained if lower prices are not associated with overall lower expected utility arising from lower expected quality. However, one issue not pursued formally in Section 4 is the consequence of paying a price for a commodity and of being able therefore to evaluate the experience characteristic q. Rather than passively accept the quality the searcher may decide to take action. If we regard q as a constant 'flow' of service per period of the commodity's life and if utility is increasing in q then there is a 'reservation quality' rule which determines the acceptability of the purchased good. In fact there are *two* reservation qualities in the model of Hey and McKenna (1981) and they arise in the following way. It appears that, at the time the good's true quality comes to light (and hence the residual uncertainty removed) the decision to dispose (cost-lessly) of the good depends on a 'reservation quality' level q_1^* such that if $q < q_1^*$ the good is thrown away immediately and search resumed whereas if $q \geqslant q_1^*$ the good is retained for its entire life-span. If $u(p,q)$ is the utility of retaining the good for its lifespan and if S is the constant return to search then for a given p, q_1^* satistifes,

$$U(p, q_1^*) = S \tag{31}$$

so that q_1^* makes the individual indifferent between not disposing of the good and continuing search. The second 'reservation quality' level q_n^* arises because although a product may have a sufficiently high quality to be kept for its lifetime (of n-periods) the quality may not be sufficiently high to warrant a repeat purchase. Thus it is shown that $q_n^* > q_1^*$ and a good chosen initially with $q_1^* < q < q_n^*$ will not be repurchased and search will resume afresh after the present good has ceased its yield of service.

As interesting as these properties of consumer search are they are couched in a framework which is far removed from the conventional model of consumer choice. The gap is bridged somewhat by a search model involving several goods [Peterson and Barron (1978)]. However the most comprehensive available integration of search with the traditional concerns of consumer choice is to be found in Manning and Morgan (1982).

The essence of the Manning and Morgan model is that of a vector of consumption goods, the price of all except one of the m goods is known. For one of the goods, however, stores operate varying discounts which are uncertain *ex ante* but distributed according to the known density $f(\cdot)$. A discount factor is defined so that the actual selling price for good l (the good to which the discount applies) is λp_1. The search rule is of the FSS type so that after n quotes

$$\hat{\lambda} = \min\{\lambda_1, \ldots, \lambda_n\} \tag{32}$$

acquired at total cost cn. The budget constraint after search is

$$\hat{\lambda} p_1 x_1 + \sum_{i=2}^{m} p_i x_i = w - cn \tag{33}$$

where w is initial wealth. Consumer's utility depends only on the quantities x_i ($i = 1, \ldots, m$) (and not on net wealth $w - cn$) which, along with n constitute the objects of choice for the consumer, giving demands as

$$x_j^*(\hat{\lambda} p_1, p_2, \ldots, p_m, w - cn) \quad j = 1, \ldots, m \tag{34}$$

optimal search intensity as

$$n^*(p_1, \ldots, p_m, c, w) \qquad (35)$$

We omit the derivation, but summarize the more interesting results.

1. n^* is homogeneous of degree zero in p_i, $i = 1, \ldots, m$, c and w.

2. n^* is non-decreasing in w, decreasing in c, and increasing in the price of a substitute good (i.e. a good which is a substitute for good 1).

7. CONCLUSION

Search theory has been put to many uses, including that of providing a microeconomic underpinning to macroeconomic equilibrium and adjustment problems. At the purely microeconomic level there are a large number of models now available reflecting the richness of the variety of assumptions which may be incorporated into a search framework. However, of the several areas which remain to be clarified (that of the uncertain recall problem, for example), the most major is still the apparently complex issue of search market equilibrium. Much attention is currently focussed on issues of this type.

REFERENCES

Axell, B. (1974). 'Price Dispersion and Information – An Adaptive Sequential Search Model', *Swedish Journal of Economics*, Vol. 76, No. 1, pp. 77-98.

Benhabib, J. and Bull, C. (1983). Job search: 'The Choice of Intensity', *Journal of Political Economy*, Vol. 91, pp. 747-64.

Borjas, G. N. and Goldberg, M. S. (1978). 'The Economics of Job Search: A Comment', *Economic Inquiry*, Vol. 16, No. 1, pp. 119-25.

Burdett, K. (1978). 'A Theory of Employee Search and Quit Rates', *American Economic Review*, Vol. 68, No. 1, pp. 212-20.

Burdett, K. (1979). Search, Leisure and Individual Labour Supply, in Lippman, S. A. and McCall, J. J. (eds.), pp. 157-70.

Cressy, R. (1983), 'Goodwill, Intertemporal Price Dependence and the Repurchase Decision', *Economic Journal*, Vol. 93, pp. 847-61.

Degroot, M. H. (1970). *Optimal Statistical Decisions*, McGraw-Hill, New York.

Gal, S., Landsberger, M. and Levykson, B. (1981). 'A Compound Strategy for Search in the Labour Market', *International Economic Review*, Vol. 22, pp. 597-608.

Gastwirth, J. L. (1976). 'On Probabilistic Models of Consumer Search for Information', *Quarterly Journal of Economics*, Vol. 90, No. 1, pp. 38-50.

Hall, J. R., Lippman, S. A. and McCall, J. J. (1979). Expected Utility Maximizing Job Search, in Lippman, S. A. and McCall, J. J. (eds.), pp. 133-55.

Hey, J. D. (1979a). 'A Simple Generalized Stopping Rule', *Economics Letters*, Vol. 2, pp. 115-20.

Hey, J. D. (1979b). *Uncertainty in Microeconomics*, Martin Robertson, Oxford.

Hey, J. D. (1982). 'Search for Rules for Search', *Journal of Economic Behaviour and Organisation*, Vol. 3, pp. 65-81.

Hey, J. D. and McKenna, C. J. (1979). 'To Move or Not to Move?', *Economica*, Vol. 46, pp. 175-85.

Hey, J. D. and McKenna, C. J. (1981). 'Consumer Search with Uncertain Product Quality, *Journal of Political Economy*, Vol. 89, No. 1, pp. 54-68.

Karni, E. and Schwartz. A. (1977). 'Search Theory: The Case of Search With Uncertain Recall', *Journal of Economic Theory*, Vol. 16, No. 2, pp. 38-52.

Kohn, M. G. and Shavell, S. (1974). 'The Theory of Search', *Journal of Economic Theory*, Vol. 9, No. 2, pp. 93-123.

Landsberger, M. and Peled, D. (1977). 'Duration of Offers, Price Structure and the Gain from Search', *Journal of Economic Theory*, Vol. 16, No. 2, pp. 17-37.

Lippman, S. A. and McCall, J. J. (1976). 'The Economics of Job Search: A Survey. Part I', *Economic Inquiry*, Vol. 14, No. 2, pp. 155-89.

Lippman, S. A. and McCall, J. J. (eds.). (1979). *Studies in the Economics of Search*, North-Holland, Amsterdam.

McKenna, C. J. (1979). 'A Solution to a Class of Sequential Decision Problems', *Economics Letters*, Vol. 3, pp. 415-18.

McKenna, C. J. (1980). 'Wage Offers, Layoffs and the Firm in an Uncertain Labour Market', *Manchester School*, Vol. 48, No. 3, pp. 255-64.

McKenna, C. J. (1985). *Uncertainty and the Labour Market*, Wheatsheaf Books, Brighton.

Manning, R. and Morgan, P. B. (1982). 'Search and Consumer Theory', *Review of Economic Studies*, Vol. 49, pp. 203-16.

Morgan, P. B. (1983). 'Search and Optimal Sample Sizes', *Review of Economic Studies*, Vol. 50, pp. 659-75.

Morgan, P. B. (1985). 'Distributions of the Duration and the Value of Search with Learning', *Econometrica*, Vol. 53, No. 5, pp. 1199-232.

Morgan, P. B. and Manning, R. (1985). 'Optimal Search', *Econometrica*, Vol. 53, pp. 923-44.

Peterson, R. L. and Barron, D. P. (1978). 'Multi-Factor and Multi-Commodity Search', *Southern Economic Journal*, Vol. 44, No. 3, pp. 516-25.

Rosenfield, D. and Shapiro, R. (1981). 'Optimal Adaptive Search', *Journal of Economic Theory*, Vol. 25, pp. 1-20.

Rothschild, M. (1974). 'Searching for the Lowest Price When the Distribution of Prices is Unknown', *Journal of Political Economy*, Vol. 82, pp. 689-711.

Salop, S. (1973). 'Systematic Job Search and Unemployment', *Review of Economic Studies*, Vol. 40, No. 2, pp. 191-202.

Seater, J. J. 'A Unified Model of Consumption, Labour Supply and Job Search', *Journal of Economic Theory*, Vol. 14, No. 2, pp. 349-72.

Siven, C-H. (1974), 'Consumption, Supply of Labour and Search Activity in an Intertemporal Perspective', *Swedish Journal of Economics*, Vol. 76, No. 1, pp. 44-61.

Stigler, G. J. (1961). 'The Economics of Information', *Journal of Political Economy*, Vol. 69, No. 3, pp. 213-25.

Stigler, C. J. (1962), 'Information in the Labour Market', *Journal of Political*

Economy, Vol. 70, No. 5, S. 94-S. 105.

Weitzman, M. L. (1979). 'Optimal Search for the Best Alternative', *Econometrica*, Vol. 47, No. 3, pp. 641-54.

Whipple, D. (1973). 'A Generalized Theory of Job Search', *Journal of Political Economy*, Vol. 81, No. 5, pp. 1070-88.

Wilde, L. L. (1977). 'Labour Market Equilibrium Under Nonsequential Search', *Journal of Economic Theory*, Vol. 16, No. 2, pp. 373-93.

Wilde, L. L. (1979). An Information-Theoretic Approach to Job Quits, in Lippman, S. A. and McCall, J. J. (eds.).

Wilde, L. L. and Schwartz, A. (1979). 'Equilibrium Comparison Shopping', *Review of Economic Studies*, Vol. 40, pp. 543-53.

MODELS OF SEARCH MARKET EQUILIBRIUM

C. J. McKenna

ABSTRACT

It is both desirable and necessary that individual search behaviour be placed in a market setting. This survey brings together the more important results of exercises of this type and reviews the literature. We consider both the adjustments which lead to equilibrium price distributions and more generally the efficiency of search equilibrium. Although the entire area is relatively new we pay particular attention to recent contributions.

1. INTRODUCTION

In an earlier paper I presented a survey of the key results of theories of individual search behaviour (McKenna, 1986c). In this, the sequel, I focus on the market equilibrium implications of individual search decisions. This enables us to see to what extent the models of individual behaviour lead to market outcomes consistent with the market environment which is treated as parametric in the partial equilibrium context. For example, internal consistency of the consumer search problem requires as a minimum that equilibrium is characterized by a stable non-degenerate price distribution. This particular question is taken up in section 3(a).

The equilibrium analysis also serves two rather deeper purposes. In the first place it forces us to consider the price and quantity adjustment mechanisms, and their consequences, in a decentralized market framework. In a market with a large number of imperfectly informed traders, firms are left to set prices to which consumers respond through their search. It has been recognized for some time that this leaves firms with some local monopoly power which may lead in the limit to the market price converging to the monopoly price or joint profit-maximizing price (Diamond, 1971; Hey, 1974). These contributions, along with the work of Fisher,[1] may be regarded

---

[1] See Fisher (1970, 1973, 1983).

as part of the literature on the dynamic stability of markets in the absence of the Walrasian 'auctioneer'. Their aim on the whole is not to explore the circumstances under which price distributions and hence search could be sustained – a necessary exercise (Rothschild, 1973), pursued with much vigour by later writers, if search was to be seen as anything other than a purely transitory feature.

The market analysis also enables us to ask questions about the efficiency of equilibrium. Do the private decisions of unco-ordinated agents lead to outcomes which all individuals acting in concert would prefer, or do individuals' decisions impose costs on others? This is a complex but very interesting issue and it is approached here in the following way. We identify two potential sources of inefficiency as being two 'stages' of a search process. First, search involves locating a partner with complementary interests. A pre-requisite for exchange is a type of 'double coincidence of wants' which simply means in this context that agents see a mututal benefit from entering into an agreement. By studying models in which there are no perceived *ex ante* differences in asking prices or wage offers we are able to focus attention on efficiency problems from 'pure' co-ordination difficulties. This is done in section 2.

Further efficiency issues arise when resources are used to locate better contractual terms and when information about opportunities is acquired. These are discussed in the context of price dispersion in section 3(b).

There are some important differences in the way product markets and labour markets work. Training and turnover costs create bonds between workers and firms, where no such ties typically exist between buyers and sellers of everyday goods. These special factors indicate that equilibrium in the labour market is worthy of separate attention. We look very briefly at models in this vein in section 4. Section 5 offers some conclusions.

If not already apparent it should be made clear that there is no universally applicable theory of search market equilibrium. There are important and recurrent themes but some of these are more apparent in, and applicable to, certain market environments than others. The organization of this survey hopefully captures this.

2. MODELS OF MATCHING EQUILIBRIUM

We start by seeing how trades take place in a decentralized market framework. Initially we abstract from the problems of the next section, those associated with price distributions which must ultimately be explained endogenously, and we consider the process which brings individuals together to make mutually beneficial bilateral trades. The central ingredients of these models are: (i) the matching technology, or the process which brings agents together; (ii) the production technology or the purpose of the match; (iii) the determination of the contractual terms. The available models of matching equilibrium differ in one or more of these areas, and also in less important aspects such as how matches break up. These three features of matching models combine to determine the number of matches formed and, in parallel, the amount of search for matches to be undertaken.[2] The emphasis is not on the individuals' decisions but on the consèquences of individual decisions for the overall amount of matching and searching taking place in the market.

One of the aims of this section is to show that in general individuals' decisions on forming matches are inefficient in the sense that such private decisions place unaccounted-for costs and benefits on other market participants.

The core of matching models is the matching technology. The models developed so far concentrate on matches of two individuals with no multiple partnerships. Hence there are during any period two groups of unattached searchers – in fact suppose there are l in one group and v in the other (both l and v are 'large'). Individuals in both groups search randomly so that in any period x matches are formed, $x \leqslant \min(l, v)$, which has the effect of reducing the total number of searchers by $2x$, x from each group. The most plausible assumption is that x depends on the number of participating searchers of both tyes so we write:

$$x = x(l, v) \tag{1}$$

Furthermore it seems plausible that the number of matches will be greater the more of each type of participant there are and so, $x_l > 0$, $x_v > 0$.

Now consider the matching process as viewed from each 'side' of the market. Let p denote the probability that one of the l-searchers will locate a partner in a particular period, and q the probability that a v-searcher will do so, then the number of matches per period is

$$x = pl = qv \tag{2}$$

In addition we are required to make assumptions about the determinants of p and q. One possibility is particularly attractive; that the matching probabilities depend on the relative number of one type of searcher to the other. Defining $\theta \equiv l/v$, gives,

$$x(l, v) = p(\theta) l \tag{3}$$

[2] See also Pissarides (1979) for an equilibrium matching model in which searchers *choose* the method of search–random search or registration at a centralized employment agency.

or alternatively,

$$x(l, v) = q(\theta) v \qquad (4)$$

both of which imply constant returns or linear homogeneity of $x(l, v)$. The presumption is that l-searchers see their probability of finding a match, p as being reduced by an increase in their own number and increased by larger numbers of v-searchers, so that $p_l < 0$ and $p_v > 0$. Clearly $p'(\theta) < 0$. Similarly for v-workers, $q_v < 0$, $q_l > 0$ and hence $q'(\theta) > 0$. It is easily established that for x to be increasing in both l and v in this case requires that the elasticity of p with respect to θ is less than unity in absolute value.

An assumption implicit in most of the literature is that the probability of forming another match while already in a match is zero, an exception is Diamond and Maskin (1979). This does not rule out the possibility that matches break up randomly (Pissarides, 1984) or as a result of a disappointing match (Jovanovic, 1984; McKenna, 1986a), and in these cases search is resumed.

Apart from determining the dynamics of matching models, or the flows from unmatched to matched states, the matching technology also determines the stock of searchers in each group in the steady state. The steady state in these models is when the stocks of individuals in all states are constant for a constant inflow of new entrants and outflow of those leaving the market permanently. In the labour market context this leads to an exploration of the steady-state unemployment–vacancy relationship – in our notation we may associate l with the stock of searching unemployed in each period and v with the stock of vacancies, so that θ is the (endogenous) unemployment–vacancy ratio. Matching models determine the equilibrium steady-state numbers of unemployed, vacancies and matches.

However, the principal concern is whether these steady-state values which result from the individual decisions of unco-ordinated economic agents are 'efficient in the sense normally used by economists. In general they are not, and the reason is the presence of externalities. In short the matching process does not provide a mechanism by which individuals entering a new state are forced to consider the effect of their joining on the activity of existing individuals. The matching process is responsible for this, but generally the inefficiencies are not counteracted elsewhere, for example by 'appropriate' incentives generated by an 'appropriate' price structure.

To see how these inefficiencies arise, consider the 'private' decisions of l-agents. The calculation of the expected total utility from search will be based on, among other things, the probability $p(\theta)$ which individuals treat as parametric, that is $given$ the present (steady-state) value of θ. That this ratio changes as a result of their own decisions (and those of people making similar decisions) is not taken into account.

The externalities operate in two directions when the market is composed of two identifiable groups. For example, the search decision of new *l*-searchers imposes unaccounted for costs on existing *l*-searchers through 'crowding', whereas the extra *l*-searchers represent an unaccounted-for benefit on *v*-searchers because of the improved chances of locating a partner. As a consequence the net direction of the inefficiency may be ambiguous as in Pissarides (1984). When the total of searchers is not subdivided according to type the market generates too little activity since private participation decisions do not take account of the unambiguous benefit an extra searcher has on the market in improving matching opportunities, as in Diamond (1984).

Interestingly the externalities generated by the matching process are not automatically corrected for by the process determining the contractual terms. In the majority of the small number of models developed thus far, the context is the labour market and the wage results from a Nash bargain (Diamond, 1982; Mortensen, 1982) between the 'worker' and the 'employer'. The resultant wage does not in general provide a corrective 'signal' to offset the externality, though often a wage exists which would produce the (second-best) optimum amount of search and match-formation (Pissarides, 1984; McKenna, 1986b).

The bargaining approach to contractual terms seems to have appeal in models of one-to-one matching. With multiple partnerships, and as a description of many non-unionized employment contracts, a take-it-or-leave it offer by one side (the 'employer') seems more appropriate. There are very few models of this type in the matching literature, and those tend to consider the turnover implications but not the efficiency issues (Jovanovic, 1984; McKenna, 1986b). Clearly there is room for a great deal more research in this area.

Finally we note that steady-state equilibria are not only inefficient but may not be unique either. Diamond (1984) demonstrates this, and deduces that unco-ordinated exchange may not guarantee 'high' levels of economic activity in equilibrium – a lesson in the spirit of the 'microfoundations' of Keynesian macroeconomics.

3. EQUILIBRIUM WITH PRICE DISTRIBUTIONS

Early enquiries into the consequences of firms' price adjustments concluded that the only equilibrium, even with imperfectly informed consumers, involved a single price, either the perfectly competitive price (Fisher, 1970) or the monopoly price (Diamond, 1971; Hey, 1974), depending on the particular assumptions made. In a similar spirit Braverman (1980) has shown how differences in consumer search costs may sustain a single price equilibrium either at the competitive price or at a price higher than this but lower than the monopoly price. An equilibrium involving price dispersion is also shown to be possible but involving at most *two* prices, the competitive price and price somewhat lower than the monopoly price.

This largely early work on the consequences of price or wage adjustment for the durability of price dispersion generally assumed homogeneous groups of agents – firms and searchers. Much of the subsequent literature has approached the topic from a different direction, and asks what conditions are required for price distributions to be anything other than a temporary market phenomenon. The question of efficiency in markets with price dispersion and agents searching for more favourable terms has been hardly touched upon in the literature, and we postpone our discussion until the mechanics of price dispersion models have been outlined.

3.1. Sustaining price dispersion

Models of price dispersion take as their starting points one or other of the sequential search strategy or a variant of the fixed sample size strategy (McKenna, 1986c). To date there appears to be no market equilibrium analysis using the unified approach of sequential inter-period sampling and fixed sample (intensity) within-period sampling discussed in the earlier survey, and of which the model of Morgan and Manning (1985) is typical, although Burdett and Judd (1983) have a similar model in mind in their section 3.

The short answer to the question of what is required to sustain price dispersion appears to be some form of heterogeneity.[3] In consequence researchers in this area have turned to the minimal requirements or weakest assumptions about heterogeneity required for dispersion. However, the presence of many types of heterogeneity is not sufficient for sustained dispersion, and many papers contain examples of the degeneracy discovered by the early work (Diamond, 1971; Fisher, 1970; Hey, 1974), whilst at the same time indicating the possibility of non-degeneracy. Examples here are Axell (1977), Burdett and Judd (1983), Salop ad Stiglitz (1977) and Rob (1985). One distinction suggested by Burdett and Judd (1983) is between *ex ante* and *ex post* heterogeneity. The former indicates embedded

---

[3] I ignore other possible sources of dispersion such as perverse or inconsistent behaviour by firms and searchers.

differences in characteristics – for example search costs or production costs, while the latter arise only when the information-gathering
process is complete, or when uncertainties are resolved. The suggestion
is that *ex post* heterogeneity constitutes a weaker postulate, or at
least a less arbitrary assumption, than does the *ex ante* variety.

We start by presenting a particularly simple and transparent model
of price dispersion as a benchmark with which we may compare
other contributions in the literature. The model we outline is due to
Reinganum (1979), and has both *ex ante* and *ex post* heterogeneities
present. The *ex ante* heterogeneity is in a given distribution of firm's
(constant) marginal costs of production, while *ex post* consumers
purchase different quantities of a homogeneous good according to a
given demand schedule.

Consumers use a pure sequential search strategy and all face the
same price distributions $F(p)$, $p \in [\underline{p}, \bar{p}]$ which is continuous and
differentiable almost everywhere. In view of this we write the density
as $dF(p)$ which is positive for $p \in [\underline{p}, \bar{p}]$ and zero elsewhere. All
consumers have the same constant search cost $k > 0$ and search with
full recall to maximize utility $U(p)$ with $U'(p) < 0$ – lower prices
are preferred. It is easily shown that if $\hat{p} \geqslant \underline{p}$ is the lowest price
discovered to date, the net value of one more search is given by;

$$h(\hat{p}) = \int_{\underline{p}}^{\hat{p}} [U(p) - U(\hat{p})] \, dF(p) - k \qquad (5)$$

which has an obvious interpretation. Differentiation of (5) gives,

$$h'(\hat{p}) = - F(\hat{p}) \, U'(\hat{p}) \geqslant 0 \quad \text{for } \hat{p} \geqslant \underline{p}$$

A *reservation price* clearly makes $h(\cdot) = 0$. Hence p^* is a reservation
price satisfying

$$\int_{\underline{p}}^{p^*} [U(p) - U(p^*)] \, dF(p) - k = 0 \qquad (6)[4]$$

Under the assumptions all searchers have the same reservation price.
Searchers also have the same demand schedule – though actual *ex
post* demands will differ because of different fortunes in search.
Demand is given by;

$$d(p) = \begin{cases} q(p) & p \leqslant p^* \\ 0 & p > p^* \end{cases} \qquad (7)$$

Firms differ in their constant marginal cost c which has a con-
tinuous and differentiable distribution $G(c)$, $c \in [\underline{c}, \bar{c}]$, and they

---

[4] Compare this with equation (16) of the earlier survey McKenna (1986c), but recall that
there $U'(x) > 0$, whilst here $U'(p) < 0$, hence the 'reversal' is the limits of integration.

maximize expected profit given by (making use of (7));

$$\pi_j = \begin{cases} (p_j - c_j)\, q(p_j)\, E[n_j] & p_j \leqslant p^* \\ 0 & p_j > p^* \end{cases} \tag{8}$$

for each firm j. The term $(p_j - c_j)$ is profit per unit sold, $q(p_j)$ is the number of units sold to each buyer and $E[n_j]$ is the expected number of buyers. If the number of buyers and sellers is 'large' and search is truly random, then $E[n_j]$ may be replaced by $\lambda = m/n$, where m and n are the number of buyers and sellers respectively. In an 'atomistic' market we let m and n increase without limit keeping λ constant. That firms offering a price below p^* should all expect the same number of customers simply reflects the fact that search is random and that a consumer will buy at the first store j for which $p_j \leqslant p^*$. Choosing p_j in (8) gives the expected profit-maximizing price for each firm as

$$p_j = c_j e/(1 + e), \quad e = \frac{p_j}{q_j}\, q'(p_j) \tag{9}$$

for each firm j, where e is assumed constant and $|e| > 1$.

The kind of equilibrium we are looking for is a Nash equilibrium in which all firms make equal profit and therefore have no incentive to change their prices. Furthermore consumers should have no incentive to change their reservation price. Finally, equilibrium should be characterized by price dispersion. Intuitively, the price distribution is induced by the given distribution of firm's costs. In view of (9)

$$F(p) = G(p(1 + e)/e) \quad p \in [\underline{p}, \bar{p}] \tag{10}$$

is the distribution of prices induced by the cost distribution, where $\underline{p} = \underline{c}e/1 + e$, and $\bar{p} = \bar{c}e/(1 + e)$. To establish the equilibrium price distribution for a given reservation price $F^*(p)$, we first note that $h(\underline{p}) = -k$, $h(p^*) = 0$ and $h(\bar{p}) \geqslant 0$ which imply (given $h'(\cdot) > 0$) that $\bar{p} \geqslant p^* > \underline{p}$ and so $p^* \leqslant \bar{c}e/(1 + e) = \bar{p}$. This last relation raises the apparent possibility that the firm's (unconstrained) choice of p_j might exceed p^* if c_j were 'high' (sufficiently close to $\bar{c}$); in this case, however, in view of the upper bound on tolerated prices, the (constrained) best policy for the firm is $p_j = p^*$. Thus in the induced equilibrium distribution there will be a mass point at $p = p^*$. Hence, $F^*(p)$ differs from $F(p)$ given in (10) by the presence of a mass point (jump continuity) at $p = p^*$. In other words the equilibrium distribution $F^*(\cdot)$, given the reservation price p^*, differs from the initially presumed distribution $F(\cdot)$ induced by $G(\cdot)$. Surely in this case, since p^* was initially derived under $F(\cdot)$, there will be a new p^* derived under $F^*(\cdot)$ and so on? Not so. The cycle is avoided by noting that the only difference between $F(\cdot)$ and $F^*(\cdot)$ is at and above p^*. Recall that p^* is the solution to;

$$\int_{\underline{p}}^{p^*} [U(p) - U(p^*)] \, dF(p) - k = 0 \tag{11}$$

and is the same as the solution to

$$\int_{\underline{p}}^{p^*} [U(p) - U(p^*)] \, dF^*(p) - k = 0 \tag{12}$$

since at the mass point (the only point at which the difference between $F(\cdot)$ and $F^*(\cdot)$ matters) $[U(p) - U(p^*)] = 0$ in both (11) and (12). The non-degenerate price distribution in equilibrium is therefore

$$F^*(p) = \begin{cases} G(p(1 + e)/e) & p < p^* \\ 1 & p \geqslant p^* \end{cases} \tag{13}$$

No prices above p^* are observed even though costs would induce such prices were it not for the demand constraint. Notice that the role of the *ex post* heterogeneity among consumers is critical. If all consumers bought the same quantity inelastically then the best policy for all firms would be $p_j = p^*$, all j and the price distribution would disappear.

This model gives a flavour of the methodology employed in the literature, but by no means does it incorporate all the ingredients that have been used by various authors. The use of the pure sequential strategy, for example, is by no means universal. One influential model (Axell, 1977) made use of the sequential strategy but showed the possibility of dispersion in equilibrium by a different route. Briefly, it is shown that a distribution of search costs induces a distribution of reservation prices which in turn generates a distribution of price offers. Apart from *ex ante* differences in consumer search costs, however, there is also an *ex post* heterogeneity on the firm's side. This results from a rather odd, *ad hoc* price adjustment process by firms in which they 'experiment' being uncertain as to whether raising or lowering their prices will increase expected profits. In Carlson and McAfee (1983) and MacMinn (1980) there are *ex ante* heterogeneities on both sides of the market, in both search costs and production costs, but unlike Reinganum (1979) demand by each consumer is perfectly inelastic. In Rob (1985) the only source of heterogeneity is the *ex ante* distribution of search costs in a model using sequential search. This work is closely related to Axell (1977), but the conditions which sustain dispersion are weaker.

Several authors have looked at price dispersion using a modified version of the fixed sample size strategy. These include Burdett and

Judd (1983), Butters (1977), MacMinn (1980), Salop and Stiglitz (1977), Wilde (1977) and Wilde and Schwartz (1979).

In the model of Butters (1977) consumers receive a random selection of advertisements from sellers and choose the lowest price at which to buy (inelastically). All consumers are identical *ex ante*. Sellers choose which prices to advertise and how many 'ads' should be transmitted in order to reach potential buyers.[5] Each 'ad' generates a random number of sales. It appears that in this model it pays for no two sellers to advertise the same price, with the consequence that sellers spread themselves evenly along the price continuum and all earn equal (zero) profits. The reason for this is that since price quotes hit consumers randomly, sellers wish to avoid the possibility that, should their price be the minimum received by a consumer it is in competition with another firm's price quote of the same amount. The result here depends on each firm's 'ads' constituting a small (infinitesimally small) share of the total. Thus it is *ex post* hetergeneity – the outcome of the random process of the success of advertising which drives the model. Incidentally this is one of the very few models in which not only is the *sustaining* of a price distribution explained but the *generation* of such a distribution is also explained. Single-price equilibria are impossible.

Along similar lines the equilibrium in Wilde (1977) is the result of *ex post* heterogeneity resulting from the outcome of a stochastic version of the fixed sample size rule. Similarly in Burdett and Judd (1983) 'high' price firms survive because there are some consumers who discover only their price and no others.

In Salop and Stiglitz (1977) the search rule is of the non-sequential variety, but consumers differ *ex ante* in terms of their search costs such that some consumers choose to become fully informed (those with low search costs) whilst others (those with high search costs) choose to remain ignorant and sample randomly. Crucially average costs are U-shaped and given a zero profit condition for equilibrium at most two prices can persist – the low (competitive) price exploited by informed customers and a high (monopolistically competitive) price determined by the demands forthcoming from uninformed customers. Single-price equilibria and the non-existence of any equilibrium are also possible in this model.

3.2. Efficiency with price dispersion

We return to the theme of section 2, and examine what new efficiency considerations are introduced by price (or wage) dispersion.

---

[5] Firm behaviour in many of the models involves treating other competitor's decisions as given, and not influenced by its own behaviour – a Nash competitor – and yet recognizes the impact of its own price behaviour on consumer search – a Stackleberg leader.

There are no general propositions here, and claims should be made strictly within the context of one of the models discussed. However, in many search processes insufficient search takes place. A simple example illustrates. In the Salop and Stiglitz (1977) model it is the presence of consumers in the market who are willing to become fully informed which keeps the lower price 'alive' in the market, and this passes on a benefit to all uninformed search *ex ante* and in particular those uninformed who are lucky enough to find the low price *ex post*. Hence this externality implies that fewer resources than are socially warranted are being devoted to search. The discussion in Butters (1977) also comes to similar conclusions.

4. WAGES, TURNOVER AND LABOUR MARKET EQUILIBRIUM

In general the types of issues at the heart of models of price dispersion are also present in models of equilibrium wage dispersion. That is, we identify wage dispersion with some sort of heterogeneity (McKenna, 1985). However, labour markets have features of particular interest arising from the nature of contracts and turnover. We briefly examine some of these issues here.

The feature which makes labour markets different is that generally the story does not end with the discovery of an acceptable offer. A particularly simple but powerful study of the consequences is given in a recent paper by Stiglitz (1985).[6] In this paper workers engage in on-the-job search for wage improvements and quit when a higher wage is found. Wage improvements are less likely the higher is the firm's own wage offer. Firms incur turnover costs or recruitment costs and higher wages may be prompted by a desire to reduce these costs. A zero-profit condition for equilibrium gives the quit rate for any presumed wage offer. Consequently single-wage or multiple-wage equilibria are possible with firms being indifferent between being high wage–low turnover firms or low wage–high turnover firms.

Turning once more to efficiency matters it is apparent that wage dispersion serves no useful purpose in the allocation of resources[7] in this model, and since it creates turnover expenditures are made which could be eliminated by the establishment of a single wage. Furthermore a high wage firm takes account of the reduction in its

---

[6] Although the paper has only recently been published, the author has been working on the problem for some time and the ideas have been available in working paper form for some time.

[7] The first model considered by Stiglitz (1985) in some ways reverses the assumptions of the matching models discussed in section 2, for there is (the possibility of) wage dispersion but no matching problem as such.

own quit rate[8] as a consequence of pursuing a 'high wage' policy, but there is no account in the calculus of the effect this has of increasing the quit rate of low wage firms.

Finally, two early papers gave attention to wage dispersion in labour markets. In Lucas and Prescott (1974) wage dispersion is generated across spatially distinct markets and the economy receives random 'price' shocks. In Eaton and Watts (1977) the wage distribution is supported by differences in workers' *perceptions* of the distribution giving rise to a distribution of reservation wages. This model is solved by numerical simulation rather than by analytical methods.

CONCLUSIONS

Rather than go over the ground covered, I give attention here to some outstanding issues.

The models of residual uncertainty in which non-wage 'experience' characteristics contribute to the expected value of search appears to be relatively neglected. Stiglitz (1985) has given this some consideration. A market analysis here must first establish whether the non-wage characteristic is a choice-variable of the firm, i.e. that the wage and non-wage characteristics are 'joint products', or whether the non-wage element is an endowed characteristic. In either case there seems to be scope for interplay between differences in the wage/non-wage package, turnover and wage dispersion.

Finally, there is the question of the empirical relevance of the models of price dispersion. The evidence here is strongly suggestive of substantial returns to search. A review of the evidence is out of the question here, but two recent papers relating to this issue may be of interest. Pratt, Wise and Zeckhauser (1979) look at price differences facing consumers, and Lynch (1983) uses data from the labour market for young people.

Department of Economics, University College, Cardiff

---

[8] Another source of turnover is that initiated by firms. If the probability of layoff is associated with the wage in an *ex ante* distribution then we are in a market discussed by Burdett and Mortensen (1980), whilst attempts to combine the search approach to labour supply and the implicit-contract approach to labour demand.

REFERENCES

Axell, B. (1977). 'Search Market Equilibrium', *Scandinavian Journal of Economics*, Vol. 79, pp. 20-40.

Braverman, A. (1980). 'Consumer Search and Alternative Market Equilibria', *Review of Economic Studies*, Vol. 47, pp. 487-502.

Burdett, K. and Judd, K. L. (1983). 'Equilibrium Price Dispersion', *Econometrica*, Vol. 51, pp. 955-69.

Burdett, K. and Mortenson, D. T. (1980). 'Search, Payoffs and Market Equilibrium', *Journal of Political Economy*, Vol. 88, pp. 652-72.

Butters, G. R. (1977). 'Equilibrium Distributions of Sales and Advertising Prices', *Review of Economic Studies*, Vol. 44, pp. 465-92.

Carlson, J. A. and McAfee, R. P. (1983). 'Discrete Equilibrium Price Dispersions', *Journal of Political Economy*, Vol. 9, pp. 480-93.

Diamond, P. A. (1971). 'A Model of Price Adjustment', *Journal of Economic Theory*, Vol. 3, pp. 156-68.

Diamond, P. A. (1982). 'Wage Determination and Efficiency in Search Equilibrium', *Review of Economic Studies'*, Vol. 49, pp. 217-28.

Diamond, P. A. (1984). *A Search-Equilibrium Approach to the MicroFoundations of Macroeconomics*, Cambridge, Mass., MIT Press.

Diamond, P. A. and Maskin, E. (1979). 'An Equilibrium Analysis of Search and Breach of Contract, I: Steady States', *Bell Journal of Economics*, Vol. 10, pp. 282-316.

Eaton, B. C. and Watts, M. (1977). 'Wage Dispersion, Job Vacancies and Job Search in Equilibrium', *Economica*, Vol. 44, pp. 23-35.

Fisher, F. M. (1970). 'Quasi-competitive Price Adjustment by Individual Firms', *Journal of Economic Theory*, Vol. 2, pp. 195-206.

Fisher, F. M. (1973). 'Stability and Competitive Equilibrium in Two Models of Search and Individual Price Adjustment', *Journal of Economic Theory*, Vol. 6, pp. 446-70.

Fisher, F. M. (1983). *Disequilibrium Foundations of Equilibrium Economics*, Cambridge: Cambridge University Press.

Hey, J. D. (1974). 'Price Adjustment in an Atomistic Market', *Journal of Economic Theory*, Vol. 84, pp. 483-99.

Jovanovic, B. (1984). 'Matching, Turnover and Unemployment', *Journal of Political Economy*, Vol. 92, pp. 108-22.

Lucas, R. E. and Prescott, E. C. (1974). 'Equilibrium Search and Unemployment', *Journal of Economic Theory*, Vol. 7, pp. 188-209.

Lynch, L. M. (1983). 'Job Search and Youth Unemployment', *Oxford Economic Papers*, Vol. 35 (Supplement), pp. 271-83.

McKenna, C. J. (1985). *Uncertainty and the Labour Market*, Brighton, Wheatsheaf Books.

McKenna, C. J. (1986a). 'Equilibrium Wage Offers and Turnover in a Simple Search Market', *Economic Journal*, Vol. 96, pp. 785-97.

McKenna, C. J. (1986b). 'Labour Market Participation in Matching Equilibrium', Mimeo, University College, Cardiff. Forthcoming in *Economica.*

McKenna, C. J. (1986c). 'Theories of Individual Search Behaviour', *Bulletin of Economic Research*, Vol. 38, pp. 189-207.

MacMinn, R. D. (1980). 'Search and Market Equilibrium', *Journal of Political Economy*, Vol. 88, pp. 308-27.

Morgan, P. B. and Manning, R. (1985). 'Optimal Search', *Econometrica*, Vol. 53, pp. 923-44.

Mortensen, D. T. 'The Matching Process as a Noncooperative Bargaining Game', in *The Economics of Information and Uncertainty*, McCall, J. J. (ed.), pp. 233-54, Chicago, NBER/University of Chicago Press.

Pissarides, C. A. (1979). 'Job Matchings with State Employment Agencies and Random Search', *Economic Journal*, Vol. 89, pp. 818-33.

Pissarides, C. A. (1984). 'Efficient Job Rejection', *Economic Journal*, Vol. 94, pp. 97-108.

Pratt, J. W., Wise, D. and Zeckhauser, R. (1979). 'Price Differences in Almost Competitive Markets', *Quarterly Journal of Economics*, Vol. 93, pp. 189-211.

Reinganum, J. T. (1979). 'A Simple Model of Equilibrium Price Dispersion', *Journal of Political Economy*, Vol. 87, pp. 851-8.

Rob, R. (1985). 'Equilibrium Price Distributions', *Review of Economic Studies*, Vol. 52, pp. 487-504.

Rothschild, M. (1973). 'Models of Market Organisation with Imperfect Information: A Survey', *Journal of Political Economy*, Vol. 81, pp. 1283-308.

Salop, S. and Stiglitz, J. E. (1971). 'Bargains and Ripoffs: A Model of Monopolistically Competitive Price Dispersion', *Review of Economic Studies*, Vol. 44, pp. 493-510.

Stiglitz, J. E. (1985). 'Equilibrium Wage Distributions', *Economic Journal*, Vol. 95, pp. 595-618.

Wilde, L. L. (1977). 'Labor Market Equilibrium under Nonsequential Search', *Journal of Economic Theory*, Vol. 16, pp. 373-93.

Wilde, L. L. and Schwartz, A. (1979). 'Equilibrium Comparison Shopping', *Review of Economic Studies*, Vol. 40, pp. 543-53.

THE SIMPLE ANALYTICS OF IMPLICIT LABOUR CONTRACTS

*Mark P. Taylor**

ABSTRACT

This paper outlines the development and exposits some of the central ideas of implicit contract theory using only basic mathematics (mainly Lagrangeans) and diagrams.

1. INTRODUCTION

Traditional neoclassical economics predicts that profit maximizing firms will pay workers a real wage equal to their marginal product. This in turn implies that competitive firms will vary both employment and the real wage over the business cycle in response to fluctuations in product demand. However, the observed normal practice in most western economies is to lay off workers as product demand contracts, paying the rest of the workforce a fairly unchanged wage. Laid-off workers may even be later re-hired by the same firm at the same wage as before the layoff (Feldstein (1975), Lilien (1980), Katz (1984)). Given that labour is in less than perfectly elastic supply, this is something of an anomaly.

One response to this empirical phenomenon has been to abandon the idea of short-run market clearing altogether and to take sticky wages and prices as parametric – see for example Clower (1965), Leijonhufvud (1968), Barro and Grossman (1976).

A rather different response has generated a body of literature which sees the employer–employee relationship as being rather more complex than that suggested by more traditional models, and in which sticky wages and layoffs may be the outcome of jointly optimizing behaviour on the part of agents. Seminal papers in this literature are Baily (1974), Gordon (1974) and Azariadis (1975), the

* I am grateful to Mike Waterson and an anonymous referee for helpful comments on a previous version of this paper. The usual disclaimer applies. Any views expressed are mine and not necessarily those of the Bank of England.

124

last of which apparently coined the phrase 'implicit contract'.[1] One way of thinking about the theory of implicit labour contracts is to note that if employers are less risk averse than employees, then it may be optimal for them both to enter into an optimal risk-sharing agreement whereby the firm in effect insures the worker against the risk of wage variations. In fact, one can think of wages in such models as 'varying', but when the wage is below 'average', the shortfall is made up by an indemnity paid to the worker, whilst when it is above average the excess is paid as a premium to the firm. The net effect is an observationally sticky wage.

There is now a large and growing literature on implicit contract theory, and a number of good surveys are available which document it – see for example Azariadis (1979), Azariadis and Stiglitz (1983), Hart (1983) and Rosen (1985). The object of the present essay is rather more modest than that of any of these. The implicit contracts literature is technically quite demanding and is hence rather inaccessible to students and non-specialist economists who wish to acquire a grasp of the topic. This paper aims to outline the development and exposit some of the main ideas of implicit contract theory using only basic mathematics (mainly Lagrangeans) and diagrams. (Readers requiring an exhaustive literature survey should refer to Hart (1983) or Rosen (1985).) Because we try to spell out rather than skate over the arguments, the analysis is limited to a treatment of various aspects of symmetric information contracts – those where both employers and employees have the same information. In a related paper (Taylor (1987)) we extend the analysis to consider the nature of implicit labour contracts when firms are risk averse and information is asymmetric, and also when the workforce is heterogeneous.

In the next section we set up our basic model and examine the variability of wages over the business cycle with full employment. Section 3, which forms the core of the analysis, examines the nature of the optimal labour contract when both wages and employment are allowed to vary. Section 4 considers the nature of unemployment in implicit contracts models – whether in some sense it may be considered involuntary, and how it compares to the corresponding levels of unemployment which would prevail in a Walrasian spot auction. A final section summarizes and concludes.

---

[1] Hart (1983) argues that contracts in these models should be thought of as explicit rather than implicit, since otherwise there may be problems of enforceability once the state of nature is observed. It might be argued that reputation considerations force the firm to be 'time consistent', but a formal model embodying such considerations has yet to be advanced. As far as workers are concerned, Grossman (1977, 1978) suggests that senior workers are recognized as less likely to renege on contracts and hence are given preferential treatment during layoffs.

2. THE VARIABILITY OF WAGES WITH FULL-EMPLOYMENT CONTRACTS

The belief that wages should vary (counter-cyclically) over the business cycle is implicitly based on a view of the labour market as a spot auction. The insight of implicit contract models is that labour is not in fact auctioned off at each point in time in quite the same way as, say, fresh fruit or vegetables are, but is rather more complex. In particular, the wage for a particular job will generally be only one element of an overall package which a job offers. Other factors which the worker might consider are, for example, whether there is a staff canteen, how sociable the hours are, how congenial the working environment is, and so on (you can make your own list). A chief item which most workers will be looking for in a job is job security – whether or not there is a risk of redundancy or layoff at some point, and how regular the wages are. The theory of implicit labour contracts models the labour market not as a spot auction but as one where employers and workers enter into mutually advantageous, unwritten, long-term contracts. Such contracts will indicate the wage that will be paid and the probability of being laid off at various phases over the business cycle (as well as other factors in the job package which we can ignore for a first approximation).

The starting point for most implicit contract models is that employers are less risk-averse than workers. In fact, we shall assume in this paper that employers are risk-neutral.[2] By this we mean that employers stand ready to accept (actuarially) fair bets in unlimited quantities. One way in which this might be rationalized is to argue that entrepreneurs, as a self-selecting group, are inherently less risk-averse than workers. Probably a more convincing argument (advanced in Baily (1974)) is based on the observation that shareholders rather than entrepreneurs are in fact the ultimate owners of most modern firms. The majority of shareholders are either wealthy individuals or large institutions such as pension funds or insurance companies. These agents are able to hold large, diversified portfolios and to employ or take advice from financial experts. On the other hand, a typical worker's assets might consist of durable goods, a small cash balance, and human capital – he may even have outstanding consumer credit liabilities. He cannot diversify his 'portfolio' by holding several jobs simultaneously, and is also far less likely to have a good knowledge of the capital markets or to be able to employ someone else who does. Hence, by utilizing their greater wealth and financial expertise, shareholders are much more able to bear risk than workers. This difference in characteristics suggests that there may be gains from trade.

---

[2] In Taylor (1987) we consider the possibility that employers may be risk averse.

By agreeing to accept some of the risk of wage variation, employers implicitly offer an insurance service to workers. This is attractive to workers because of their risk aversion and is relatively costless to the firm because of its risk neutrality. Thus, 'Risk-reducing policies are the cheapest and hence most profitable way of attracting any given work force' (Baily (1974), p. 37). We start the analysis by considering a much simplified version of the model in Azariadis (1975). Initially, we assume that the firm holds employment constant over the business cycle but may or may not vary wages. In the next section we relax this assumption and allow the firm to vary or hold constant both real wages and employment.

We assume a competitive firm that can sell all of its output at a given price. At any point in time, one of two states of nature will prevail – state one ('boom') or state two ('slump').[3] The known probability of state one occurring is ρ_1 and of state two $(1 - \rho_1)$. Both workers and employers are able to observe which state of the world is prevailing (information is symmetric).

Corresponding to the state of nature there will be a certain output price, p_1 (for state one) or p_2 (for state two), which the firm faces and which reflects industry demand conditions ($p_2 < p_1$). An important assumption we make is that the firm and industry are small in the sense that variations in the product price do not affect the overall, exogenous price level, which is fixed. Thus, variations in product price affect the *real* value of output which can be produced with a given level of inputs. Another interpretation which could therefore be given to the states of nature is the incidence of technology shocks with fixed product price. That is, occurrence of state two can be interpreted as a decline in technological efficiency such as might result from a 'supply side' shock.

Before the state of nature is actually observed, the firm chooses a wage and employment level for each state – w_i and n_i respectively, $i = 1, 2$, where the subscript denotes the relevant state. This composes the labour contract. Formally, we can define a contract as an ordered list, or vector, (w_1, n_1, w_2, n_2), which specifies what the wage and employment prospects are for the worker for any given state of nature.

Technology is described by an increasing, monotone, strictly concave function through the origin (i.e. a standard production function):

$$y_i = f(n_i), \ f' > 0, \ f'' < 0, \ f(0) = 0, \tag{1}$$

where y_i and n_i denote output and employment respectively in state

---

[3] This is a key simplifying assumption. Azariadis (1975), for example, considers a set of discrete states $S = \{s/s = s_1, s_2, \ldots, s_J\}$

i, $i = 1$, 2. In this section and throughout we assume that there is full employment in state one. In this section only we set $n_2 = n_1$.

Since we assume the firm is risk-neutral, it is indifferent to the expected value of profit and the certainty equivalent of that expected profit. The firm's objective is therefore to maximize its expected real profit:

$$\Pi = \rho_1(p_1 y_1 - w_1 n_1) + (1 - \rho_1)(p_2 y_2 - w_2 n_1). \tag{2}$$

At first sight this may appear to be expected nominal rather than real profit. Recall, however, that the overall price level is fixed and independent of the output price of the firm, so that changes in the firm's product price therefore reflect changes in the real value of output.

Now consider the typical worker. He is endowed with a von Neumann–Morgenstern utility function with real wage income and leisure as arguments. We shall assume that each worker supplies labour in an indivisible unit, so that wage income is strictly proportional to the wage rate. It makes no difference therefore if we treat the utility function as a function of the wage rate rather than wage income. Further, since we initially assume full employment in boom and slump, the amount of leisure enjoyed is the same over the business cycle. Thus, utility can only vary in the wage dimension. We can therefore think of the worker's utility in state i as an increasing, strictly concave, monotone function of w_i:

$$U = u(w_i), \quad u' > 0, \quad u'' < 0. \tag{3}$$

The concavity of the utility function is of course due to the worker's risk aversion. The worker maximizes his expected utility:

$$U = \rho_1 u(w_1) + (1 - \rho_1) u(w_2). \tag{4}$$

We assume that the firm cannot drive down both w_1 and w_2 indefinitely without losing its workforce. There will be a certain level of expected utility, $\tilde{U}$, say, which is determined by market forces and which workers could get by working for other firms. Hence, the firm's problem is to choose w_1 and w_2 to maximize (2) subject to:

$$\rho_1 u(w_1) + (1 - \rho_1) u(w_2) > \tilde{U}. \tag{5}$$

A contract which satisfies (5) is termed feasible (Azariadis (1975)). We should expect a profit-maximizing firm (knowing $u(\cdot)$ and $\tilde{U}$) to force (5) to an equality. A contract which is feasible and yields a higher level of expected profit than any other feasible contract will be termed optimal (Azariadis (1975)).

Since state one is 'boom', let us assume the firm is considering paying $w_1 > w_2$.[4] The worker's utility function will then look some-

---

[4] Since $p_1 > p_2$ implies a higher marginal product for the firm, wages vary procyclically at the firm level.

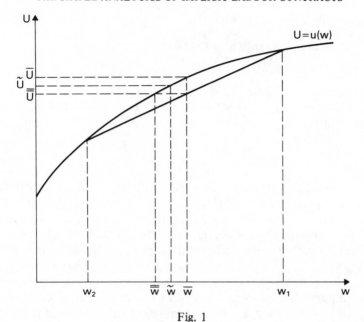

Fig. 1

thing like Figure 1. The expected utility obtained by the worker is $\bar{U} = \rho_1 u(w_1) + (1-\rho_1)u(w_2)$. Clearly, the worker would prefer to receive a constant real wage of $\bar{w} = \varrho_1 w_1 + (1-\rho_1)w_2$ which confers a level of expected utility of $\bar{U} > \bar{U}$. This is a consequence of the concavity of u which itself reflects the risk aversion of the worker.

However, the worker would in fact be content with a fixed wage of $\tilde{w}$, which yields a level of expected utility, $\bar{U}$, just sufficient to retain him. If we had $\tilde{U} < \bar{U}$, the fixed wage could be further reduced to $\bar{w}$ before the worker would prefer variable to fixed wages. It is clear, therefore, that the firm will in general be able to make the worker better off by paying him a state-invariant real wage which is slightly less than the expected value of the state-variable wage. Say this fixed wage is in fact $\tilde{w}$, the minimum wage the worker will accept, or his 'acceptance wage'.

Now, because the firm is risk-neutral, it is indifferent to paying out a constant wage of $\bar{w} = \rho_1 w_1 + (1-\rho_1)w_2$, or w_1 with probability ρ_1 and w_2 with probability $(1-\rho_1)$. To see this, simply rearrange equation (2):

$$\rho_1(p_1 y_1 - w_1 n_1) + (1-\rho_1)(p_2 y_1 - w_2 n_1)$$
$$= (\rho_1 p_1 + (1-\rho_1)p_2) y_1 - (\rho_1 w_1 + (1-\rho_1) w_2) n_1$$
$$= (\rho_1 p_1 + (1-\rho_1) p_2) y_1 - \bar{w} n_1. \qquad (6)$$

Moreover, since $\tilde{w} < \bar{w}$, (6) implies:

$$\rho_1(p_1 y_1 - \tilde{w} n_1) + (1 - \rho_1)(p_2 y_1 - \tilde{w} n_1)$$

$$> \rho_1(p_1 y_1 - w_1 n_1) + (1 - \rho_1)(p_2 y_1 - w_2 n_1), \qquad (7)$$

i.e. it is more profitable on average to pay a fixed wage of $\tilde{w}$ than to vary it. Since $\tilde{w}$ is the lowest wage which can be paid before workers quit to find employment elsewhere, the solution to the firm's maximization problem is clearly:

$$w_1 = w_2 = \tilde{w}. \qquad (8)$$

So the profit-maximizing, feasible, full-employment contract is $(\tilde{w}, n_1, \tilde{w}, n_1)$. Indeed, it is clear that this contract is Pareto-optimal (in this partial equilibrium context). From Figure 1 we can see that $(w_1 - \tilde{w})$ is the maximum insurance premium that the worker would be willing to pay in order to have his wage made up to w_1 (i.e. receive indemnity of $(w_1 - w_2)$ should state two occur). Note that this is less than $(w_1 - \bar{w})$ which is the maximum premium the worker would pay in the absence of expected utility opportunities of $\bar{U}$ elsewhere. Hence we can see that the firm is in effect offering insurance to the worker against variations in the real wage. The firm is happy to do this because it is less risk-averse than the worker. Put slightly differently, the risk is transferred from wages to profits and hence to the capital market, and so the firm implicitly acts as a financial intermediary. Given the attitudes toward risk of the worker and the firm, this is an optimal risk-sharing equilibrium.

3. THE EXISTENCE OF LAYOFFS

So far we have been able to gain some insight into why real wages may be sticky by examining the nature of the full-employment contract. But we have yet to provide an explanation for the existence of layoffs. We now relax the assumption of constant (full) employment and allow the firm to choose what levels of employment to offer simultaneously with wages.

We shall in fact continue to assume that everyone is employed during state one ('boom'), but there may now be layoffs during state two ('slump'). Hence, n_1 still denotes full employment but $(n_1 - n_2)$ workers will be randomly laid off should state two occur. So if state one occurs, workers are certain of finding employment. If state two occurs, workers will find employment with conditional probability n_2/n_1 and will be laid off with conditional probability $(1 - n_2/n_1)$.

In the discussion in Section 2 workers were never laid off, so we did not have to explicitly consider leisure as an argument in the utility function. Now suppose that if workers are employed they have leisure l_e whilst if they are laid off they have leisure l_u, $l_u > l_e$. We now have to redefine the utility function to take explicit account of leisure, l:

$$U = v(w, l), \; \partial v/\partial w > 0, \; \partial^2 v/\partial w^2 < 0, \; \partial v/\partial l > 0, \; \partial^2 v/\partial l^2 < 0. \quad (9)$$

In fact, the discussion in Section 2 can be made consistent with (9) by defining $u(\cdot)$ appropriately:

$$u(w) = v(w, l_e). \quad (10)$$

Now suppose that when the worker is unemployed he receives real unemployment benefit of b paid from an economy-wide fund. Further, let c be the value that the worker attaches to having leisure l_u rather than l_e, i.e. c is just enough to compensate for the loss of leisure $(l_u - l_e)$.[6] Then if we define r:

$$r = c + b, \quad (11)$$

r is the real wage that will make the worker indifferent between working (and receiving r) and not working (and receiving b):

$$v(b, l_u) = v(r, l_e) = u(r). \quad (12)$$

In the light of (12) we can continue to use $u(\cdot)$ as before, so long as we take care in its interpretation.

Now workers know that there is probability ρ_1 of a boom occurring, in which case they derive a utility of $u(w_1)$. There is probability of $(1 - \rho_1)$ of a slump occurring. Given that a slump occurs, with a homogeneous workforce there is a probability of n_2/n_1 of finding employment and deriving utility $u(w_1)$, and a probability of $(1 - n_2/n_1)$ of being laid off and deriving utility $u(r)$. Hence, the expected utility for the worker is:

$$U = \rho_1 u(w_1) + (1 - \rho_1)[(n_2/n_1) u(w_2) + (1 - n_2/n_1) u(r)]. \quad (13)$$

We again assume that there is some market-determined level of expected utility $\tilde{U}$ which the worker could obtain by accepting a contract elsewhere.

The firm's expected real profit is similar to (2) except that output and employment can now vary between states:

$$\Pi = \rho_1(p_1 f(n_1) - w_1 n_1) + (1 - \rho_1)(p_2 f(n_2) - w_2 n_2). \quad (14)$$

As before, the firm maximizes expected real profit, now with respect to n_2 as well as w_1 and w_2, subject to the worker achieving a level of

---

[6] Note that c will itself generally be a positive function of b. However, the results below require only that r be an increasing function of b. At a less general level, we could assume perfect substitutability between income and leisure (see Section 4, footnote 8).

expected utility of at least $\tilde{U}$. This is equivalent to unconstrained maximization of the Lagrangean:[5]

$$\pounds = \rho_1(p_1 f(n_1) - w_1 n_1) + (1 - \rho_1)(p_2 f(n_2) - w_2 n_2)$$
$$+ \lambda [\rho_1 u(w_1) + (1 - \rho_1)(n_2/n_1) u(w_2)$$
$$+ (1 - \rho_1)(1 - n_2/n_1) u(r) - \tilde{U}] \qquad (15)$$

where λ is a Lagrange multiplier. The necessary first-order conditions for maximization of (15) are:

$$\frac{\partial \pounds}{\partial n_2} = (1 - \rho_1)(p_2 f'(n_2) - w_2) + \lambda(1 - \rho_1)(1/n_1)(u(w_2) - u(r)) = 0$$
$$(16)$$

$$\frac{\partial \pounds}{\partial w_1} = -\rho_1 n_1 + \lambda \rho_1 u'(w_1) = 0 \qquad (17)$$

$$\frac{\partial \pounds}{\partial w_2} = -(1 - \rho_1) n_2 + \lambda(1 - \rho_1)(n_2/n_1) u'(w_2) = 0 \qquad (18)$$

$$\frac{\partial \pounds}{\partial \lambda} = \rho_1 u(w_1) + (1 - \rho_1)(n_2/n_1) u(w_2) + (1 - \rho_1)(1 - n_2/n_1) u(r) - \tilde{U}$$
$$= 0. \qquad (19)$$

Equation (17) can be written:

$$-\rho_1 n_1 = -\lambda \rho_1 u'(w_1) \qquad (20)$$

and equation (18) can be written:

$$-(1 - \rho_1) n_2 = -\lambda(1 - \rho_1)(n_2/n_1) u'(w_2). \qquad (21)$$

Dividing (20) by (21):

$$\frac{-\rho_1 n_1}{-(1 - \rho_1) n_2} = \frac{\rho_1 u'(w_1)}{(1 - \rho_1)(n_2/n_1) u'(w_2)}. \qquad (22)$$

Now $-\rho_1 n_1$ is the marginal expected profit accruing to the firm from an increase in w_1 – i.e. total expected profits would fall by $-\rho_1 n_1$ if w_1 rose one unit. Similarly, $-(1 - \rho_1) n_2$ is the marginal expected profit of wages in state two. Hence, the left-hand side of (22) is the firm's marginal rate of substitution between real wages in different states of nature, or (minus) the slope of an iso-profit line in (w_1, w_2) space, holding n_1 and n_2 constant. (To prove that the left-hand side of (22) is a marginal rate of substitution for the firm, totally differentiate (14), set $d\Pi = 0$, $dn_1 = 0$, $dn_2 = 0$ and solve for dw_2/dw_1.)

---

[5] We assume that the firm forces the worker's expected utility to its lowest feasible level, $\tilde{U}$, and that an interior solution is obtained to (15).

Similarly, $\rho_1 u'(w_1)$ is the marginal expected utility to the worker of an increase in w_1 and $(1-\rho_1)(n_2/n_1)u'(w_2)$ is the marginal expected utility of an increase in w_2. This implies that the right-hand side of (23) is the worker's marginal rate of substitution of income in state two for income in state one, or (minus) the slope of an indifference curve in (w_1, w_2) space, holding n_1 and n_2 constant. (To prove that this is so, totally differentiate (13), set $dU = 0$, $dn_1 = 0$, $dn_2 = 0$ and solve for dw_2/dw_1.)

Thus, (22) simply says that real wages in boom and slump should be chosen so as to equalize marginal rates of substitution between incomes in different states for the firm and the worker. This condition for optimal risk sharing is a special case of a result due to Borch (1962) and Arrow (1971).

But (22) can be written, after cancelling common factors and rearranging:

$$u'(w_1) = u'(w_2), \tag{23}$$

i.e. the slope of the worker's utility curve at w_1 is the same as at w_2. But we assumed that u is a strictly concave function – i.e. its slope is continuously falling, $u'' < 0$. This implies that it cannot have the same slope at two points, i.e. (23) cannot be satisfied for $w_1 \neq w_2$. Thus, we must have:

$$w_1 = w_2 = w \tag{24}$$

– the optimal risk-sharing wage is state-invariant.

We can view this diagrammatically. Note that the preceding discussion implies that the firm's iso-profit curves will be straight lines in (w_1, w_2) space for given n_1, n_2, whilst the worker's indifference curves will be convex. Thus, as Figure 2 illustrates, maximizing expected profit Π, for a given level of the worker's expected utility $\bar{U}$, will result in a tangency solution. But, as equation (22) implies, tangencies only occur when $w_1 = w_2$, i.e. on a $45°$ ray through the origin.

Therefore, the result derived earlier that firms will be willing to absorb the risk of variation in wages, by essentially acting as a financial intermediary to the worker, carries over to the case where the firm is free to vary employment. Although relaxing the assumption of state-invariant employment apparently complicates matters, the same arguments as in the previous section go through as before. The firm is still willing to absorb the risk of wage variation, since it is risk-neutral. But will it be optimal for the firm to vary employment over booms and slumps?

In order to answer this question we pose it slightly differently. Given that the optimal contract will be one with a fixed wage, the question is whether or not it is optimal to reduce employment in

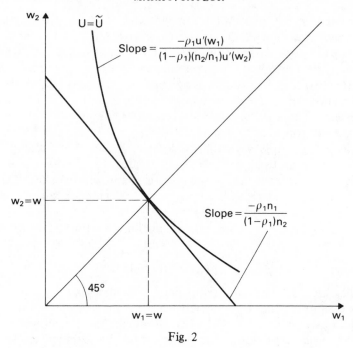

Fig. 2

slumps, or to maintain full employment (perhaps with a lower fixed wage). In other words, are full-employment contracts optimal?

Firstly, we examine how, starting from a position of state-invariant full employment ($n_2 = n_1$) changes in n_2/n_1 below unity affect the firm. We have already shown that it is optimal for the firm to set a state-invariant wage, regardless of whether employment is state-invariant or not. From the previous section, we know that, in a full-employment contract, this wage will be $\tilde{w}$, the worker's acceptance wage.

Taking the expression for the firm's expected real profit, (14), and differentiating totally:

$$d\Pi = -(\rho_1 n_1 + (1-\rho_1) n_2) \, dw$$
$$+ \rho_1(p_1 f'(n_1) - \tilde{w}) \, dn_1$$
$$+ (1-\rho_1)(p_2 f'(n_2) - \tilde{w}) \, dn_2. \qquad (25)$$

Since we are starting from a position of state-invariant employment ($n_2 = n_1$), and are only interested in variations in n_2, we can set $n_2 = n_1$, $dn_1 = 0$:

$$d\Pi = -n_1 \, dw + (1-\rho_1)(p_2 f'(n_1) - \tilde{w}) \, dn_2. \qquad (26)$$

Now the firm will be indifferent to changes in w and n_2 which leave its expected real profit constant, i.e. such that $d\Pi = 0$ in (26), which implies:

$$\frac{dw}{dn_2} = \frac{(1-\rho_1)}{n_1}(p_2 f'(n_1) - \bar{w})$$

or

$$\frac{dw}{d(n_2/n_1)} = (1-\rho_1)(p_2 f'(n_1) - \bar{w}), \qquad (27)$$

since $d(n_2/n_1) = (1/n_1)dn_2$ when $dn_1 = 0$. Since $p_2 < p_1$ and $\bar{w}$ is state-invariant, we might suspect that (27) is negative. That this is in fact the case can be seen by noting that (17) can be written as:

$$\lambda = n_1/u'(w) \qquad (28)$$

which, when substituted into (16) yields, after rearrangement:

$$p_2 f'(n_1) - \bar{w} = -\frac{(u(\bar{w}) - u(r))}{u'(\bar{w})} < 0. \qquad (29)$$

So the firm pays a real wage greater than the value of the marginal product in state two at full employment. Therefore it would like to reduce employment in that state.

Now the probability that a worker will be unemployed is

$$(1-\rho_1)(1-n_2/n_1) = \phi,$$

say. Since $(1-\rho_1)$ is fixed, $d\phi = -(1-\rho_1)d(n_2/n_1)$, so that (27) may be alternatively expressed as:

$$\left.\frac{dw}{d\phi}\right|_{n_2=n_1}^{F} = \bar{w} - p_2 f'(n_1) \; (>0). \qquad (30)$$

Equation (30) says that the marginal increment to the state-invariant wage that the firm is willing to pay to the worker in return for a tiny reduction in the probability of employing him, is just equal to the excess of the real wage over the slump value of the full-employment marginal product – i.e. the amount real profit would rise if one worker were laid off in state two. The vertical bar is to remind us that this expression is computed at full-employment and relates to the firm's behaviour.

How will changes in the level of slump employment and the state-invariant real wage affect workers? To answer this, we start by totally differentiating the expression for the worker's expected utility, (13), setting $n_2 = n_1$ and $w_2 = w_1 = \bar{w}$:

$$dU = u'(\bar{w})dw + (1-\rho_1)(u(\bar{w}) - u(r))d(n_2/n_1). \qquad (31)$$

If the firm wishes to lay off workers during the slump, state two, it will have to increase the state-invariant real wage in order to compensate the worker for an increase in the probability of unemployment, i.e. it will have to pay an 'underemployment premium' (Azariadis (1975)). Otherwise, expected utility would fall below U and workers would quit (the contract ceases to be feasible).

In order to find the marginal underemployment premium demanded for a marginal increase in the probability of unemployment in slump, evaluated at the full-employment contract, we set $dU = 0$ in (31) and solve for $dw/d(n_2/n_1)$:

$$\frac{dw}{d(n_2/n_1)} = -(1-\rho_1)\frac{(u(\tilde{w})-u(r))}{u'(\tilde{w})}$$

or

$$\left.\frac{dw}{d\phi}\right|_{n_2=n_1}^{W} = \frac{(u(\tilde{w})-u(r))}{u'(\tilde{w})} \quad (>0) \tag{32}$$

where the vertical bar is to remind us that this expression relates to the behaviour of the worker and is computed at the full-employment contract. The right-hand side of (32) is the marginal underemployment premium, $z(\tilde{w}, r)$ say:

$$z(\tilde{w}, r) = \frac{u(\tilde{w})-u(r)}{u'(\tilde{w})}. \tag{33}$$

This is the amount the worker would have to be paid in order to compensate him for an infinitessimally small probability of unemployment. If the worker stands to lose a lot by being unemployed (i.e. $(u(\tilde{w}) - u(r))$ is large), then this will be reflected in the size of $z(\tilde{w}, r)$. If marginal utility is low ($u'(\tilde{w})$ is small), then a larger increase in the wage is necessary in order to compensate for the risk of unemployment. Given that there is diminishing marginal utility ($u'' < 0$), z will clearly be increasing in w and decreasing in r:

$$\frac{\partial z(\tilde{w}, r)}{\partial w} = 1 - \frac{(u(\tilde{w})-u(r))\,u''(\tilde{w})}{(u'(\tilde{w}))^2} > 0 \tag{34}$$

$$\frac{\partial z(\tilde{w}, r)}{\partial r} = -\frac{u'(r)}{u'(\tilde{w})} < 0. \tag{35}$$

The question that remains is whether, by reducing n_2/n_1 below unity and increasing the state-invariant wage above $\tilde{w}$, the firm can increase its expected profit whilst keeping the worker's expected utility constant (i.e. keeping the contract feasible). This will clearly be the case if expression (30) is greater than expression (32):

$$\tilde{w} - p_2 f'(n_1) > z(\tilde{w}, r)$$

i.e.

$$p_2 f'(n_1) < \tilde{w} - z(\tilde{w}, r). \qquad (36)$$

For then the marginal increase in the wage that the firm is willing to concede for a marginal increase in ϕ is actually greater than the marginal underemployment premium demanded by the worker. This means that, for a tiny increase in ϕ, the firm can pay an increase in the wage which will increase rather than merely hold constant its expected profit, whilst keeping the contract feasible. Viewed slightly differently, $p_2 f'(n_1)$ is the marginal cost of laying off one worker in state two (the value of his marginal product), whilst $\tilde{w} - z(\tilde{w}, r)$ is the marginal benefit to the firm of such an action (the wage saving of $\tilde{w}$ less the marginal underemployment premium which has to be paid to keep contracts feasible). Clearly, the firm will wish to lay off workers in state two so long as marginal benefit exceeds marginal cost.

Inequality (36) is a necessary and sufficient condition for the suboptimality of full-employment contracts.

Under what conditions is (36) more likely to hold? From (35) we can see that the right-hand side of (36) will be bigger the bigger r is. But r, the wage that would have to be paid in order to make the worker indifferent between working and not working, is an increasing function of the level of unemployment compensation and the worker's valuation of extra leisure (see (11)). Hence, layoffs will be more likely to occur the higher is the level of unemployment benefit. This makes intuitive sense since unemployment benefit serves to cushion the impact of being laid off.

The Arrow–Pratt measure of (absolute) risk aversion is:

$$Q(w) = -\frac{u''(w)}{u'(w)}.$$

To see how Q relates to (34), expand $u(r)$ in a Taylor series about $\tilde{w}$:

$$u(r) = u(\tilde{w}) + (r - w)\, u'(\tilde{w}) + \tfrac{1}{2}(r - \tilde{w})^2 u''(\tilde{w}) + \dots$$

Ignoring terms in derivatives of u higher than the second (assuming r is fairly close to $\tilde{w}$), this gives us:

$$\frac{u(\tilde{w}) - u(r)}{u'(\tilde{w})} = (\tilde{w} - r) + \tfrac{1}{2}(r - \tilde{w})^2 Q(\tilde{w}) = z(\tilde{w}, r). \qquad (37)$$

So that the marginal underemployment premium is an increasing function of Q, for given r. This makes sense intuitively since the more risk-averse the worker is the more he will have to be compensated for the probability of unemployment. But (37) implies:

$$\tilde{w} - z(\tilde{w}, r) = r - \tfrac{1}{2}(r - \tilde{w})^2 Q(\tilde{w}), \qquad (38)$$

so that the right-hand side of (34) is a decreasing function of the worker's risk aversion. Hence, layoffs are less likely to occur the more risk-averse workers are.

The left-hand side of (34) will obviously be smaller for lower p_2. Therefore the inequality is more likely to hold the more volatile are industry demand shifts over the business cycle and the more inelastic that demand is. Recall from (29) that the firm pays a real wage in excess of the value of marginal product in slump. This excess increases as p_2 falls, making the firm more anxious to lay workers off.

Having derived the necessary and sufficient condition for layoffs to occur and the conditions under which this condition is likely to hold, we can now characterize the optimal level of employment in slump n_2. Recall that the probability a worker will be unemployed is $(1-\rho_1)(1-n_2/n_1) = \phi$. Given that $\phi \neq 0$, i.e. that there are layoffs, we can compute the marginal increase in the wage that the worker would require to compensate him for a tiny increase in ϕ. Going through the same steps as in the derivation of (32) but with $n_2 \neq n_1$, we can derive:

$$\left.\frac{dw}{d\phi}\right|^W_{n_2 \neq n_1} = \frac{u(\tilde{w}) - u(r)}{(\rho_1 + (1-\rho_1)(n_2/n_1))\, u'(\tilde{w})}. \tag{39}$$

Similarly, we can derive the marginal increase in the wage that the firm is willing to pay for a tiny increase in ϕ, given that $n_2 \neq n_1$, this will be the analogue of (30):

$$\left.\frac{dw}{d\phi}\right|^F_{n_2 \neq n_1} = \frac{\tilde{w} - p_2 f'(n_2)}{(\rho_1 + (1-\rho_1)(n_2/n_1))}. \tag{40}$$

It will be in the firm's interest to keep refashioning the contract with w higher and n_2 lower so long as (40) exceeds (39), i.e.

$$\frac{\tilde{w} - p_2 f'(n_2)}{(\rho_1 + (1-\rho_1)(n_2/n_1))} > \frac{u(\tilde{w}) - u(r)}{(\rho_1 + (1-\rho_1)(n_2/n_1))\, u'(\tilde{w})}$$

or equivalently:

$$p_2 f'(n_2) < \tilde{w} - z(\tilde{w}, r). \tag{41}$$

But as n_2 falls, the left-hand side of (41) rises because of diminishing returns. As $\tilde{w}$ rises, the right-hand side falls (see (34)). This implies that an 'equilibrium' level of layoffs will be reached and at this point:

$$p_2 f'(n_2) = \tilde{w} - z(\tilde{w}, r). \tag{42}$$

Of course, the firm could run out of workers to lay off before (42) could be satisfied – i.e. (41) may hold with $n_2 = 0$. This situation could be avoided by assuming that the marginal product of labour becomes infinite as the production function approaches the origin –

$$\lim_{n \to 0} f'(n) = \infty.$$

To summarize the results developed so far, implicit contract theory develops the observation that labour is not generally sold in a spot auction but will be traded subject to implicit long-term commitments by the firm and workers. The firm, being less risk-averse than workers, will in effect insure workers against real wage variation. This implies that the equilibrium real wage is no longer equal to the marginal product of labour at each point in time, but will instead differ from this value by a premium paid to the firm in favourable states of nature and by an indemnity received by the worker in adverse states of nature. Moreover, even though workers are assumed to be risk-averse, it turns out that it may be optimal for firms to pay a slightly higher fixed wage and to lay off workers over the cycle. Layoffs are more likely to occur in an industry the more of the following conditions hold: output demand shifts are volatile and/or demand is inelastic, unemployment compensation is high, workers are only 'slightly' risk-averse, there is a competitive demand for labour.

Thus, the empirically observed phenomenon of sticky real wages and layoffs may in fact be the outcome of jointly optimizing behaviour on the part of workers and firms who enter into long-term, unwritten agreements. This is the invisible handshake at work!

4.   THE NATURE OF UNEMPLOYMENT UNDER IMPLICIT CONTRACTS

Is the unemployment generated under implicit labour contracts involuntary? By 'involuntary' we normally mean that unemployed workers would be willing to work at the going wage but are unable to do so. Clearly, unemployment in slump is voluntary at the time the contract is negotiated, since it is freely agreed to. But this is before the true state of nature materializes, so unemployment might be said to be voluntary in an *ex ante* sense. However, after the state of nature, say slump, materializes, laid-off workers would presumably envy their working colleagues and would wish to work at the going rate. Does this constitute involuntary unemployment, in an *ex post* sense perhaps?

'The fact that laid-off workers would gladly exchange places with their employed colleagues is not in itself sufficient to establish a misallocation of resources. After all, accident victims may very well envy more fortunate individuals without any implication that the insurance industry works poorly.' (Azariadis and Stiglitz (1983), p. 8)

Implicit in this quotation is the idea that the existence of involuntary unemployment constitutes a market failure. We know that if labour was auctioned off by the Walrasian auctioneer at each point in time then this market would by definition clear, i.e. Walrasian unemployment is purely voluntary. Therefore, one way of judging whether contractual unemployment is voluntary is to compare its magnitude with that predicted by a Walrasian spot auction.

We shall return to this idea presently. For the moment, we can show that even the *ex post* notion of involuntary unemployment can be precluded if we allow the firm to pay unemployment compensation directly to the worker. In the above discussion we were careful to point out that any unemployment compensation was paid out of an economy-wide fund which did not directly affect the firm's behaviour. Now assume that the firm can make a payment to laid-off workers without affecting their entitlement to dole from the central fund.[7] Alternatively, let the economy-wide dole payment be zero ($b = 0$ in (11)). To simplify matters, we shall assume that consumption and leisure are perfect substitutes. Since there is no saving and labour is supplied in an indivisible unit, this is equivalent to saying that wages and leisure are perfect substitutes. We can do this by letting the utility function v take the form:

$$u = v(w + Rl), \quad v' >, \quad v'' < 0 \tag{43}$$

where l is leisure as before. R is a scale factor which puts w and Rl into the same units of measurement. Recall that leisure for the laid-off worker is l_u and is l_e otherwise. Also, r is the wage payment that makes the worker indifferent between working and not working, so:[8]

$$b + Rl_u = r + Rl_e$$

or, setting $b = 0$ for simplicity:

$$Rl_u = r + Rl_e. \tag{44}$$

Now suppose the firm is free to pay the worker an amount w_3 if he is laid off during slump. Adding this to both sides of (44):

$$w_3 + Rl_u = w_3 + r + Rl_e. \tag{45}$$

Now recall the definition of our equivalent utility function, u:

$$u(w) = v(w, l_e)$$

[7] Since the model we are using is essentially timeless (compare Baily (1974)), firm-paid unemployment compensation can be interpreted as redundancy pay or 'severance pay'.

[8] In terms of equation (11), the perfect substitutability assumption implies $c = R(l_u - l_e)$.

or

$$u(w) = v(w + Rl_e). \tag{46}$$

From (45) we have:

$$v(w_3 + Rl_u) = v(w_3 + r + Rl_e)$$
$$= u(w_3 + r). \tag{47}$$

So, if the firm pays w_3 to laid off workers, they derive utility of $u(w_3 + r)$, where r is the wage payment that makes the worker indifferent between working and not working.

The firm now designs a contract $(w_1, n_1, w_2, n_2, w_3)$ by maximizing the following Lagrangean:

$$£ = \rho_1(p_1 f(n_1) - w_1 n_1) + (1 - \rho_1)(p_2 f(n_2) - w_2 n_2 - w_3(n_1 - n_2))$$
$$+ \lambda[\rho_1 u(w_1) + (1 - \rho_1)(n_2/n_1) u(w_2)$$
$$+ (1 - \rho_1)(1 - n_2/n_1) u(w_3 + r) - \tilde{U}]. \tag{48}$$

The only difference between (48) and (15) is that the firm's profits in state two are now reduced by the total amount of the payment to laid-off workers, $w_3(n_1 - n_2)$, and that the utility of a laid-off worker is $u(w_3 + r)$ rather than $u(r)$.

The first-order conditions with respect to w_1 and w_2 are identical to (17) and (18):

$$-\rho_1 n_1 + \lambda \rho_1 u'(w_1) = 0 \tag{49}$$

$$-(1 - \rho_1) n_2 + \lambda(1 - \rho_1)(n_2/n_1) u'(w_2) = 0. \tag{50}$$

The first-order condition with respect to w_3 is:

$$-(1 - \rho_1)(n_1 - n_2) + \lambda(1 - \rho_1)(1 - n_2/n_1) u'(w_3 + r) = 0. \tag{51}$$

Equations (49), (50) and (51) can be written respectively:

$$n_1 = \lambda u'(w_1) \tag{52}$$

$$n_1 = \lambda u'(w_2) \tag{53}$$

$$n_1 = \lambda u'(w_3 + r) \tag{54}$$

which imply:

$$w_1 = w_2 = w_3 + r, \tag{55}$$

by the concavity of u. Therefore, if the firm is allowed to pay unemployment compensation, the worker bears no risk whatsoever. He receives a state-invariant wage when he is working and, when he is laid off, the firm pays him just enough money (w_3) to make him indifferent between working at the going wage (w_2) and being laid off. In this case, involuntary unemployment in the *ex post* sense discussed above would be precluded.

A similar result would follow if unemployment compensation from the firm was not allowed but work sharing was. In the above analysis, the worker's leisure is l_e when he is employed and l_u when he is unemployed. Therefore, he supplies labour in an indivisible unit of $(l_u - l_e)$. Suppose that hours of work could vary so that instead of having to supply either zero or eight hours per day, the worker could supply anywhere between zero and eight hours. If the wage was paid at an hourly rate and w_3 was constrained to zero, an analysis similar to that in Section 3 would lead to the following contract. The hourly wage rate would be state-invariant with each worker supplying $(l_u - l_e)$ units of labour in state one and $\beta(l_u - l_e)$ units of labour in state two where $\beta(<1)$ was such that total wage income for the worker in state two, plus the value of the extra leisure, was just equal to total wage income in state one. As in the case of discrete labour and unemployment compensation, each worker would be just as well off in both states in both the *ex ante* and *ex post* sense – all risks would be traded to the firm.[9]

Let us now return to the discussion of whether contractual employment is more variable than 'Walrasian' employment (Akerlof and Miyazaki (1980)). In a Walrasian spot auction, the labour market clears with the real wage set equal to the value of the marginal product of labour. We have assumed that labour is supplied inelastically at n_1 above a wage of r, but workers would prefer to be unemployed if the going wage in the auction was below r (i.e. supply is perfectly elastic at r). In state one, the firm's labour demand schedule is its marginal product schedule, $p_1 f'(n)$, and in state two it is $p_2 f'(n)$.

This situation is depicted in Figure 3. A Walrasian auction in state one would determine full employment at a wage of w_1^q (where the superscript is to denote the auction variable). An auction in state two would determine employment of n_2^q at a wage equal to r. Note that unemployment in the Walrasian model, $n_2^q < n_1$, can only occur if the full-employment value of the marginal product in state two is less than r. If this was not the case then the $p_2 f'(n)$ schedule would intersect the vertical part of the labour supply schedule and there would be full employment at a wage at or above r. Hence, a necessary and sufficient condition for Walrasian unemployment is:

$$p_2 f'(n_1) < r. \tag{56}$$

Now consider unemployment under an implicit contract. Initially, constrain w_3 to be zero – the firm pays no unemployment compen-

---

[9] The proof of this assertion is left as an exercise.

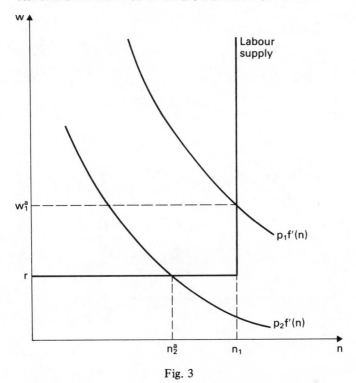

Fig. 3

sation. Suppose the fixed-wage optimal contract is (w, n_1, w, n_2) with $n_2 < n_1$. So if state one occurs the worker derives utility of $u(w)$. If state two occurs, the worker derives utility of $u(w)$ with probability n_2/n_1 and utility of $u(r)$ with probability $(1-n_2/n_1)$. Hence, *given* that state two occurs, the expected utility of the worker is

$$(n_2/n_1) u(w) + (1 - n_2/n_1) u(r).$$

Given that the worker is risk-averse, he would in fact prefer to be employed in state two and paid a lower wage of

$$w^0 = (n_2/n_1) w + (1-n_2/n_1) r.$$

This contract will only be blocked if it reduces the firm's expected profit – i.e. if:

$$\rho_1(p_1 f(n_1) - w n_1) + (1-\rho_1)(p_2 f(n_2) - w n_2)$$
$$> \rho_1(p_1 f(n_1) - w n_1) + (1-\rho_1)(p_2 f(n_1)$$
$$- ((n_2/n_1) w + (1-n_2/n_1) r) n_1). \tag{57}$$

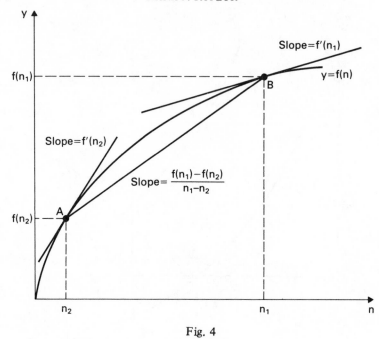

Fig. 4

But after rearrangement and cancelling, (57) reduces to:

$$\frac{f(n_1) - f(n_2)}{(n_1 - n_2)} < \frac{r}{p_2}. \tag{58}$$

If (58) holds then a full-employment contract, even with a varying wage, will not be optimal. Consider Figure 4, which is a graph of the production function. The left-hand side of (58) is the slope of a chord joining A and B. This is clearly greater than the slope of a tangent at B, i.e. $f'(n_1)$. Therefore:

$$f'(n_1) < \frac{f(n_1) - f(n_2)}{(n_1 - n_2)}. \tag{59}$$

This is due to the concavity of f. Expressions (58) and (59) jointly imply:

$$p_2 f(n_2) < r. \tag{60}$$

If (60) holds then full-employment contracts are never optimal and some contractual unemployment will occur over the business cycle. But (60) is identical to (56), the necessary and sufficient condition for Walrasian unemployment. Therefore, we have the result that unemployment will never occur under an implicit contract unless it would also occur under the corresponding Walrasian spot auction.

We can in fact go further than this. Recall from Section 3 that the equilibrium condition for layoffs in state two is:

$$p_2 f'(n_2) = w - z(w, r) \tag{61}$$

so that employment in state two under the optimal contract, n_2, can be found by solving (61). From the definition of z:

$$z(w, r) = \frac{u(w) - u(r)}{u'(w)} \tag{62}$$

where w is the optimal state-invariant wage. In Figure 5 using (62), $z(w, r)$ is easily seen to be equal to the horizontal distance AB so that, clearly:

$$w - z(w, r) \leqslant r, \text{ for } w \geqslant r. \tag{63}$$

Using (63), we can see from Figure 6 that the contractual level of state two employment, n_2 will generally be greater than the Walrasian level, n_2^a. This gives us the interesting result that, provided that r, p_1 and p_2 are the same for each regime and the firm cannot pay unemployment compensation, unemployment under an implicit contract

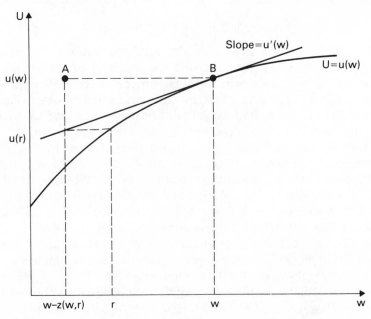

Fig. 5

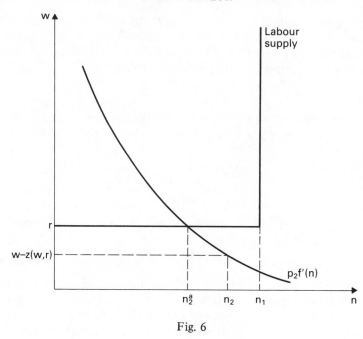

Fig. 6

regime cannot exceed the corresponding level of unemployment under a standard neoclassical regime of Walrasian labour auctions:

$$(n_1 - n_2) \leqslant (n_1 - n_2^a). \tag{64}$$

That is to say, compared with the spot auction regime, implicit labour contracts tend to stabilize both the level of wages *and* employment. As is well known, Walrasian outcomes generally define the social optimum at each point in time under fairly weak (Pareto) criteria. In this sense, implicit labour contracts may lead to 'socially excessive' volumes of employment in some states of the world.

Would this result be changed if firms were allowed to pay unemployment compensation (Grossman and Hart (1981))? We showed above that such an institution would lead to workers obtaining complete insurance – they derive the same utility in all states of the world. The worker is indifferent between working for a fixed wage w or being laid off with compensation w_3, where $w_3 = w - r$. Now if the firm lays off a worker at the margin in state two, it loses the value of that worker's marginal product and has to pay him unemployment compensation, the total marginal cost is therefore $p_2 f'(n_2) + w_3$. On the other hand, there is a marginal saving equal to the worker's (employed) wage, w. The equilibrium level of employment is therefore given by solving the condition that marginal benefit equals marginal cost:

$$w = p_2 f'(n_2) + w_3. \tag{65}$$

But since $w = r + w_3$, (65) implies:

$$p_2 f'(n_2) = r. \tag{66}$$

But the value of n_2 which solves (66) is precisely the level of employment which would transpire in a Walrasian spot auction, n_2^a in Figures 3 and 6. This means that, if the firm is allowed to pay unemployment compensation, the same amount of employment would occur in each state of the world regardless of whether the prevailing regime was one of implicit contracts or Walrasian spot auctions – i.e. any contractual unemployment is 'Walrasian' and in that sense is not involuntary.

5. SUMMARY, CONCLUSION AND EXTENSION

The theory of implicit contracts was developed largely as an antidote to the empirical anomaly that cyclical output fluctuations tend to be associated with high employment variability and low real wage variability, in defiance of competitive wage theory. The central insight of the theory is that it may be optimal for less risk-averse employers to effectively insure more risk-averse employees against real wage variability. Real wages are shown to differ from the marginal product of labour by an insurance indemnity paid to the worker in adverse states of nature and by a premium paid by the worker in favourable states. Given this optimal risk sharing agreement concerning wage payments, it is natural to wonder why the firm does not offer the worker insurance against employment variation also. It turns out that, if the firm is allowed to pay the worker unemployment compensation (redundancy pay), this is exactly what happens. Given their unemployment compensation, laid-off workers are just as well off as their working colleagues – all risks are traded to the firm. In this sense, contractual unemployment is not involuntary. Moreover, implicit contracts tend to stabilize the level of employment in the sense that unemployment under an implicit contract cannot be greater than it would have been under a Walrasian spot auction, so that any unemployment that does occur is Walrasian.[10]

An important assumption in the basic model of this paper is that the firm is completely risk-neutral. Whilst it is hard to provide a

---

[10] This is only true of the simple, symmetric information contracts considered in this paper – see Akerlof and Miyazaki (1980), Taylor (1987).

convincing argument as to why firms should be *more* risk-averse than workers, this is perhaps rather a strong assumption.

Given that firms are less than completely risk-neutral, it is easy to show that optimal contract wages cease to be state-invariant — the firm will absorb some, but not all of the risks. Thus, the real wage paid will be lower in adverse states of nature, but not as low as it would be under a Walrasian spot auction (see Taylor (1987)).

Another assumption of the present analysis is that of symmetric information — both the firm and the worker are able to observe which state of the world is prevailing. This again may be a somewhat strong assumption. For example the firm may be a producer of intermediate goods or other specialized equipment which may not appear directly in the High Street shops. In such cases, the worker may very well have to take the firm's word for it that times are either good or bad — information is asymmetric. So long as firms are risk-neutral, informational asymmetry does not make very much difference (that is, as long as the firm does not pretend to be risk-averse). However, as argued above, wages will tend to be state-contingent when firms are risk-averse. Calvo and Phelps (1977) were the first to point out that if wages are state-contingent and information is asymmetric it may be in the firm's interest to lie about the state of nature — for example by claiming that times are bad when in fact they are good and thereby reducing the wage bill. Such models open up special kinds of principal–agent problems (Arrow (1985), Rees (1985a, b)). Azariadis (1982) and Grossman and Hart (1981, 1983) have shown that implicit contracts in models displaying informational asymmetry and firm risk-aversion will generate levels of unemployment greater than those which would prevail under a corresponding Walrasian spot auction. This is because the firm has to convince workers that times really are bad before they will agree to a wage cut in adverse states. It can do this by reducing employment as well as wages when times are bad. Thus, employment will be more variable 'simply because this is the only way the firm can get wages down' (Hart (1983), p. 3).

In Taylor (1987) we extend the present analysis to consider a heterogeneous workforce, firm risk-aversion and informational asymmetry.

REFERENCES

Akerlof, G. and Miyazaki, H. (1980). 'The Implicit Contract Theory of Unemployment Meets the Wage Bill Argument', *Review of Economic Studies*, Vol. 47, pp. 109–28.

Arrow, K. J. (1971). *Essays in the Theory of Risk Bearing*, Chicago: Markham.

Arrow, K. J. (1985). 'The Economics of Agency', in Pratt, J. W. and Zeckhauser, R. (eds.), *Agency: The Structure of Business*, Cambridge, Mass., Harvard Business School Press.

Azariadis, C. (1975). 'Implicit Contracts and Underemployment Equilibria', *Journal of Political Economy*, Vol. 83, pp. 1183-202.

Azariadis, C. (1979). 'Implicit Contracts and Related Topics: A Survey', in Hornstein, Z., Grice, J. and Webb, A. (eds.), *The Economics of the Labour Market*, London, HMSO.

Azariadis, C. and Stiglitz, J. E. (1983). 'Implicit Contracts and Fixed Price Equilibria', *Quarterly Journal of Economics*, Vol. 98 (supplement), pp. 1-22.

Baily, M. N. (1974). 'Wages and Employment under Uncertain Demand', *Review of Economic Studies*, Vol. 41, pp. 37-50.

Barro, R. J. and Grossman, H. I. (1976). *Money, Employment and Inflation*, Cambridge, Cambridge University Press.

Borch, K. (1962). 'Equilibrium in a Reinsurance Market', *Econometrica*, Vol. 30, pp. 424-44.

Calvo, G. A. and Phelps, E. S. (1977). 'Indexation Issues: Appendix', *Journal of Monetary Economics*, supplementary series, Vol. 5, pp. 160-8.

Clower, R. W. (1965). 'The Keynesian Counter-Revolution: A Theoretical Appraisal', in Hahn, F. H. and Brechling, F. (eds.), *The Theory of Interest Rates*, London, Macmillan.

Feldstein, M. (1975). 'The Importance of Temporary Layoffs: An Empirical Analysis', *Brookings Papers on Economic Activity*, Vol. 3, pp. 725-44.

Gordon, D. F. (1974). 'A Neo-Classical Theory of Keynesian Unemployment', *Economic Inquiry*, Vol. 12, pp. 431-59.

Grossman, H. I. (1977). 'Risk Shifting and Reliability in Labor Markets', *Scandinavian Journal of Economics*, Vol. 79, pp. 187-209.

Grossman, H. I. (1978). 'Risk Shifting, Layoffs and Seniority', *Journal of Monetary Economics*, Vol. 4, pp. 661-86.

Grossman, S. J. and Hart, O. D. (1981). 'Implicit Contracts, Moral Hazard and Unemployment', *American Economic Review*, Vol. 71, pp. 301-7.

Grossman, S. J. and Hart, O. D. (1983). 'Implicit Contracts under Asymmetrical Information', *Quarterly Journal of Economics*, Vol. 98 (supplement), pp. 123-56.

Hart, O. D. (1983). 'Optimal Labour Contracts under Asymmetric Information: An Introduction', *Review of Economic Studies*, Vol. 50, pp. 3-35.

Katz, L. (1984). 'Layoffs, Uncertain Recall and the Duration of Unemployment', Massachusetts Institute of Technology, mimeo.

Leijonhufvud, A. (1968). *On Keynesian Economics and the Economics of Keynes*, New York, Oxford University Press.

Lilien, D. (1980). 'The Cyclical Pattern of Temporary Layoffs in United States Manufacturing', *Review of Economics and Statistics*, Vol. 62, pp. 24-31.

Rees, R. (1985a). 'The Theory of Principal and Agent: Part I', *Bulletin of Economic Research*, Vol. 37, pp. 3-26.

Rees, R. (1985b). 'The Theory of Principal and Agent: Part II', *Bulletin of Economic Research*, Vol. 37, pp. 77-95.

Rosen, S. (1985). 'Implicit Contracts: A Survey', *Journal of Economic Literature*, Vol. 23, pp. 1144-75.

Taylor, M. P. (1987). 'Further Developments in the Theory of Implicit Labour Contracts', Chapter 8 in Hey, J. D. and Lambert, P. J. (eds.), *Surveys in the Economics of Uncertainty*, Oxford, Basil Blackwell.

FURTHER DEVELOPMENTS IN THE THEORY OF IMPLICIT LABOUR CONTRACTS

Mark P. Taylor[1]

1. INTRODUCTION

This paper is designed as an extension to Taylor (1987) (see previous chapter, this volume) in which we survey some of the central ideas of the theory of implicit labour contracts under symmetric information. Firstly, in section 2 we see how relaxing the assumption of labour homogeneity allows us to use contract theory to explain the relative incidence of layoffs on skilled and unskilled workers. In sections 3 and 4 respectively we explore how allowing employer risk-aversion and informational asymmetries raises interesting principal–agent problems in contracting models. A final section summarizes and concludes, ending with some very brief remarks concerning the relationship between implicit contract theory and Keynesian economics.[2]

2. CONTRACTS WITH HETEROGENEOUS LABOUR

The simple model of implicit labour contracts analysed in Taylor (1987) treats all workers as if they were identical. In the real world labour is heterogeneous in the sense that a firm usually employs a range of different skill grades – from highly skilled craftsmen to basic labourers. Historically, labour statistics show that unskilled workers tend to bear the brunt of unemployment over the business cycle. Why this should be so is not immediately obvious – after all, skilled labour is generally more expensive than unskilled labour. Oi (1962) attempts to explain this phenomenon by arguing that the higher human capital embodied in skilled labour may be the result of past investment on the part of the firm – for example through

---

[1] I am grateful to Mike Waterson and an anonymous referee for helpful comments on a previous version of this paper. The usual disclaimer applies.

[2] In order to facilitate cross-referencing, equations and diagrams are numbered consecutively following Taylor (1987), i.e. starting with equation (67) and Figure 7. References to equations (1)–(66) and figures 1–6 are, therefore, implicit references to Taylor (1987).

apprenticeship schemes. This investment is amortized over time by paying the skilled worker a real wage slightly less than the value of his marginal product. The firm will then be reluctant to reduce the return on its investment through temporary layoffs of the skilled workforce, and will be happier to lay off unskilled workers in whom no comparable investment has been made. However, this line of reasoning does not explain why such layoffs should occur in the first place. There is no reason why the firm could not amortize its investment in skilled labour with a variable wage level.

Grossman (1977, 1978), within a risk-shifting contract framework, argues that skilled, or more particularly, senior, workers will be able to effect more complete insurance against the variations of the business cycle since they will be seen by the firm as being more 'reliable'. Reliable workers are desirable to the firm because they keep down hiring and training costs. In particular they are seen as being less likely than more junior or unskilled workers to renege on their contract during good times when the demand, and hence the market rate, for their labour is high. Therefore the firm will tend to lay off junior or unskilled workers in preference to senior or skilled grades. Reasons for the existence of such layoffs are precisely analogous to those outlined in our model with homogeneous labour.

Azariadis (1976) shows how his basic model can be extended to explain preferential layoffs when allowance is made for heterogeneous labour. The reason that unskilled labour is laid off in preference to skilled labour in this model is, it turns out, not because of reliability considerations, but because skilled workers demand a relatively high underemployment premium for bearing the risk of unemployment. This in turn is related to the fact that skilled workers will generally command a higher wage than unskilled workers (see (34)).

We now extend our simple model by allowing two skill grades of labour — skilled and unskilled. We largely retain the previous notation except that a superscript of u or s now implies that the relevant variable pertains to unskilled or skilled labour respectively (e.g. w_1^u is the real wage paid to unskilled workers in state one). We assume that workers have identical preferences and the same value of leisure, and draw the same amount of unemployment benefit when unemployed. This means that the utility function for each type of worker is as defined in (10) and (9). In fact the only difference between skilled and unskilled workers is that the former are more productive in the production process. Specifically, we assume that skilled and unskilled workers are infinitely substitutable, but that a skilled worker is worth α (> 1) unskilled men. Output in state i is now governed by:

$$y_i = f(\alpha n_i^s + n_i^u), \ f' > 0, \ f'' < 0, \ f(0) = 0, \ \alpha > 1 \qquad (67)$$

where n_i^s and n_i^u denote the amount of skilled and unskilled labour hired in state i respectively. In particular, (67) implies that the marginal product of a skilled worker is α times that of an unskilled worker:

$$\frac{\partial y_i}{\partial n_i^s} = \alpha f'(\alpha n_i^s + n_i^u) > \frac{\partial y_i}{\partial n_i^u} = f'(\alpha n_i^s + n_i^u). \tag{68}$$

Given the greater productivity of skilled labour, it seems reasonable to assume that skilled workers will have a higher fixed acceptance wage than unskilled workers. Equivalently, the market-determined 'utility floor' for the skilled worker, $\bar{U}^s$, is greater than that of the unskilled worker, $\bar{U}^u$:

$$\bar{U}^s = u(\bar{w}^s) > \bar{U}^u \Rightarrow u(\bar{w}^u) = \bar{w}^s > \bar{w}^u. \tag{69}$$

We assume that there is full employment of both skill grades in state one.

The firm now offers two contracts – one for each type of worker – $(w_1^s, n_1^s, w_2^s, n_2^s)$ and $(w_1^u, n_1^u, w_2^u, n_2^u)$. To determine the optimal pair of contracts the firm maximizes its expected profit subject to each type of worker obtaining their minimum expected utility level. This is equivalent to unconstrained maximization of the Lagrangean:

$$\begin{aligned}
\pounds = &\, \rho_1(p_1 f(\alpha n_1^s + n_1^u) - w_1^s n_1^s - w_1^u n_1^u) + (1 - \rho_1)(p_2 f(\alpha n_2^s + n_2^s) \\
&- w_2^s n_2^s - w_2^u n_2^u) + \lambda[\rho_1 u(w_1^s) + (1 - \rho_1)(n_2^s/n_1^s) u(w_2^s) \\
&+ (1 - \rho_1)(1 - n_2^s/n_1^s) u(r) - \bar{U}^s] + \mu[\rho_1 u(w_1^u) \\
&+ (1 - \rho_1)(n_2^u/n_1^u) u(w_2^u) + (1 - \rho_1)(1 - n_2^u/n_1^u) u(r) - \bar{U}^u]
\end{aligned} \tag{70}$$

where λ and μ are Lagrange multipliers. Among the first-order conditions for the maximization of (70) we have:

$$\frac{\partial \pounds}{\partial w_1^s} = -\rho_1 n_1^s + \lambda \rho_1 u'(w_1^s) = 0 \tag{71}$$

$$\frac{\partial \pounds}{\partial w_2^s} = -(1 - \rho_1) n_2^s + \lambda(1 - \rho_1)(n_2^s/n_1^s) u'(w_2^s) = 0 \tag{72}$$

$$\frac{\partial \pounds}{\partial w_1^u} = -\rho_1 n_1^u + \mu \rho_1 u'(w_1^u) = 0 \tag{73}$$

$$\frac{\partial \pounds}{\partial w_2^u} = -(1 - \rho_1) n_2^u + \mu(1 - \rho_1)(n_2^u/n_1^u) u'(w_2^u) = 0. \tag{74}$$

From which it is easy to derive, as in Taylor (1987) the optimal risk-sharing conditions:

$$\frac{-\rho_1 n_1^s}{-(1 - \rho_1) n_2^s} = \frac{\rho_1 u'(w_1^s)}{(1 - \rho_1)(n_2^s/n_1^s) u'(w_2^s)} \tag{75}$$

$$\frac{-\rho_1 n_1^u}{-(1-\rho_1)\,n_2^u} = \frac{\rho_1 u'(w_1^u)}{(1-\rho_1)\,(n_2^u/n_1^u)\,u'(w_2^u)} \tag{76}$$

These conditions in turn imply $u'(w_1^s) = u'(w_2^s)$ and $u'(w_1^u) = u'(w_2^u)$, or

$$w_1^s = w_2^s = w^s,\ \ w_1^u = w_2^u = w^u, \tag{77}$$

analogously to the homogeneous labour case, so the sticky wage result goes through when we have two grades of labour exactly as before. Once we move away from state-invariant full employment there are no analytic reasons why the fixed wage paid to skilled workers should exceed that paid to unskilled workers. Nevertheless, it seems reasonable to assume that institutional and other considerations will ensure that this is so. In fact, if this were not the case then, after the state of nature becomes known (i.e. boom or slump materialises), skilled workers would have an extremely strong incentive to renege on their contract by quitting and then seeking re-employment with the same firm at the lower skill grade. We therefore assume that:

$$w^s > w^u. \tag{78}$$

By methods exactly similar to those employed in Taylor (1987) we can derive conditions for the suboptimality of full-employment contracts for each type of labour precisely analogous to (36). Full employment contracts for skilled labour will be suboptimal if:

$$p_2 \alpha f'(\alpha n_1^s + n_1^u) < \bar{w}^s - z(\bar{w}^s, r) \tag{79}$$

whilst unskilled-labour full-employment contracts will be suboptimal if:

$$p_2 f'(\alpha n_1^s + n_1^u) < \bar{w}^u - z(\bar{w}^u, r) \tag{80}$$

where, as before, $z(\bar{w}^x, r)$ denotes the marginal underemployment premium:

$$z(\bar{w}^x, r) = \frac{u(\bar{w}^x) - u(r)}{u'(\bar{w}^x)},\ \ x = s, u. \tag{81}$$

Now

$$\frac{\partial(w^x - z(w^x, r))}{\partial w^x} = \frac{(u(w^x) - u(r))\,u''(w^x)}{(u'(w^x))^2} < 0\ \ \text{for } w^x \geqslant \bar{w}^x,$$

$$x = s, u. \tag{82}$$

Given (78), i.e. that skilled workers command a higher wage than unskilled workers, (82) implies:

$$w^s - z(w^s, r) < w^u - z(w^u, r),\ \ \text{for all } w^x \geqslant \bar{w}^x,\ \ x = s, u. \tag{83}$$

and in particular,

$$\bar{w}^s - z(\bar{w}^s, r) < \bar{w}^u - z(\bar{w}^u, r). \tag{84}$$

Expression (83) is extremely important for our explanation of preferential layoffs. When (83) is evaluated at the acceptance wages we have (84), which is extremely suggestive since it says that the marginal cost of keeping a skilled worker employed over the business cycle is actually less than that of keeping on an unskilled worker. This is so because although the skilled worker commands a higher full-employment wage than the unskilled worker, the increase in the wage he requires to compensate him for the probability of unemployment (i.e. $z(\bar{w}^s, r)$) more than offsets the apparent saving to be made by not paying his wage when he is laid off. This is because $z(w, r)$ is increasing in w (see (34)). Intuitively, the skilled worker stands to lose more in terms of income by being laid off. Also, he requires a greater marginal increase in the wage to compensate for the risk of losing one unit of income because his marginal utility is lower (see (33)).

We can use (84) to prove the relatively weak proposition that contracts will not be struck such that the skilled labour force suffers layoffs in slump whilst unskilled labour is fully employed over the cycle. For suppose that this was the case. Then, from (79) and (80) we would have:

$$p_2 \alpha f'(\alpha n_1^s + n_1^u) < \bar{w}^s - z(\bar{w}^s, r) \tag{79}$$

and

$$p_2 f'(\alpha n_1^s + n_1^u) \geq \bar{w}^u - z(\bar{w}^u, r). \tag{85}$$

Since $\alpha > 1$, (55) and (61) together imply:

$$\bar{w}^s - z(\bar{w}^s, r) > \bar{w}^u - z(\bar{w}^u, r) \tag{86}$$

which contradicts (84) and proves that (79) and (85) cannot hold simultaneously — i.e. proves the proposition.

We can in fact prove a much stronger proposition using (83). This is that the *whole* of the unskilled labour force will be laid off in state two before even *one* skilled labourer is. To prove this, note that for an 'equilibrium' level of layoffs of both skill grades the optimal pair of contracts would have to specify a pair of conditions precisely analogous to (42):

$$p_2 f'(\alpha n_2^s + n_2^u) = w^u - z(w^u, r) \tag{87}$$

$$p_2 \alpha f'(\alpha n_2^s + n_2^u) = w^s - z(w^s, r). \tag{88}$$

Now if contracts are agreed to such that both $0 < n_2^s/n_1^s < 1$ and $0 < n_2^u/n_1^u < 1$ then both (87) and (88) must hold. But since $\alpha > 1$,

(87) and (88) jointly imply:

$$w_2^s - z(w^s, r) > w_2^u - z(w^u, r) \qquad (89)$$

which contradicts (83). This means that we cannot have an equilibrium level of layoffs for both skill grades. One or both of (87) and (88) must be turned into an inequality. If we make both (87) and (88) inequalities:

$$p_2 \alpha f'(\alpha n_2^s + n_2^u) < w^s - z(w^s, r) \qquad (90)$$

$$p_2 f'(\alpha n_2^s + n_2^u) < w^u - z(w^u, r) \qquad (91)$$

then (83) is not contradicted. This would be the case if the optimal contracts were such that *all* workers were laid off in slump ($n_2^s = n_2^u = 0$) — the firm ran out of workers to lay off before it reached the equilibrium. As in Taylor (1987) the possibility of zero production in slump can be precluded by assuming that the production function has the limit property

$$\lim_{n \to 0} f'(n) = \infty.$$

If this was the case then some workers of one type of skill grade would be employed in state two. However, even without this limit property, the firm will never lay off all its skilled workers in state two whilst keeping some unskilled labour on; for then we would have:

$$p_2 f'(\alpha n_2^s + n_2^u) = w^u - z(w^u, r) \qquad (87)$$

and

$$p_2 \alpha f'(\alpha n_2^s + n_2^u) < w^s - z(w^s, r). \qquad (90)$$

Since $\alpha > 1$, this contradicts (83). We could, however, have:

$$p_2 \alpha f'(\alpha n_2^s + n_2^u) = w_2^s - z(w^s, r) \qquad (88)$$

and

$$p_2 f'(\alpha n_2^s + n_2^u) < w^u - z(w^u, r) \qquad (91)$$

without contradiction of (83).

In short, only (88) and (91) or (if we allow zero production) (90) and (91) can hold simultaneously. But this means that, if just one skilled worker is laid off, the whole of the unskilled labour force will be laid off. The intuition behind this result is that skilled workers are always more expensive to lay off because, although they command a higher state-invariant wage, they require more compensation than unskilled workers for a given increase in the probability of unemployment.

It should be noted that this result depends to some extent on the assumption we made of the infinite substitutability of skilled and unskilled workers. If for example we replaced (67) with the more general production function $y_i = f(n_i^s, n_i)$ and retained an inequality similar to (68), then the preceding results would be harder to prove.

Apart from suggesting why unskilled labour is more readily shed over the business cycle, the preceding analysis also explains another empirical phenomenon. This is the countercyclical nature of the unskilled-to-skilled wage ratio. Evidence from both the US (Bell, 1951) and the UK (Knowles and Robertson, 1961) has shown that unskilled wages tend to rise relative to skilled wages in boom, and to fall in slump. To explain this phenomenon, imagine an economy in which all industries except one experience little cyclical fluctuation. In one industry cyclical fluctuations are important and cause large fluctuations in unskilled employment in that industry. Moreover, unskilled workers extract an underemployment premium in this industry, so that the economy-wide average unskilled wages rises during boom and falls during slump. If skilled wages and employment are relatively stable in this industry and the economy as a whole over the cycle, then the economy-wide (average) occupational wage differential will show a counter-cyclical pattern.

3. RISK-AVERSE FIRMS

A central assumption of the preceding analysis is that the firm is risk-neutral. We consider the consequences of relaxing this assumption in this section. The assumption of firm risk-aversion can be motivated in a number of ways. For example, if the returns to shareholders from all firms in their portfolios are positively correlated, then they cannot 'diversify away' the income risk from any one firm in particular. Intuitively, portfolio diversification makes shareholders less risk-averse with respect to the income from any one firm because any loss is likely to be offset elsewhere in the portfolio (a little like 'putting eggs into more than one basket'). If there is a positive correlation between firms' incomes, however, losses from one firm are in fact likely to be accompanied by losses from other firms (a little like knowing that all the baskets are tied together). This will generally induce risk-averse behaviour on the part of shareholders and hence of 'firms'.

A second way in which firm risk-aversion might arise is due to the fact that, even if shareholders are risk-neutral, they generally have to rely upon a manager or managers to run the firm on a day-to-day basis. Assume that there is in fact a single manager. It seems reasonable to suppose that, other things equal, the profits of the firm will depend upon how hard the manager works. But how hard the manager works is only observable to himself. The owners of the firm and the manager are therefore in what is sometimes termed a 'principal–agent' relationship — the manager is a more informed 'agent' acting on behalf of a less informed 'principal' (the shareholders) — see, e.g. Arrow (1985), Rees (1985a, b). In order to induce the manager to work hard the owners may therefore wish to make the manager's salary an increasing function of the firm's profit (e.g. operate a bonus scheme). Since the manager is an individual he is likely to be risk-averse. An interesting but equivalent way of viewing the owner–manager relationship is as a problem of 'moral hazard'. Moral hazard normally arises in insurance markets where the risks borne by the insurer are a function of the care taken by the insured party, and the level of care cannot be directly observed by the insurer. For example, if my bicycle is fully insured I have little incentive to lock it up at night since, if it is stolen, I know the insurance firm will fully compensate me. Assuming that they are loth to charge very high premiums, the insurance company will find it better to offer me less than full coverage — i.e. I would have to pay the first £50 or so of a replacement. Having a deductible policy, i.e. less than full coverage, then induces me to take better care of my property. In the same way, even where shareholders are risk-neutral and the manager is risk-averse, the shareholders will not in general wish to fully insure the manager against variations in profit because the level of profit is itself a function of, amongst other things, the unobservable level of manager effort — i.e. there is moral hazard.

Let us assume therefore that the firm is run by a single manager who is endowed with a von Neumann–Morgenstern utility function with profit as argument:

$$V = v(\pi_i), \quad v' > 0, \quad v'' < 0, \tag{92}$$

where π_i (lower case) denotes the *ex post* level of profit in state i, e.g.

$$\pi_1 = p_1 f(n_1) - w_1 n_1.$$

What difference does this change in our assumptions make? Let us assume that the firm pays unemployment compensation. Then we know from Taylor (1987) that, if the firm is risk-neutral, the optimal contract will dictate a state-invariant wage to be paid to employed workers and a level of unemployment compensation which, when combined with the utility of additional labour, makes workers indifferent to being laid off. Further, this contract predicts exactly the same amount of employment as a Walrasian spot auction.

If the firm is risk-averse the Lagrangean (48) must be modified slightly, so the optimal contract maximizes:

$$\pounds = \rho_1 v(p_1 f(n_1) - w_1 n_1) + (1 - \rho_1) v(p_2 f(n_2) - w_2 n_2 - w_3(n_1 - n_2))$$
$$+ \lambda [\rho_1 u(w_1) + (1 - \rho_1)(n_2/n_1) u(w_2)$$
$$+ (1 - \rho_1) 1 - n_2/n_1) u(w_3 + r) - \tilde{U}]. \tag{93}$$

The first-order conditions with respect to w_1, w_2 and w_3 are respectively:

$$-\rho_1 v'(\pi_1) n_1 + \lambda \rho_1 u'(w_1) = 0$$
$$-(1 - \rho_1) v'(\pi_2) n_2 + \lambda(1 - \rho_1) n_2/n_1) u'(w_2) = 0$$
$$-(1 - \rho_1) v'(\pi_2)(n_1 - n_2) + \lambda(1 - p_1)(1 - n_2/n_1) u'(w_3 + r) = 0.$$

Or equivalently:

$$v'(\pi_1) n_1 = \lambda u'(w_1) \tag{94}$$
$$v'(\pi_2) n_1 = \lambda u'(w_2) \tag{95}$$
$$v'(\pi_2) n_1 = \lambda u'(w_3 + r). \tag{96}$$

From (95) and (96) we have:

$$w_2 = w_3 + r \tag{97}$$

by the concavity of u, as before. But (94) and (95) imply:

$$\frac{v'(\pi_1)}{v'(\pi_2)} = \frac{u'(w_1)}{u'(w_2)}. \tag{98}$$

Equation (98) is now the optimal risk-sharing condition. It states that the marginal rates of substitution between incomes in different states are equalized for the firm and the worker. Since $v'' \neq 0$, (98) implies that the optimal wage is now variable – less risk is traded to the firm because it is now risk-averse. Clearly, the less risk-averse the firm is, i.e. the smaller v'' is in absolute terms for any given level of profit, the closer the left-hand side of (98) will be to unity, and so the closer w_2 and w_1 will be. In general, though, the worker obtains less than full insurance from wage variation over the business cycle because this insurance is now costly to the firm due to its risk-aversion.

Equation (97), however, implies that, *within states*, workers obtain full insurance. That is to say, all workers are equally well off for any given state of the world. In state one all workers receive w_1. In state two, employed workers receive w_2 and derive utility $u(w_2)$ whilst laid-off workers receive w_3 and derive utility $u(w_3 + r) = u(w_2)$. The firm is willing to provide full insurance *within* states (and notably in state two) because, although it is risk-averse with respect to the overall size of the wage bill (and hence profits), it is indifferent as to how the wage bill is divided between employed and laid-off workers.

Another point worth noticing about (98) is that, because both the firm and the worker experience diminishing marginal utility $(v'' < 0, u'' < 0)$, $\pi_1 > \pi_2$ implies $w_1 > w_2$ (since $v'(\pi_1) < v'(\pi_2)$ implies $u'(w_1) < u'(w_2)$ by (98) or, more generally:

$$\pi_i > \pi_j \Rightarrow w_i > w_j, \quad i,j = 1, 2. \tag{99}$$

So the firm pays higher wages in states where profit is correspondingly high. This result is sometimes termed coinsurance.

Now consider the optimal level of layoffs. Since workers are fully compensated for being laid off, the firm can continue reducing n_2 until the marginal utility of doing so becomes zero. That is:

$$v'(\pi_2) (p_2 f'(n_2) - w_2 + w_3) = 0. \tag{100}$$

This is just the derivative of the utility of state two profit, with respect to n, set equal to zero. But since $w_2 = w_3 + r$ and $v'(\pi_2) \neq 0$, (100) implies:

$$pf'(n_2) = r. \tag{101}$$

But as we saw in Taylor (1987) the level of n_2 which solves (101) is precisely the level of employment which would occur in state two under a Walrasian spot auction (recall Figure 3). Thus, even under the assumption of firm risk-aversion, workers are never involuntarily unemployed either in the '*ex post*' sense of envying their working colleagues or in the sense of unemployment differing from the Walrasian level.

4. ASYMMETRIC INFORMATION

Now the possibility that the optimal wage may be state-variable introduces an extra complication (Calvo and Phelps, 1977). Suppose, for example, that n_2 was only slightly below n_1 but w_2 was much less than w_1. Then, if it could get away with it, the firm might be tempted to claim that times are bad (state two materializes) when in fact they are good (state one has occurred). This is because the firm would be able to make a large saving on the wage bill for only a small loss in output, and hence revenue. Of course, this situation could only arise if workers are unable to observe which state of the world occurs whilst firms *are* able to. This situation is one of *asymmetric information*, where both parties can observe the wage and employment level (and may even have knowledge of each others' utility functions) but only firms can observe the true state of nature (in this model, p_1 or p_2).

In all the preceding analysis of this chapter we have implicitly assumed symmetric information (both firm and workers can observe the state of the world). In fact, for the case of firm risk-neutrality this makes no difference. The firm will only have an incentive to lie if it can thereby make more profit than could be obtained from a contract which was freely agreed to by the workers. Now, as we have seen, firm risk-neutrality leads to a state-invariant wage for the employed and full compensation for the laid off. Since the wage is fixed, firms can only get the wage bill down by reducing employment in one state. But since workers are indifferent to working or being laid off (since they receive full compensation), they will readily enter into a contract which specifies any level of unemployment. That is, assuming the firm pays unemployment compensation, the worker's expected utility is:

$$\rho_1 u(w_1) + (1 - \rho_1)(n_2/n_1) u(w_2) + (1 - \rho_1)(1 - n_2/n_1) u(w_3 + r).$$

But, as we have seen in the case of firm risk-neutrality, the optimal contract specifies $w_1 = w_2 = w$ and $w_2 = w_3 + r$, so that the worker's expected utility becomes simply $u(w)$, i.e. it is independent of the level of employment in any state. Thus, since the firm can get workers to agree to any state-contingent level of employment, it will clearly have no incentive to tell lies in order to trick them into supplying a different level. However, this result disappears once we allow firms to become risk-averse and the wage to be state-variable.

It is not too difficult to justify the notion that firms may be better informed about demand conditions for their goods than workers are. The firm might sell largely to foreign markets, or to a different part of the country, for example; or be a producer of specialized equipment which does not appear in the High Street shops.

Now since workers know that only the firm can observe the true state of nature, and that their utility level will in general be affected if the firm lies about it, this will affect the nature of the contracts they are willing to enter into. In particular, workers will not agree to a contract in which firms have an incentive to lie. Note that this is another case of the principal–agent problem – the workers are a principal seeking to control the behaviour of a more informed agent (the firm). Again borrowing terminology from the theory of insurance, this is a problem of 'adverse selection'. An adverse selection problem is a principal–agent situation where the agent uses his superior information in making a decision, but the principal has no way of checking whether the information has been used in the way that best serves the principal's interests.

It will be convenient at this point to introduce a little extra nota-tion. Let π_{ij} be the *ex post* level of profit that accrues to the firm if state i materializes but the firm announces to the worker that state j has in fact occurred, i.e.

$$\pi_{11} = p_1 f(n_1) - w_1 n_1 \tag{102}$$

$$\pi_{12} = p_1 f(n_2) - w_2 n_2 - w_3(n_1 - n_2) \tag{103}$$

$$\pi_{22} = p_2 f(n_2) - w_2 n_2 - w_3(n_1 - n_2) \tag{104}$$

$$\pi_{21} = p_2 f(n_1) - w_1 n_1. \tag{105}$$

Assuming that a contract has been agreed to, $(w_1, n_1, w_2, n_2, w_3)$, (102) defines π_{11} as the level of profit if state one occurs (price is p_1) and the firm announces the truth (i.e. employs n_1 men at a wage of w_1). Expression (103) defines π_{12} as the level of profit if state one occurs (price is p_1), but the firm lies and announces state two to the workers (i.e. employs n_2 men at wage w_2 and pays w_3 to those laid off). Expressions (104) and (105) define π_{22} and π_{21} similarly.

Now, as we have pointed out, the worker will not enter into a contract in which the firm has an incentive to lie. In other words, the contract must satisfy the following inequalities:

$$\pi_{11} \geqslant \pi_{12} \tag{106}$$

$$\pi_{22} \geqslant \pi_{21}. \tag{107}$$

If a contract satisfies both (106) and (107) then the incentives of the firm (i.e. whether to tell the truth or to lie) are compatible with the interests of the workers. Accordingly, inequalities such as (106) and (107) are termed incentive-compatibility constraints, and contracts which satisfy them are termed incentive-compatible.

Our assumption that workers will not enter into a contract which is not incentive-compatible is unrestrictive, given that workers recognize a contract which is not incentive-compatible. This is because any non-incentive-compatible contract can be shown to be equivalent to one that is incentive-compatible. For example, consider the contract $(w_1, n_1, w_2, n_1, 0)$, where w_2 is much less than w_1. Since the contract is full-employment $(n_2 = n_1)$, firms have an incentive always to claim that they are in slump, since this allows them to keep the wage bill down without affecting the level of output. However, since workers know that the firm will lie, this is just as if they had been offered the fixed-wage, full-employment contract $(w_2, n_1, w_2, n_1, 0)$, which is quite obviously incentive-compatible. Moreover, the firm will clearly be indifferent between offering this contract and always telling the truth and offering $(w_1, n_1, w_2, n_1, 0)$ and always claiming that times are bad, since each strategy yields the same actual levels of employment and wages. This result is sometimes termed the Revelation Principle, and is due to Myerson (1979).

Contract design under asymmetric information therefore involves maximizing the firm's expected utility of profit subject to workers obtaining a minimum level of expected utility $\bar{U}$ and subject to the incentive-compatability constraints (106) and (107). Since this is similar to the symmetric information problem discussed earlier, but with the additional incentive-compatibility constraints, we might expect the firm to be generally worse off under asymmetric information since its behaviour is further circumscribed. For any given level of p_1 and p_2 and distribution of states of nature (i.e. value of ρ_1), we shall therefore term a contract which is optimal under symmetric information the first-best contract. A contract which is optimal under exactly the same conditions except that the state of nature is not directly observable by workers (i.e. information is asymmetric) we shall term the second-best contract (Azariadis and Stiglitz, 1983). If the optimal, symmetric-information contract satisfies the incentive-compatibility constraints (106) and (107) then the first-best and second-best coincide.

Before we write down the maximization problem which determines the second-best contract, we can make a simplification. As we showed above, the firm is risk-averse to the overall size of the wage bill but indifferent to its composition. This means that it is willing to offer full insurance to workers within states and, in particular, sets $w_2 = w_3 + r$. This allows us to substitute out for w_3 and maximize with respect to one less variable. Specifically, instead of writing the state two wage bill as:

$$w_2 n_2 + w_3(n_1 - n_2),$$

we shall write it as:

$$w_2 n_1 + r(n_1 - n_2).$$

Also, instead of writing the typical worker's expected utility as:

$$\rho_1 u(w_1) + (1 - \rho_1)(n_2/n_1) u(w_2) + (1 - \rho_1)(1 - n_2/n_1) u(w_3 + r),$$

it can be written as:

$$\rho_1 u(w_1) + (1 - \rho_1) u(w_2).$$

Since w_3 need not be specified, contracts may now be designated by a vector excluding this term — e.g. (w_1, n_1, w_2, n_2).

The maximization problem facing the firm can now be explicitly written down:

Maximize: $\rho_1 v(p_1 f(n_1) - w_1 n_1) + (1 - \rho_1) v(p_2 f(n_2)$
$$- w_2 n_1 - r(n_1 - n_2))$$

subject to: $\rho_1 u(w_1) + (1 - \rho_1) u(w_2) \geqslant \bar{U}$,

$$p_1 f(n_1) - w_1 n_1 \geqslant p_1 f(n_2) - w_2 n_1 - r(n_1 - n_2),$$

$$p_2 f(n_2) - w_2 n_1 - r(n_1 - n_2) \geqslant p_2 f(n_1) - w_1 n_1.$$

Note that the last two inequalities are just the incentive-compatibility constraints (106), (107), where we have substituted for the π_{ij} using (102)–(105) and the fact that $w_2 = w_3 + r$.

The second-best contract then defines a saddlepoint of the Lagrangean:

$$\begin{aligned}
\pounds = &\ \rho_1 v(p_1 f(n_1) - w_1 n_1) + (1 - \rho_1) v(p_2 f(n_2) - w_2 n_1 - r(n_1 - n_2)) \\
&+ \lambda[\rho_1 u(w_1) + (1 - \rho_1) u(w_2) - \bar{U}] \\
&+ \gamma_1 [p_1 f(n_1) - w_1 n_1 - p_1 f(n_2) + w_2 n_1 + r(n_1 - n_2)] \\
&+ \gamma_2 [p_2 f(n_2) - w_2 n_1 - r(n_1 - n_2) - p_2 f(n_1) + w_1 n_1]
\end{aligned} \qquad (108)$$

where λ, γ_1 and γ_2 are non-negative Lagrange multipliers. The necessary Kuhn–Tucker conditions for this optimization problem are, assuming an interior solution, (i.e. $w_1, w_2, n_1, n_2 > 0$):

$$\frac{\partial \pounds}{\partial w_1} = \rho_1 v'(\pi_{11}) n_1 + \lambda \rho_1 u'(w_1) - \gamma_1 n_1 + \gamma_2 n_1 = 0 \qquad (109)$$

$$\frac{\partial \pounds}{\partial w_2} = -(1 - \rho_1) v'(\pi_{22}) n_1 + \lambda(1 - \rho_1) u'(w_2) + \gamma_1 n_1 - \gamma_2 n_1 = 0 \qquad (110)$$

$$\frac{\partial \pounds}{\partial n_2} = (1 - \rho_1) v'(\pi_{22}) (p_2 f'(n_2) - r) - \gamma_1 (p_1 f'(n_2) - r)$$
$$+ \gamma_2 (p_2 f'(n_2) - r) = 0 \qquad (111)$$

$$\lambda[\rho_1 u(w_1) + (1 - \rho_1) u(w_2) - \bar{U}] = 0, \quad \lambda \geqslant 0 \qquad (112)$$

$$\gamma_1 [\pi_{11} - \pi_{12}] = 0, \quad \gamma_1 \geqslant 0 \qquad (113)$$

$$\gamma_2 [\pi_{22} - \pi_{21}] = 0, \quad \gamma_2 \geqslant 0 \qquad (114)$$

where we have used (102)–(105) to simplify as much as possible. We have also again imposed full employment in state one, so that n_1 is not a choice variable.

The first question we shall seek to answer is whether a second-best contract will generally predict employment levels any different from those which would prevail under a neoclassical Walrasian auction regime. In order to make this answer interesting we shall assume that a Walrasian auction would predict full employment in state one and unemployment in state two. As we saw in Taylor (1987) this implies:

$$p_1 f'(n_1) > r \qquad (115)$$

and

$$p_2 f'(n_1) < r, \tag{116}$$

(recall Figure 3). The level of Walrasian employment in state two then solves:

$$p_2 f'(n_2^a) = r \tag{117}$$

We can now distinguish between four cases concerning whether or not the incentive-compatibility constraints (106) and (107) are binding. They can either both be slack (i.e. (106) and (107) are satisfied for strict inequality), both be binding ((106) and (107) are satisfied for equality) or any one of them can be binding.

If both of the incentive-compatibility constraints are slack, then the first-best contract is incentive-compatible. Intuitively, if we do not have to impose the constraint that firms tell the truth then they become irrelevant, as in the symmetric information case. Formally, if both (106) and (107) are slack, then from (113) and (114) we must have $\gamma_1 = 0$ and $\gamma_2 = 0$, so that the Lagrangean (108) is formally identical to (93). In this case, therefore, the second-best coincides with the first-best, and since we have already characterized the first-best, this is an uninteresting case.

What if both of the incentive-compatibility constraints are binding, i.e. $\pi_{11} = \pi_{12}$ and $\pi_{22} = \pi_{21}$? In that case we have:

$$p_1 f(n_1) - w_1 n_1 = p_1 f(n_2) - w_2 n_1 + r(n_1 - n_2) \tag{118}$$

and

$$p_2 f(n_2) - w_2 n_1 + r(n_1 - n_2) = p_2 f(n_1) - w_1 n_1. \tag{119}$$

After rearrangement, (118) and (119) become respectively:

$$p_1(f(n_1) - f(n_2)) = n_1(w_1 - w_2) + r(n_1 - n_2)$$

$$p_2(f(n_1) - f(n_2)) = n_1(w_1 - w_2) + r(n_1 - n_2)$$

which imply:

$$p_1(f(n_1) - f(n_2)) = p_2(f(n_1) - f(n_2)). \tag{120}$$

Since $p_1 > p_2$, (120) can only be satisfied if $n_2 = n_1$. Substituting this into the first-order condition (111) and rearranging:

$$(1 - \rho_1) v'(\pi_{22}) + \gamma_2 = \gamma_1 \frac{(p_1 f'(n_1) - r)}{(p_2 f'(n_1) - r)}. \tag{121}$$

Now in general, γ_1 and γ_2 will be positive for binding incentive-compatibility constraints (see (113) and (114)). Therefore the left-hand side of (121) is positive. But, using (115) and (116), the right-hand side of (121) will be negative, so (111) cannot be satisfied. This means that, if a Walrasian auction regime would result in full employment in state one and unemployment in state two, both of the incentive-compatibility contracts cannot be binding simultaneously for the second-best contract.

A third possibility is that (107) is binding but (106) is slack, i.e. $\pi_{22} = \pi_{21}$ and $\pi_{11} > \pi_{12}$. This means that, in the absence of the incentive-compatibility constraints, the firm would announce the correct state only if state one occurred – i.e. it would generally claim that times were good even if they were bad. One might suspect that this will not generally be the case. This possibility can be ruled out formally quite straightforwardly. Firstly, $\pi_{11} > \pi_{12}$ implies $\gamma_1 = 0$, by the Kuhn–Tucker condition (113), whilst γ_2 will in general be positive. Substituting $\gamma_1 = 0$ into (111) and rearranging slightly:

$$(1 - \rho_1) v'(\pi_{22}) (p_2 f'(n_2) - r) = -\gamma_2 (p_2 f'(n_2) - r). \qquad (122)$$

Now since $(1 - \rho_1) v'(\pi_{22}) > 0$ whilst $-\gamma_2 \leqslant 0$, (122) can only be satisfied for $(p_2 f'(n_2) - r) = 0$, i.e.

$$r = p_2 f'(n_2). \qquad (123)$$

Now

$$f'(n_2) > \frac{f(n_1) - f(n_2)}{n_1 - n_2} \qquad (124)$$

by the concavity of f (recall Figure 4). Combining (123) and (124):

$$r(n_1 - n_2) > p_2(f(n_1) - f(n_2)). \qquad (125)$$

Since $\pi_{22} = \pi_{21}$,

$$p_2 f(n_2) - w_2 n_1 + r(n_1 - n_2) = p_2 f(n_1) - w_1 n_1$$

or

$$r(n_1 - n_2) = p_2(f(n_1) - f(n_2)) + (w_2 - w_1) n_1. \qquad (126)$$

Expressions (125) and (126) are only compatible if $(w_2 - w_1) n_1 > 0$, i.e.

$$w_1 < w_2. \qquad (127)$$

Intuitively, firms only have an incentive to claim times are good when in fact they are bad if the wage is lower in the best state of the world.

However, $\pi_{11} > \pi_{21}$ (clearly, $p_1 f(n_1) - w_1 n_1 > p_2 f(n_1) - w_1 n_1$, since $p_1 > p_2$), so that if $\pi_{22} = \pi_{21}$, then $\pi_{11} > \pi_{22}$ – i.e. profits are higher in state one than state two when the firm tells the truth. The coinsurance result discussed earlier would therefore suggest that w_1 should be greater than w_2. This is easily seen to be the case since, setting $\gamma_1 = 0$ and letting $\gamma_2 \geqslant 0$ in (109) implies:

$$v'(\pi_{11}) \, n_1 \geqslant \lambda u'(w_1) \tag{128}$$

and similarly, from (110):

$$v'(\pi_{22}) \, n_1 \leqslant \lambda u'(w_2). \tag{129}$$

Hence

$$\frac{v'(\pi_{11})}{v'(\pi_{22})} \geqslant \frac{u'(w_1)}{u'(w_2)}. \tag{130}$$

By diminishing marginal utility ($v'' < 0$), $\pi_{11} > \pi_{22}$ implies that the left-hand side (and hence the right-hand side) of (13) is less than unity, i.e.

$$u'(w_1) < u'(w_2). \tag{131}$$

But given diminishing marginal utility, ($u'' < 0$), (131) implies:

$$w_1 > w_2 \tag{132}$$

which contradicts (128). This contradiction rules out the possibility that $\pi_{11} > \pi_{12}$ and $\pi_{22} = \pi_{21}$ for the second-best contract.

The only remaining possibility is $\pi_{11} = \pi_{12}$ and $\pi_{22} > \pi_{21}$. This seems the most intuitively plausible case, since one can easily imagine a situation where the firm would find it profitable to claim that times are bad when in fact they are good, but not vice-versa. From the Kuhn–Tucker conditions (113), (114) we have in this case $\gamma_2 = 0$ and $\gamma_1 \geqslant 0$. Substituting into condition (111) yields:

$$(1 - \rho_1) \, v'(\pi_{22}) \, (p_2 f'(n_2) - r) = \gamma_1 (p_1 f'(n_2) - r). \tag{133}$$

Now, since we assumed state one Walrasian full employment, $p_1 f'(n_1) > r$ ((115)), and since $f'(n_2) > f'(n_1)$ for $n_1 > n_2$ by diminishing returns, we have $p_1 f'(n_2) > r$. Therefore, the right-hand side of (133) is non-negative. But the left-hand side will only be non-negative if $(p_2 f'(n_2) - r)$ is, i.e.

$$p_2 f'(n_2) \geqslant r. \tag{134}$$

Except under very special circumstances, the Lagrange multiplier γ_1 will in fact be strictly greater than zero, so that (134) can in general be strengthened to a strict inequality:

$$p_2 f'(n_2) > r. \tag{135}$$

Comparing (135) with (117) (which gives the level of Walrasian state two employment), we can see that a second-best contract will generate a lower level of employment in slump than would occur under a Walrasian regime (or indeed under a first-best contract – see (101)). This is illustrated in Figure 7, in which n_2 denotes the level of state

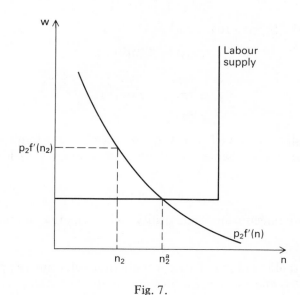

Fig. 7.

two employment under a second-best contract, and n_2^a the corresponding Walrasian level. Since $n_2 < n_2^a$, this means that implicit labour contracts under asymmetric information will in general create socially deficient levels of employment in some states of nature (Azariadis, 1983; Grossman and Hart, 1981, 1983).

What is the intuition underlying this under-employment result? Since workers do not trust firms to truthfully report the state of nature, they will not enter into a contract in which the wage is purely a function of which state prevails. Instead, wages will effectively be made to depend on variables which the worker can observe, such as the level of employment. Thus, reductions in the wage will only be allowed in the contract if the firm also reduces the level of employment enough to convince the workers that times actually are bad, and this is not just a ploy to cut the wage bill. Thus, in adverse states of nature the firm may have to reduce employment below the socially efficient level purely because this is the only way it can get wages down.

Will optimal risk-sharing occur under asymmetric information? Substituting $\gamma_2 = 0$ and assuming γ_1 strictly positive in (109) yields, after rearrangement:

$$v'(\pi_{11}) n_1 - \lambda u'(w_1) = -\gamma n_1/\rho_1 < 0$$

which implies:

$$v'(\pi_{11})\, n_1 < \lambda u'(w_1). \tag{136}$$

Similarly, from (110):

$$v'(\pi_{22})\, n_1 > \lambda u'(w_2). \tag{137}$$

Expression (136) and (137) imply:

$$\frac{v'(\pi_{11})}{v'(\pi_{22})} < \frac{u'(w_1)}{u'(w_2)} \tag{138}$$

Since (138) is an inequality, the optimal risk-sharing condition is violated − marginal rates of substitution between incomes in different states are not equalized for the firm and the worker. However, optimal risk sharing could be achieved by reducing w_2 a little and increasing w_1, holding n_1 and n_2 constant. This would have the effect of reducing π_{11} and increasing π_{22}. Given diminishing marginal utility for the firm and the worker, juggling with w_1 and w_2 in this way could clearly turn (138) into an equality. What is precluding this result? Again, the firm would have to reduce employment further in state two if it were to cut w_2, in order to convince the worker that its intentions are honourable. Given that output would fall in state two (and total unemployment compensation rise), π_{22} would not rise enough to prevent (138) holding as an inequality (indeed, π_{22} may even fall).

Let us summarize the main results of this section. There are good reasons for believing that employers may not be completely risk-neutral. Once we allow the possibility of firm risk-aversion, optimal risk-sharing dictates state-variable wages − the worker can pass some, but not all, of the risk of wage variation to the employer. In the case where the firm is risk-neutral, and wages are hence state-invariant, it makes no difference whether or not the worker as well as the firm can observe which state of the world is prevailing (i.e. whether information is symmetric or asymmetric). However, once it is conceded that wages may be state-variable, an interesting principal−agent problem arises when information is asymmetric, because it may sometimes be in the interests of the employer to lie to the worker about the state of the world. In such a situation, employers will have to convince workers that times really are bad before they will accept a wage cut. The only other variable observable to the worker is the level of employment, and so employment in adverse states of nature will actually be lower than it would be under a Walrasian spot auction or a symmetric information contract simply because this is the only way the firm can get wages down. Moreover, we also showed that second-best contracts will not in general allocate risks optimally (i.e. the Arrow−Borch optimal risk-sharing condition is violated).

5. SUMMARY AND CONCLUSION

This paper extends Taylor (1987) to consider the consequences for implicit contract theory of allowing heterogeneous labour, firm risk-aversion and informational asymmetry.

Allowing the firm to hire different skill grades of labour certainly yields further interesting insights into the employment process. In particular, we saw that there will be a tendency for firms to lay off less skilled workers in preference to more skilled workers in adverse states. Intuitively, although there might appear to be a larger saving to be had from laying off skilled workers (since they command a higher wage), skilled workers will demand a much higher state-invariant wage in order to compensate them for the risk of unemployment, thereby inflating the overall expected wage bill.

If we abandon the idea that firms are completely risk-neutral, then the optimal risk-sharing condition (i.e. that the marginal rate of substitution between income in different states of nature should be the same for the firm and worker) no longer dictates a state-invariant wage. However, so long as the firm is less risk-averse than the worker, optimal risk-sharing will still impart some degree of stickiness to the wage, the less so the more risk-averse the firm is.

If, in addition to firm risk-aversion, we allow the possibility that there may be an informational asymmetry – only the firm can observe which state of nature is prevailing – a rather interesting principal–agent problem opens up. Firms then have to convince workers that times really are bad before the latter will accept a wage cut in the down phase of the business cycle. Since the only other variable observable to workers is the level of employment, the firm can do this by reducing employment as well as wages in adverse states of nature. In contrast, therefore, to the symmetric information case, employment will be more variable under an asymmetric information contract regime than under a Walrasian spot auction regime, because this is the only way the firm can get wages down. Using employment as a signal in this fashion will also generally cause risks to be shared less than optimally – the Arrow–Borch condition is violated.

Finally, given the wage stickiness generated within implicit contract models of the employment process it is natural to ponder whether they can be used as a rationalization of Keynesian macroeconomics, as opposed to monetarist or new classical macroeconomics which assumes flexible wages and prices. The first point to note is that Keynesian economics of the traditional variety, once wealth effects are allowed, requires stickiness of *nominal* rather than real wages, and it is the stickiness of the latter that implicit contract theory seeks to explain.[3] Moreover, as the discussion of the nature of contractual unemployment in Taylor (1987) makes clear, contract theory cannot be used to explain 'involuntary' unemployment – the apparent rigidities engendered by contractual agreements do not necessarily signal market failure. Staggered nominal wage contract models of the kind discussed, for example, by Fischer (1977) are rather different from those discussed in this paper, and do not appear to have a microeconomic foundation more rigorous than a rather vague appeal to the costs of wage setting and the difficulties of contract writing.

Economics Division, Bank of England, and Department of Economics, The University, Newcastle upon Tyne

REFERENCES

Arrow, K. J. (1985). 'The Economics of Agency', in *Agency: The Structure of Business*, Pratt, J. W. and Zeckhauser, R. (eds.), Cambridge, Mass., Harvard Business School Press.

Azariadis, C. (1976). 'On the Incidence of Unemployment', *Review of Economic Studies*, Vol. 43, pp. 115-25.

Azariadis, C. (1983). 'Employment with Asymmetric Information', *Quarterly Journal of Economics*, Vol. 98 (supplement), pp. 157-72.

Azariadis, C. and Stiglitz, J. E. (1983). 'Implicit Contracts and Fixed Price Equilibria', *Quarterly Journal of Economics*, Vol. 98 (supplement), pp. 1-22.

Bell, P. W. (1951). 'Cyclical Variations and Trend in Occupational Wage Differentials in American Industry Since 1914', *Review of Economics and Statistics*, Vol. 33, pp. 329-37.

Calvo, G. A. and Phelps, E. S. (1977). 'Indexation Issues: Appendix', *Journal of Monetary Economics*, supplementary series, Vol. 5, pp. 160-8.

Fischer, S. (1977). 'Long-term Contracts, Rational Expectations and the Optimal Money Supply', *Journal of Political Economy*, Vol. 85, pp. 191-205.

Grossman, H. I. (1977). 'Risk Shifting and Reliability in Labor Markets', *Scandinavian Journal of Economics*, Vol. 79, pp. 187-209.

Grossman, H. I. (1978). 'Risk Shifting, Layoffs and Seniority', *Journal of Monetary Economics*, Vol. 4, pp. 661-86.

Grossman, S. J. and Hart, O. D. (1981). 'Implicit Contracts, Moral Hazard and Unemployment', *American Economic Review*, Vol. 71, pp. 301-7.

Grossman, S. J. and Hart, O. D. (1983). 'Implicit Contracts Under Asymmetrical Information', *Quarterly Journal of Economics*, Vol. 98 (supplement), pp. 123-56.

---

[3] Sargent (1979) appears to say that implicit contract theory can be used to bolster nominal wage rigidities. However, his analysis is misleading in this respect, since he makes the workers' utility a function of the *nominal* wage – i.e. it is *money illusion* rather than contracting which is driving the nominal wage rigidity in his model. Sutton (1979) argues that nominal wage rigidities may arise if workers and employers fail to agree on a common price index.

Knowles, K. G. and Robertson, D. J. (1961). 'Difference Between the Wages of Skilled and Unskilled Workers, 1880–1950', *Bulletin of the Oxford Institute of Statistics*, Vol. 13, pp. 109–27.

Myerson, R. (1979). 'Incentive Compatibility and the Bargaining Problem', *Econometrica*, Vol. 47, pp. 61–74.

Oi, W. Y. (1962). 'Labor as a Quasi-Fixed Factor of Production', *Journal of Political Economy*, Vol. 70, pp. 538–55.

Rees, R. (1985a). 'The Theory of Principal and Agent: Part I', *Bulletin of Economic Research*, Vol. 36, pp. 3–26.

Rees, R. (1985b). 'The Theory of Principal and Agent: Part II', *Bulletin of Economic Research*, Vol. 37, pp. 77–95.

Sargent, T. J. (1979). *Macroeconomic Theory*, New York, Academic Press.

Sutton, J. (1979). 'Comment on Azariadis' Paper', in *The Economics of the Labour Market*, Hornstein, A., Grice, J. and Webb, A. (eds.), London, HMSO.

Taylor, M. P. (1987). 'The Simple Analytics of Implicit Labour Contracts', *Bulletin of Economic Research*, Vol. 39, pp. 1–27.

THE ECONOMIC ANALYSIS OF TAX EVASION

Frank A. Cowell

'The income tax has made more liars
out of the American people than
golf has' — Will Rogers

1. INTRODUCTION

Like pornography, the subject of tax evasion seems to arouse a mixture of outrage, guilty curiosity and incredulous admiration. It is an area about which one knows little but suspects much, and which perhaps one simply ignores in the majority of economic and social activities. One has had one's own personal experiences (minor, of course) or word-of-mouth accounts concerning the practice, and one is led to believe that there are people who are involved in it in a big way, yet one is not entirely clear how to fit it into the general pattern of life's above-board experiences. Official statistics are rare and it is not clear whether they should be believed anyway.

The principal question which one must address of course is whether the topic of illegitimate tax dodging is in its own right a legitimate subject for academic discussion. Some would argue that it scarcely merits such attention either because they view the analytical questions that it raises as being neither novel nor particularly interesting, or because the phenomenon is trivial in terms of its quantitative importance, or because the inherent inaccessibility and unreliability of data makes empirical modelling an extremely difficult task. Of these three negative views it seems to me that only the last has any force, since there is sufficient evidence to suggest that tax evasion is quantitatively a non-negligible problem in advanced Western-style economies,[1] and some of the analytical work done on the subject has uncovered some intriguing issues which economists are

*My thanks go to A. B. Atkinson, J. C. Baldry, E. L. Feige, A. Sandmo who provided helpful comments on an earlier draft. Errors and omissions are my responsibility.
[1] For a general introduction see Bawly (1982), Heertje *et al.* (1982), Simon and Witte (1982), Smith (1981), Tanzi (1983); an interesting historical perspective for the UK is given by Smithies (1984).

only beginning to address. But seeking hypotheses on the shadow economy with nebulous data clearly does present some disquieting problems.

In fact one might view the whole topic of tax evasion as being rather disturbing from the standpoint of traditional economic analysis. Much of the theory of Public Economics is based on the premiss of virtually an all-knowing and all-powerful State implementing policy to maximize Social Welfare – whatever that might be taken to be. Admittedly in practice there are likely to be some limitations on the scope and effectiveness of the State's activities – for otherwise first-best policies with lump sum taxation would always be practicable and the entire subject of Public Economics could have been summarized in two-and-a-half pages. But in the main the theory of taxation and public expenditure presupposes that the State has a number of levers it can pull with determinate, predictable results in order to achieve its objectives of revenue raising and redistribution. If there is widespread evasion this simple, comforting view of the world – which I do not share – will no longer be adequate.

Accordingly we shall examine some of the main questions in roughly this order. What is the nature of the problem? What role can standard economic theorizing play in helping one to analyse the phenomenon of evasion? How far can one test the theories from the patchy evidence available? What are the policy implications for the structure and enforcement of tax systems?

2. THE BOUNDARIES OF EVASION

One of the problems that one must confront immediately is that it is not self evident what a sensible definition of 'tax evasion' should be. This is not solely a definitional issue: several questions of economic analysis are raised. The national income accountant may reasonably wish to incorporate certain types of concealed or illicit activities within his ideal 'production boundary' for the economy. Models of the microeconomic behaviour of tax evaders may well be indistinguishable from models of other criminal activities, so that the formal analysis of tax evasion is hardly worth discussing as a problem on its own. The social welfare interpretation of different activities, which might loosely be categorized under the same heading of 'evasion', may nevertheless be markedly different. Let us see if it is possible to draw a clear and useful line round the set of activities which we shall term 'evasion'. To do this we shall consider three 'boundaries' which have often been discussed in the literature and which obviously overlap to some extent: the boundary between evasion and avoidance, that between evasion and other activities in the 'informal sector'; that between evasion and other criminal activities.

Can tax evasion be distinguished from tax avoidance and is there any point in trying to do so? The answers given to this question in the literature seem to fall into three categories:

(i) The distinction is purely a legal one. Evasion is beyond the law; avoidance isn't.

(ii) The argument is a moral one: certain types of avoidance are 'just as bad' as evasion and should not be treated as any different.[2]

(iii) Evasion and avoidance are just two arbitrary segments of a continuum that stretches from tax planning for the kiddies' education to the fringes of extortion.[3]

In fact each of the above views has some force – and we shall be discussing later some of the problems which are raised by them – but to some extent they miss the point as far as the positive economic analysis of tax evasion is concerned. The legal boundaries differ in the specification and interpretation from country to country,[4] moral views are difficult to translate from vague generalities to specific concepts of economic analysis, and the 'continuum' thesis may be pressed to the point of vacuity. But nevertheless there still appears to be a distinct economic problem which we may label 'tax evasion'. The essential distinction which I shall make in this survey can be expressed in terms of the agent's perceived budget constraint.

'Avoidance' in its strict sense implies certainty on the part of the tax payer at the time when he makes his decisions about the deployment of his assets and his report to the tax authority. 'Evasion' activities shall be taken to involve a decision or decisions made under uncertainty with respect to the tax payer's eventual tax liability.[5] The logic of this is as follows. If the law effectively

[2] Of course this point can be stood on its head in a very obvious fashion. Certain types of officially designated evasion are really not all that bad... See the discussion by Bracewell-Milnes (1979).

[3] See Seldon et al. (1979) who introduced the term 'tax avoision' or Cross and Shaw (1981, 1982) with their more emotive term 'tax aversion'.

[4] See Boidman (1983), International Bar Association (1982).

[5] A nice distinction between avoidance and evasion has been made by Kay (1980). 'The incidence of evasion is therefore a function of the mechanisms by which tax is assessed and collected, and the extent to which they can be controlled or monitored; the incidence of avoidance is a function of the tax base and depends on the extent to which legislation is successful in expressing the underlying economic concepts. Avoidance depends on the base: evasion on the assessment procedures'. However he points out that there still remains an area of transactions which lies 'in between the two': here the intention or reason for the taxpayer's action – as perceived by the authority – becomes important. 'Intention or motive is remarkably hard to translate into specific economic terms so once again the next definition breaks down. For our purposes what is important is how the tax-payer perceives the situation. 'The problem of avoidance and the definition of income is discussed further in Feldman and Kay (1981) using the Simons (1938) approach.

turns a blind eye to a particular form of tax evasion then, as far as the consequences to the individual taxpayers are concerned, engaging in that form of evasion is no different from legitimate tax avoidance; conversely, if a particular 'avoidance' scheme is actually the subject of legal doubt, or liable to substantial arbitrary penalty, then, as far as the economic consequences to the tax payer are concerned, engaging in that scheme is equivalent to participation in manifestly illicit tax evasion.

The second type of boundary to be considered is that between evasion activities and other activities in the 'informal' or 'irregular' sector. This sector includes household production and barter.[6] The boundary is one that is of great interest to the national income accountant, but essentially raises no new problems for the analysis of economic behaviour beyond those discussed above concerning the distinction between avoidance and evasion.[7]

The third boundary to be considered is that between the economic analysis of pure tax evasion and the economic analysis of criminal activities in general. This issue appears to be virtually a taxonomic one: is it worth attempting to isolate the analysis of tax evasion as a distinct economic problem? It is tempting to see the tax evasion problem embedded within the general problem of economic incentives for, and control of crime. One may then read off analytical results on the behaviour of tax evaders as a special case of the rational economic behaviour of criminals.[8] This is misleading for two reasons. Firstly in many cases, as Reinganum and Wilde (1984) have made clear, tax evasion implicitly involves the potential malefactor in making a report – conveying information to the authorities – a feature which is absent from crimes such as theft. Secondly the issue of evasion is, unlike other illegal activities, inseparably bound up with the instruments of fiscal control that the government attempts to use in carrying out its economic policy. The quest for effective taxation and public expenditure policy itself makes the topic of evasion interesting in its own right.

Finally we turn to the question of whether tax evasion is quantitatively important enough to matter. Here we may draw on the numerous studies of the size of the black economy.

The consensus view appears to be that this is of the order of magnitude of 5 to 10 per cent of GNP in Western style industrialized

---

[6] Some writers would want to include criminal production activities such as prostitution and the narcotics industry here as well. For further introductory discussion on this point see Henry (1978) and the paper by Gershuny and Pahl in Henry (1981).

[7] For an excellent discussion of these issues see Blades (1985).

[8] For surveys of the economics of crime and a discussion of the relationship of tax evasion to this field see Anderson (1976), Heineke (1978) and Pyle (1984).

economies.[9] This conclusion has to be heavily qualified, since the quantitative answer at which one eventually arrives depends on the way in which the question is framed, on the type of estimation method used, and above all, on the social institutions of the country in question. But clearly the problem of tax evasion cannot be dismissed as either conceptually or quantitatively trivial; accordingly we turn to the ways in which economists have attempted to model the behaviour of tax evaders.

3. THE BASIC MODEL

We begin with the standard approach, the analysis of the behaviour of an isolated tax-payer using the conventional economic theory of the household: a kind of black economy Robinson Crusoe. As far as such an individual is concerned Life can be described by a simple Bernoulli random variable: you either get caught cheating the system (with probability p) or you escape (probability $1 - p$).[10] Getting caught entails a forfeit which depends in some way upon the gravity of one's cheating. The situation can be illustrated simply in Figure 1. Along the horizontal axis measure c', consumption if the individual escapes detection, along the vertical axis c'', consumption if the individual is caught. Assuming a non-negative forfeit for cheating the wedge-shaped area bounded by the horizontal axis and the 45° ray through the origin is the subset of the diagram that is relevant to our discussion. Any point in this area represents a stochastic consumption prospect c with realizations c', c'' respectively in the two states. The subset of this area that represents the individual's budget set will be determined by (i) the person's original income,[11] (ii) the tax system, (iii) the penalty system in force. Let us begin by making extremely simple assumptions about all three items namely:

A1   The person has a fixed income Y which is liable to tax.

A2   There is a proportional income tax at rate t.

---

[9] O'Higgins (1984) suggests that 5 per cent is probably a reasonable figure for the UK. US Dept. of the Treasury (1979) suggested 6 to 8 per cent for the USA which is probably underestimated; and Hansson (1980) reports an estimate of 8 to 15 per cent by the Riksskatteverk for Sweden. Detailed surveys of the empirical literature are provided in Carter (1984) and Feige (forthcoming). A partial annotated listing of empirical work in this are as given in the expanded version of this paper: Cowell (1985c).

[10] There is a very unfortunate notation problem in the literature. The symbols p and π have been variously used to mean the probability of detection, the probability of non-detection, the penalty premium if detected, the penalty tax rate ...

[11] I shall continue to assume the official tax base as 'income'; but it only requires relatively small adjustments to the argument to make it applicable to wealth, expenditure, or some other base.

A3(a) There is a fixed probability p of tax evasion being discovered.
A3(b) The tax on any income found to have been concealed from the authorities is subject to surcharge at a rate s.

For each dollar of gross income, then, you would receive \$$[1 - t]$ if you were honest and declare it, \$1 if you were dishonest, did not declare it and escaped detection, and \$$[1 - t - ts]$ if you were dishonest and got caught. Accordingly the budget set will look something like the shaded area in Figure 1. Point A represents the situation of Absolute honesty: the distance OA' $(= A'A)$ is $[1 - t]Y$. Point B represents the situation of Blatant dishonesty: the distance OB' is simply Y, total income, and the distance BB' is $[1 - t - ts]Y$. The slope of AB in absolute terms is obviously s. We would expect to find a greedy, amoral individual somewhere in the closed line segment AB: the exact location, of course, depends on the shape of his preferences.

We shall make one of the simplest possible assumptions about preferences, namely:

A4　The individual has a von Neumann-Morgenstern utility function that is concave in consumption.

Accordingly we can write down the equation of a particular indifference curve at utility level U_0 as:

$$[1 - p]u(c') + pu(c'') = U_0 \tag{1}$$

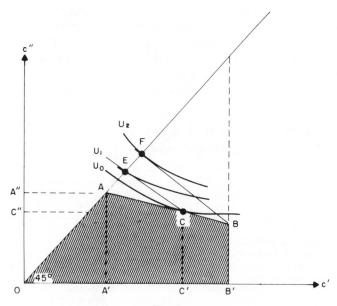

Fig. 1.

Observe that the Neumann-Morgenstern assumptions rule out state-dependent utility, so that we have no phenomena of regrets, shame, or intrinsic delight at cheating the tax man. If one wished to do so, such features could easily be incorporated. Observe that at the point where any indifference curve cuts the 45° ray through the origin, the marginal rate of substitution of consumption-if-caught (c'') for consumption-if-escape (c') is exactly $(1 - p)/p$[12] (the odds on your getting away with your dishonesty). One may now simply find the individual's expected-utility-maximizing optimum at point C where an indifference curve is tangent to AB. Then we easily see that for this particular person, out of an income of OB' he pays $C'B'$ in tax and evades an amount $A'C'$ of tax leaving him with consumption equal to OC' if his dishonesty goes undetected. If they catch up wih him, however, he pays the full tax ($A'B'$) *plus* a surcharge equal to $A''C''$ and ends up with consumption equal to OC''. His expected consumption, given this strategy, is represented by point E on the 45° ray: note that EC forms the tangent to an indifference curve at E.

Quick-witted readers will already have spotted that this is in essence a very simple 'portfolio selection' problem.[13] And indeed, with one exception, virtually all the comparative static results can be deduced directly from the standard literature on taxation and risk taking in wealth allocation models. But let us briefly look at the workings of the model in intuitive terms.

Some results from this diagram are intuitively obvious. Rotate the budget line AB through A downwards (clockwise) and the distance $A'C'$ must fall. In other words, increasing the penalty must reduce tax evasion. Alternatively, reduce the marginal rate of substitution of consumption-if-caught for consumption-if-escape everywhere ('rotate' the indifference curves anticlockwise) and again the distance $A'C'$ must fall. In other words, increasing the probability of detection must also reduce tax evasion.[14] Now consider a 'mean-preserving spread' of the returns to evasion activity. Elementary reasoning on the theory of portfolio selection by risk averse individuals gives the result that such a change results in less evasion activity.[15] Let us look at this intuitively in terms of the diagram. There are several examples of such mean preserving spreads which might be interesting. For instance Figure 2 illustrates a decrease in the tax rate and an increase in the surcharge with an unchanged

[12] Indeed in general the marginal rate of substitution at any point on the diagram includes a factor $(1 - p)/p$.

[13] See, for example, Ahsan (1974), Cowell (1975), Mossin (1968), Stiglitz (1969).

[14] See Allingham and Sandmo (1972).

[15] See Rothschild and Stiglitz (1970, 1971). Observe that our problem is a simple special case of their discussion since there are only two possible outcomes: hence a mean preserving spread has an unambiguous effect on the demand for risky assets.

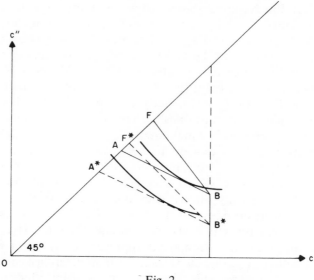

Fig. 2.

detection probability such that the expected return per dollar of tax evasion, namely $t[1-p-ps]$, remains unaltered. The budget line shifts from AB to A^*B^*, the distance $AF-A^*F^*$ (which is proportional to the expected return per dollar) stays constant and tax evasion must decrease. Other examples are less easy to represent diagrammatically, but nevertheless follow immediately from the same result – for instance an increase in the surcharge accompanied by a decrease in the probability of detection so as to keep constant the expected returns to a dollar of tax evasion.[16]

All of the above results can be formally established on the basis of very rudimentary assumptions – risk averse, von Neumann-Morgenstern preferences and free choice of evasion activities subject to a linear constraint. If one allows the structure of the indifference map to be a little more restricted, further results are available. Suppose that the individual displays *decreasing absolute risk aversion* in the sense of Pratt (1964) and Arrow (1965): this implies indifference curves such that as a person's overall resources are increased (without any change in the probability distribution on the returns to the various assets) his demand for risky assets increases in absolute terms. This has a simple interpretation in terms of Figure 1.

Cut the tax rate t, without making any alterations to the penalty structure or the person's pre-tax income. This moves the budget line AB outward, with unchanged slope (equal to $-s$) and with the abscissa of the point B unaltered (equal to Y): accordingly AB

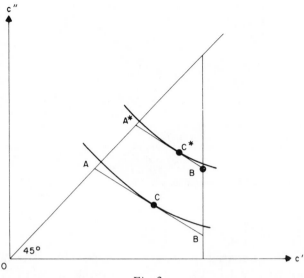

Fig. 3.

moves to $A*B*$ in Figure 3. Assuming that the original solution to the optimization problem was at C, somewhere in the interior of the segment AB, the assumption of diminishing absolute risk aversion then implies that the new solution must be at a point such as $C*$ in $A*B*$, to the right of C. Tax evasion has increased both in absolute terms and as a proportion of taxable income Y.[17]

It is also obvious that, conditional on this assumption of decreasing absolute risk aversion, an increase in income Y will shift the budget line outwards with unchanged slope *and unchanged length* (so that in this case both A *and* B move to the right as well as upwards). Hence whilst it is obvious that such an income increase must increase the absolute amount of tax evasion, we cannot say anything definite about the *proportion* of taxable income that is being concealed,

---

[16] Increasing s whilst keeping Y and t constant moves B vertically downwards toward B', thus also rotating the line AB clockwise around A. The indifference curves are also shifted as p is reduced. In order to keep the expected return to evasion constant the line FB must still be tangent to an indifference curve at F. Hence the rotation of the line FB as B slides down towards B' gives the extent to which the MRS is everywhere rotated clockwise. Tax evasion decreases, because of the mean preserving spread – see Christiansen (1980).

[17] This is the essence of Yitzhaki (1974). Allingham and Sandmo (1972) failed to get a clear-cut result because, instead of keeping the surcharge s constant, they kept the penalty tax rate $t[1 + s]$ constant which means that as you cut t you have to increase s and so segment AB becomes steeper as it is moved outwards. Which type of exercise is relevant depends, of course, on the specification of the penalty structure in the economy under investigation. McCaleb (1976) extends this analysis slightly to the case of differential taxation on capital and labour income.

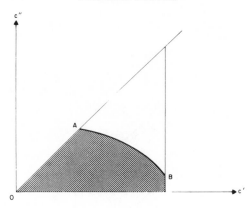

Fig. 4.

unless we are prepared to restrict the possible structure of the indifference map yet further. By definition an increase in resources will increase/leave unchanged/decrease the *proportion* of those resources devoted to risky assets according as *relative risk aversion* is, respectively, decreasing/constant/increasing:[18] in our case for the words 'resources' read 'income', and for the words 'devoted to risky assets' read 'concealed from the tax-man'.

Of course this basic model can be elaborated on in all sorts of ways. You can introduce a progressive tax system and progressive system of penalties as in Figure 4. The model will be less tractable than the linear one discussed above, but will retain many of the convenient properties.[19] It is easy to see that under pretty weak conditions there will be a unique interior solution, and that a transformation that increases the marginal penalty or increases the probability of detection will reduce evasion.[20] Two more promising directions of development are examined in the next two sections.

---

[18] Choose whichever assumption seems reasonable to you.

[19] See Srinivasan (1973) and Sproule et al. (1980). Fishburn (1981), discusses the effect of price inflation in such a model by examining, in effect, the exogenous deflation of real income with $T(\cdot)$ fixed in nominal terms. Nayak (1978) investigates the opposite case of regressive taxes and suggests that the results come out very similarly. However in this case the budget set may be convex which can lead to problems of nonuniqueness of the solution and difficulties in interpreting the comparative statics.

[20] Ali (1976) and Koskela (1983a) discuss an appealing special case where the progressive tax has a constant marginal rate (compare Ahsan (1974), Cowell (1975)). Koskela shows that, for a given p and s, if you assume decreasing absolute risk aversion then an increase in the marginal tax rate and the minimum income guarantee such that *either* (i) expected government revenue *or* (ii) expected utility is held constant will reduce tax evasion. Case (ii) can be read off directly from Figure 1 and does not need the restriction on risk aversion: constant s and constant utility imply that equilibrium must stay at C (AB stays put); thus evaded tax stays unchanged as the marginal tax rates rises; hence evaded income must have fallen.

4. EXTENSIONS: INTERACTION AMONGST AGENTS

The analysis of section 3 concentrated on the behaviour of an isolated individual playing a 'game against nature'. But this is obviously unsatisfactory in some respects. We may need to examine the inter-action between the individual and other agents – the tax authority and other tax payers. On page 169 above we noted that the formal analysis of the simple tax evasion problem was identical to that of portfolio selection *with one exception*. The exception concerns the nature of the risk involved. In portfolio analysis it is reasonable to assume that, as far as any one investor is concerned, the uncertainty is exogenous: there is some given distribution function of rates of return to any particular financial asset which is independent of any action that the investor may take. Of course it is possible to think of certain exceptions to this where the investor is 'large' relative to the market, but these are often not particularly relevant. However in the tax evasion case the distribution of returns to engaging in this risky activity (summarized in the parameters p and s) depends to a great degree on government diktat. A change of investigation policy on the part of the taxation authority can instantaneously alter the distribution of returns for different tax-payers: the individual is playing against the authority – not 'nature'. This suggests a number of possibilities. (1) The tax authorities may use the information provided by the tax-payers' reports to 'tailor' the distribution for different classes of tax-payers. (2) The tax-payer may recognize that the distribution of returns is influenced by his actions and respond accordingly.

In order to incorporate the first of these features it is also analyti-cally straightforward – but diagrammatically intractable – to intro-duce a variable detection probability that depends on the amount of income declared, for example. As long as the individual may be assumed to be informed about the investigation rule the authorities are applying, the analysis goes through much as before. Several models[21] have made use of this device, but have not really pushed the analysis much further than discussion of the simple portfolio allocation problem. However Graetz *et al.* (1984) and Reinganum and Wilde (1984, 1985) exploit the possibility of endogenizing the probability of detection p in a particular interesting fashion. They examine the possibility that by adopting a particular investigation rule that is contingent upon the 'signal' provided by the tax-payers' report, the authorities may actually be able to enforce truthful reporting. We shall examine this type of rule further in section 7.

---

[21] For example Srinivasan (1973), Nayak (1978), Sproule *et al.* (1980).

Corchon (1984) examines the interrelationship between tax-payer and authority in an attractively simple framework, that of a game with two players with two pure strategies: evade/not evade and investigate/not investigate respectively.[22] He shows that there is no equilibrium in pure strategies but that at a Nash equilibrium in *mixed* strategies the expected payments by the tax payer actually equal official tax burden and government revenue is strictly increasing with the tax burden.

Benjamini and Maital (1985)[23] and Schlicht (1985) concern themselves with the interaction between the individual tax-payer and the rest of the community. Their approach is prompted by the observation that a person's propensity to engage in tax evasion or work in the black economy seems to be strongly affected by the number of other people who are already doing the same. Let E be the proportion of income evaded, $0 \leqslant E \leqslant 1$. Then, from the discussion of section 3, we may write the objective function (1) as $V(E)$ where V is a function of the decision variable E that obviously depends also on the tax and enforcement parameters p, s, t. Now, suppose that the value of the objective function also depends on the evasion activity engaged in by everybody else. Then instead of $V(E)$, the appropriate specification of the objective function may be $V(E, \Sigma E')$ where $\Sigma E'$ denotes evasion by everyone else.

It is difficult to sign all the first and second derivatives of V *a priori* but perhaps $V(E, 0) < 0$ (stigma if no one else is evading), $V_{12} > 0$ (evasion becomes less conscience-searing the more that other people do it) seem reasonable. Benjamini and Maital suggest also that $V_2 (0, \Sigma E') > 0$: under these circumstances the model may have multiple stable equilibria. This is illustrated in Figure 5 for the case where E is taken to be a dichotomous variable (equal to either zero or one). Everybody is either at point O, where no-one evades, or at point K, where all evade. It is not hard to see that more realistic versions of this interesting idea may be easily constructed, the policy implications will be discussed in section 7.

5.   EXTENSIONS: ENDOGENOUS INCOME

The model in section 3 also rested crucially on the assumption of an exogenously given income. For some manifestations of the tax

---

[22] Corchon's modelling of the strategy options differs from Reinganum-Wilde in an important respect. Reinganum-Wilde require that a *report* be made by the tax payer to the authority, stating an amount of income; Corchon lets each 'player' choose a dichotomous decision variable in the absence of *any* further information from the other. The former approach seems to be slightly more appropriate for self-declared income on tax returns, and the latter for decisions whether or not to work in the 'black economy'.

[23] See also Maital (1982).

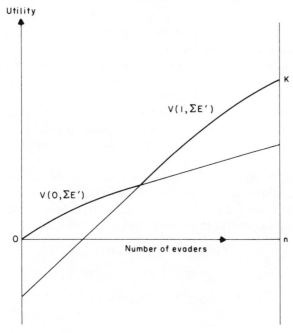

Fig. 5.

evasion problem this planly will not do. The situation of the moon-lighter or of the dishonest self-employed worker seems to combine the decision on the amount of evasion activity closely with the decision on the proportion of available time to be spent in work (of any sort) as opposed to leisure. The economic model that is required is essentially one of labour supply and labour allocation under uncertainty.[24]

The difficulty with this version of the tax-evasion model is that one has a portfolio allocation problem combined with a conventinal labour supply model which together may give perverse or ambiguous results. To see this consider what happens if the tax system is made locally more progressive by increasing the person's marginal rate of tax and adjusting his average tax rate so that the expected revenue raised by the government remains the same. Such a shift in the tax schedule is likely to (i) increase the demand for risky assets in a pure portfolio model, but (ii) reduce hours worked

[24] For an elementary treatment see Block and Heineke (1973). A fuller treatment allowing for substitution between activities is given in Cowell (1981a) and Tressler and Menezes (1980). The analysis of taxation in this context is given in Cowell (1981b). The application of this to general models of criminal behaviour is discussed in Block and Heineke (1975), Block and Lind (1975a, b) and Heineke (1978).

in a pure labour supply model. So what happens in the combined case – say the self-employed house-painter who is evading taxes and thus faces a random budget constraint? Effect (i) suggests that he engages in more 'black economy' work as a response to increased progression (the 'portfolio' here represents time to be allocated: 'black economy' work is risky); effect (ii) suggests that he engages in less. Given these contrary forces in response to changes in the conventional income tax, it is not all that surprising to find that perverse results can arise when the evasion parameters p and s are altered.[25]

Let us examine this by using the outline of a formal model. Denote the time supplied by a worker to the regular sector be h_0 and time supplied to the illegal sector h_1 where total time available per period is unity. Individual utility is now given by

$$[1 - p]u(c', l) + pu(c'', l) \qquad (2)$$

where $l \equiv 1 - h_0 - h_1$ represents leisure; consumption is given by:

$$c' = w_0 h_0 + w_1 h_1 - T(w_0 h_0) \text{ with probability } 1 - p \qquad (3)$$

or

$$c'' = w_0 h_0 + w_1 h_1 - T(w_0 h_0 + w_1 h_1) [1 + s] \text{ with probability } p$$

$$(4)$$

where w_0, w_1 are the wage rates in the legal and illegal sector respectively.

By substituting from (3) and (4) into (2) and differentiating with respect to h_0 and h_1 one can derive the first-order conditions for a maximum in the usual fashion. The difficulty that arises with the model expressed in this general form is that when one inverts these equations to find the solution for h_0 and h_1, each is an unilluminating function of all the parameters (p, s, and the parameters of $T(\cdot)$). When one examines the impact of any parameter change on evasion activity h_0 one has to consider what happens on both the h_0/h_1 margin and the consumption/leisure margin simultaneously: the two may be difficult to sort out.

The situation can be illustrated in Figure 6. Quadrant I is much the same as Figure 1 above; Quadrant II depicts the consumption/leisure choice; Quadrant III is used merely to reflect the 'hours of work axis'; Quadrant IV depicts the division of total hours between legal (h_0) and evasion (h_1) activities. Suppose the surcharge s is altered in Quadrant I. Obviously this rotates the line AB as before; but it may also affect the marginal rate of substitution between

[25] See Baldry (1979), Pencavel (1979).

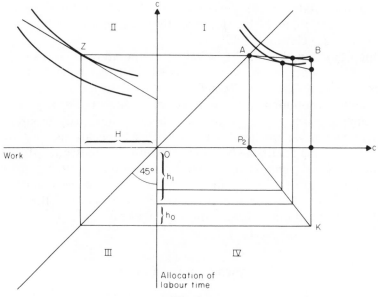

Fig. 6.

leisure and consumption so that the indifference curves in Quadrant II are shifted, total work hours change and the length and position of AB in Quadrant I also change.

However some progress can be made if one explicitly models legal and illegal work as distinct non-substitutable activities or imposes some further structure on the utility function.[26] In the first case the problem becomes similar to that of Block and Heineke (1973) and Cowell (1981b): h_0 is kept fixed and the only *effective* variable is h_1. In the second case the utility function is structured such that the decision about how much labour to supply overall is effectively 'separated' from that of how to divide the labour between legal and evasion activities.[27] This involves a specification such that total work supplied can be written

$$h_0 + h_1 = H(w_0, T(\cdot))$$ (5)

where the function H may also have non-labour income as an argument. With either specification one can usually read off definitive

[26] See Cowell (1985b), Isachsen and Strøm (1980), Isachsen, Samuelson and Strøm (1985).

[27] This should be carefully distinguished from separability of the function u in consumption and leisure as discussed by Andersen (1977) which does not assist very greatly in simplifying the problem. The 'separable decisions' case was originally discussed in the context of savings under uncertainty by Drèze and Modigliani (1972). Its application in the case of labour supply is discussed by Cowell (1981a, 1985b). The utility function u may be written $u(c, l) = \alpha(\beta(l)c + \gamma(l))$ where α, β, γ are increasing functions.

comparative static results given a few readily-interpretable conditions on risk aversion and the slope of the conventional labour-supply function – see Cowell (1985b).

One objection that might be raised to the above analysis is that it assumes the workers to be price takers. In order to deal with this point one may draw on Marelli's (1984) contribution. His model is actually expounded in the context of an expected-utility-of-profit maximizing monopolistic firm: but this can obviously be modified to a price-making worker, or indeed other applications. One of the more interesting results is that, for a uniform p, the degree of shifting of the tax is *independent* of the level of evasion activity.

Finally, note that whilst all the papers on the tax evasion problem with endogenous factor supply have dealt with labour, the analysis could easily be applied to, say, the supply of savings.

6. EMPIRICAL APPLICATIONS

By the very nature of the problem that we noted in section 1 above – chronic data unreliability or non-availability – empirically-based models are difficult to come by. However, there are some ways through the problem.

In the first place one may construct an *econometric model* of evasion where one has to hand data such as the IRS's TCMP as a base. This is what Clotfelter (1983) does. He finds that there is a significant difference in evasion behaviour between recipients of various *types* of income. Personal taxpayers have a fairly low value of the income-elasticity of underreporting (about 0.3) compared with that for farm business income (about 0.65). Clotfelter's work also tentatively suggests that there may be a significant positive elasticity of evasion with respect to the tax rate. Married people seem to evade more than single persons, and younger people more than the old. There are several problems with Clotfelter's methodology: there may be multicollinearity amongst some of the regressors, and he does not model the 'rationing' of evasion – individuals' opportunities for participating in evasion can obviously differ greatly. General problems of model specification are discussed in Baldry (1984b).

Isachsen, Samuelson and Strøm (1985) have estimated a version of the model with endogenous labour supply outlined in section 5 above based on interview data.[28] The dependent variables are labour

---

[28] The response rate was surprisingly high. Of 1,041 persons contacted, 70 per cent complied with the questionnaire in tax evasion.

in the black economy, labour in the legitimate economy, and tax under-reported; the authors do attempt to deal with obvious 'corner solution' problems where certain individuals do not participate in evasion *at all* on the grounds of morals, or lack of opportunity. The conventional effects on evasion activity of tax and tax-enforcement parameters are confirmed. Black labour market activity is greater amongst craftsmen, those in mid life cycle, those with non working spouses; expected hours of work in the black economy appear to *decrease* with income;[29] and men are more likely to be involved than women.

Attitude surveys on tax evasion find their intellectual root in Schmölders' (1959) approach to fiscal psychology in which one attempts to analyse people's views as to their tax liability. They[30] have attempted to formalize such vague notions as taxpayers' perceptin of the structure of taxation, their views as to its purpose, their views on the opportunities for avoidance, and the seriousness of the crime of evasion. Youth, greater perceived opportunities for evasion, 'negative attitudes' (for example on the inequity of the tax system) seen to predispose individuals towards evasion. The evidence on the effect of tax rates and of personal income as predisposing factors is ambiguous.

The *experimental* approach is a variant of the artificial exercises that have been used for several years to examine.[35] The problems with this type of approach are self-evident: one has to be extremely cautious in experiment design (for example the postulated probability of audit may not satisfactorily represent the likely action of a tax authority, actual or as perceived by the taxpayer); people may act in special ways simply because they know it is an experiment: the 'Hawthorne effect'. However, in a field such as this where relevant data are hard to come by, such experiments may throw light on the determinants of evasion behaviour in a broad sense. For example, if certain theoretical predictions cannot be confirmed in the laboratory, it may perhaps be that they would be likely to be confirmed by 'hard' data, were such available.

The experimental results can be briefly summarized as follows: Friedland *et al.* (1978) found that large fines may be more effective than a high probability of audit. However Schwartz and Orleans

---

[29] This appears to be at variance with a previous Norwegian interview study on tax reporting, discussed in Mork (1975) – tax evasion as a proportion of income *increased* with evasion.

[30] See, for example, Dean *et al.* (1980), Groenland and van Veldhoven (1982), Laurin (1983), Lewis (1978, 1979, 1982), Mason and Calvin (1978), Schmölders (1980), Song and Yarborough (1978), Spicer and Lundstedt (1976), Vogel (1974), Warneryd and Walerud (1982). The study by Geeroms and Wilmots (1984) is of special interest since it attempts to incorporate tax avoidance as well, (using Belgian official definitions) – avoidance and evasion were found to be close substitutes.

(1967) experiments suggest that appeals to conscience and civic responsibility may be much more effective than legal sanctions. Spicer and Becker (1980) found that evasion was high for those who perceive substantial inequities in the tax system. Spicer and Thomas (1982) suggest that whilst increasing the subjective probability of audit may reduce the probability that a person evades it may not have a significant impact on the actual amount of tax paid. Benjamini and Maital (1985) found that higher tax rates led to more evasion and that women evaded more than men. But perhaps the flavour of the literature on this point to date can be conveniently summarized by Spicer's (1975) note which drew attention to the importance, and difficulty, of measuring attitudes and which noted that

> the choice between compliance and evasion is far more complex than just a form of gambling.

7. POLICY PROBLEMS

Thus far we have given little attention to the question of how the parameters such as the probability of detection and the evasion surcharge *ought* to be set. Simple manipulation of the theoretical apparatus introduced above can lead to some pretty strange results. For example, suppose the tax gatherers take as their objective the maximization of expected revenue given the system of tax rates, allowances and exemptions laid down by the legislature. Then a fairly simple policy rule suggests itself. 'The anti-evasion parameters should be set so that the expected revenue raised by a marginal change in each parameter should exactly equal the marginal cost of changing that parameter'.[31] But this has dire consequences. For when one examines the mechanics of all of the formal models cited above one remarkable feature stands out for attention of the ruthless policy maker or manically efficient tax collector with influential friends in the legislature. Increasing either the detection probability p, or the surcharge s will reduce evasion. The first may reasonably be taken to be costly in terms of scarce resources, whilst the second is not. So, *if* tax evasion is *per se* a bad thing, then total compliance could – presumably – be ensured costlessly, as long as individual utilities are unbounded below.[32] Million-dollar fines or hanging for convicted tax evaders should provide a pretty

---

[31] See Collard (1984), Reinganum and Wilde (1984b).

[32] See Kolm (1973), Fishburn (1979), Kemp and Ng (1979), Koskela (1983b), Polinsky and Shavell (1979), Singh (1973); see Goode (1981) for some interesting comments on this approach.

effective deterrent: and if such dire penalties *are* effective then they never actually have to be applied, so you don't even have to incur the small cost of paying the wages of the hangman.

Of course it is not difficult to pick holes in this argument – even on purely economic grounds. (i) There may be costs to increasing the penalty surcharge other than the perhaps trivial costs of administering the penalty. (ii) Even if an apparent fraud is detected it may be very difficult to establish conclusive proof that an offence has been committed so that heavy penalties may impose severe welfare losses *ex post*.[33] (iii) No account is taken of whether other parameters under government control – for example tax rates – are to be varied at the same time as the penalty parameters.[34] (iv) No coherent reason is advanced as to why one is interested in eliminating tax evasion in the first place, and what should be accorded to this target relative to other social goals.

As a first step towards putting the normative analysis on a more satisfactory footing, then, let us suppose that we adopt the kind of utilitarian framework that is used in conventional cost-benefit analysis.

The costs and benefits which one ought to allow for may be itemized as follows:

(a) administrative costs incurred by the tax authority
(b) resource costs of concealment incurred by the tax-payer
(c) incentive effects on factor supply
(d) the benefits of consumption private and public goods
(e) the burden of risk confronted by individual taxpayers.

The utilitarian Social Welfare Function can easily be written down using (2) above. Let all tax revenue be spent on public goods or on direct costs of tax enforcement and let utility of private goods (c and l) be additively separable from utility of public goods. Writing R as the net revenue raised (after deduction of enforcement costs) then utility of public goods can be written $v(R)$ where v is

---

[33] Establishing whether or not punishable evasion has occurred may present some curious problems. Under the title 'Big Bang Theory' the journal *Taxation* noted: 'The Internal Revenue Service of the United States of America has published a study considering the tax collection problems that will arise in the event of a nuclear war. It concludes that taxpayers inconvenienced by the hostilities will have to be excused interest and penalties should they file their returns late'. On a more realistic note the reader may care to consult Bingham (1980) on the UK practice.

[34] This point is very important when one sees tax evasion in context with other illegal activities. One reason we do not have million dollar fines is of course that punishment of evasion must be 'in line with' punishment of other crimes. The overall structure of penalties for crimes (and charges for legitimate services) must be such as to provide deterrence at the margin – see Stigler's (1970) comment on Becker's (1968) seminal piece. Polinsky and Shavell (1984) show that under fairly weak conditions fines should be higher for high wealth groups than for low wealth groups.

an increasing concave function. For simplicity let there be the same gross wage w for legal and illegal work, a proportional tax at rate t, full employment of resources, no government transfers and let individuals be regarded as essentially identical[35] in tastes and resource ownership. Then, if there are n people in the community, and if the cost of enforcement with detection probability p is $\phi(p)$ the tax authority's objective is to maximize the Lagrangian

$$n[\mathscr{E}u + v(R)] + \lambda[nwh_0 t + pnwh_1 t[1 + s] - R - n\phi(p)] \quad (6)$$

where λ is the Lagrange multiplier for the revenue constraint and $\mathscr{E}u$ is shorthand for expression (2) above.

Consider the effect of increasing the probability of detection on social welfare. Differentiate (6) with respect to p, and we find the result to be n times

$$-\Delta u \, dp - \lambda wt \, dl - \lambda wr \, dh_1 + \lambda[wh_1 t[1 + s] - \phi_p] \, dp \quad (7)$$

where Δu is the (positive) utility difference $u(c', l) - u(c'', l)$, r equals $t - pt - pst$, the (positive) rate of return on a switch of an hour from legal to evasion activities and ϕ_p is the first derivative of ϕ.[36] Putting (7) equal to zero we find that at an optimum

$$\phi_p = wh_1 t[1 + s] - wr \frac{\partial h_1}{\partial p} - wr \frac{\partial l}{\partial p} - \frac{\Delta u}{\lambda} \quad (8)$$

Equation (8) gives the utilitarian rule for tax enforcement. On the left hand side we have the marginal cost of increasing the detection probability. The first term on the right hand side is the direct marginal yield from doing so. But this is modified by three other terms: the indirect yield from increasing p as taxpayers are 'persuaded' to be more honest – $wr \, (\partial h_1)/\partial p$ (positive); the impact of the implicit change in the effective expected real wage on labour – $wt \, \partial l/\partial p$ (ambiguous sign); the direct impact on individual utility – $\Delta u/\lambda$ (negative). This last term will be greater in absolute size the greater is individual risk aversion, since this increases Δu, and the smaller is the marginal valuation of public goods λ, which will equal $\partial v/\partial R$.

The presence of both positive and negative terms on the right hand side of (8) suggest that the impact on Social Welfare of an

---

[35] For the moment, relaxing any of these assumptions just leads to a notational mess without fresh insights. Sandmo (1981), using a richer version of this sort of model, examines wider issues, including the optimal choice of the tax rate t. In an economy with less than full employment Pandit (1977) and Peacock and Shaw (1982) discuss the impact of evasion on aggregate demand. Feige and McGree (1982a, b, 1983) show the implications of evasion activities for the Laffer curve.

[36] There may be additional private costs from a marginal increase in p which would not arise if it were the *penalty* s that were being increased: tax-payers may have to devote more resources to concealment at the margin as the snoopers become more effective; see for example the model in Hansson (1985).

increase in detection probability is in general not clear cut *even if there were no marginal enforcement costs* ϕ_p. That this is so is evident from (7) which, assuming $\phi_p = 0$, contains two positive terms one negative term and one ambiguous term. The problem is that (dishonest) taxpayers' expected utility is being taken as a criterion: increasing p lowers this (the Δu term). So the government may be able to increase social welfare from the status by actually *encouraging* dishonesty since the dishonest evaders are citizens whose utility is being respected.[37]

Thus the utilitarian approach to evasion policy does *not* imply that it is socially beneficial to reduce tax evasion wherever this can be done without resource cost,[38] nor does it imply that evasion should be eliminated were there to be no other constraints on the rates at which penalties may be set. This is in part due to the structure of the second-best problem which one is solving: if taxes are distortionary and evasion provides a way of overcoming such distortions then the social value of reducing evasion becomes ambiguous. Also surcharge made on evasion activity can be seen as a distortionary tax which may itself lead to inefficient resource allocation, so that increasing the probability of detection to reduce evasion may increase this inefficiency.

This point has also been established in the analysis of the evasion of excise taxes:[39] eliminating tax evasion by suppliers of goods completely appears to be an unambiguous welfare improvement only if the marginal costs of production for evaders are always strictly greater than for non evaders. Unless there is some perversity of technology or of temperament by which dishonest traders always turn out to be less competent and efficient than legitimate traders (a proposition which arm-chair evidence suggests is false) the only reason for such a special cost structure to obtain seems to be that evasion activities might *per se* imply higher marginal costs of production because of all the tedious business of having to hide the stuff when the King's Men call.

---

[37] There is a second utilitarian argument for encouraging evasion. Let labour supply be endogenous, the tax base be labour income, and the tax be proportional at a rate t. Assuming absolute honesty, realized utility U and revenue raised R may be written as functions of t. Using this plot U as a function of R: if U is non-concave in R then it can be shown that for a given R there may be some *randomized* tax rate which would produce the same expected revenue but yielding higher expected utility – see Stiglitz (1982), Weiss (1976). The application to tax evasion policy is obvious. Under the conditions specified above the Benthamite Utilitarian Tax Authority should *not* enforce compliance (even if it were administratively costless to do so).

[38] This point has been made by Baldry (1984a) and Cowell (1985a) who show that given the revenue constraint faced by the tax authority a reduction in the probability of detection may increase the sum of expected utilities in a simple fixed-income model.

[39] See Schweizer (1984).

The above type of marginalist, utilitarian approach to tax evasion might be considered to be unsatisfactory in two respects. On the one hand problem (iv) cited at the beginning of the section – the motive for one's being interested in eliminating evasion – has not been directly addressed; rather than allowing tax-law enforcement to emerge casually from the exercise of maximization of individual expected utilities (where the tax authority itself fixes the probabilities on which expectations are calculated, remember), it may seem more reasonable to incorporate tax law compliance as a *specific* social objective. On the other hand the constraints facing the tax authority in taking action to discharge its duty may have been rather crudely specified: an intelligent authority may be able to perform better than we have so far supposed. Let us deal with each point in turn.

Clearly simple utilitarianism may be an inadequate principle on which to analyse anti-evasion policy. One modification of the utilitarian approach which might be useful is to model evasion as an *externality* which affects others' utility directly, in a manner similar to that of Benjamini and Maital, although the normative implications of this have not yet been fully investigated. One obvious result of their model is that there may be a very strong 'watershed' effect. If one keeps evasion largely under control, then few people will know of others who are evading and will, therefore, be somewhat disinclined to evasion themselves (see the equilibrium at 0 in Figure 5). But if you let matters get out of hand it becomes very much harder to dissuade any one individual from evasion ('everyone else does it, so why shouldn't I?' – the equilibrium at K), so that starkly different policies may be appropriate depending on which type of evasion equilibrium is appropriate for the economy in question.

However, if compliance with tax law is to be included *per se* as a social objective,[40] independently of utilitarian objectives, one has to answer the questions of why one is specifically opposed to evasion, and what social ranking the crime of evasion should occupy relative to other crimes.

Prominent amongst the non-utilitarian social objectives for which tax compliance is considered desirable are presumably the criteria of vertical and horizontal equity. The vertical equity criterion itself is, in principle, easily incorporated by using a modification of the utilitarian Social Welfare Function – for example one in which

---

[40] Collard (1984) does this by suggesting a sample social welfare function which has the extent of evasion activity as an argument along with items such as output in the private sector legal economy, output in the shadow economy and output of the government sector. However his note highlights the problems that the derived policy rules are extremely sensitive to the precise weights one attaches to these various arguments of the welfare function. See also the discussion by Wertz (1979) who examines the comparative statics of a number of simplified *ad hoc* models of optimization by an administrative agency, and by Laffont (1975), who discusses non-utilitarian objectives in related areas of fiscal policy making.

individual utilities are weighted or transformed in a nonlinear fashion before summation. The implications have been surprisingly neglected in the tax evasion literature.[41] But vertical equity alone is insufficient grounds for wanting to enforce tax compliance. If the poor had more opportunity of evading taxes than the rich, or were better at it (however likely one considers such suppositions in practice) then the egalitarian policy maker might have good reason to smile indulgently on evasion: up to a point anyway. Considerations of horizontal equity[42] – which connote *ex post* 'fairness' in the tax treatment of individuals – or simple retribution thus seems to be an essential prop to the anti-evasion argument.

Another obvious defect with the simple policy rules outlined above is the crudeness of the structure of penalties and system of enforcements. Certainly heavy penalties or comprehensive ruthless investigation will ensure compliance. But it is apparent that the sketch provided above is of a pretty blunt policy instrument: applying a uniform probability of detection in conjunction with a swingeing penalty may be a clumsy way of getting people to pay their taxes.[43] Assuming, for whatever reason, the government or tax authority *does* want to ensure compliance, this simplistic approach may well be demonstrably inefficient, in that it may prove possible to design a scheme that induces a higher degree of tax-compliance with no loss of private expected utility.

The principal way in which structural improvements in policy design have been analysed has been in the direction of *discretionary* as opposed to uniform investigation schemes. A discretionary investigation scheme works like this. Let the authority categorize people into different groups and assign to each group an audit probability. The authority has to decide how to allocate individuals to these groups or – which amounts to the same thing in a model that runs for many periods – on what basis recategorize people from one group to another. Basically it can use two pieces of information – (1) the individual's current report and (2) his history – and one, possibly incorrect, assumption: that individuals are well-informed and rational. This assumption is important because, in virtually all of the formal work that has been done on constructing such investi-

---

[41] One exception is the paper by Persson and Wissen (1984). They show that whether true income is more or less unequal than reputed income, and whether a reduction in evasion would reduce inequality depends not only on the behaviour of risk aversion with respect to income, but on a complex interplay of the tax and enforcement parameters. Sandford (1980) also discussed some of the general issues involved.

[42] Note the incompatibility of this with expected utilitarianism, as highlighted by Stiglitz (1982).

[43] Even quite simple modifications of the tax authority's options can produce remarkable improvements. For example Rickard *et al.* (1982) show that allowing retroactive penalties is much more effective at deterring evasion in a multi-period model.

gation schemes, the authorities are assumed to build the expected response of tax payers to the way the scheme will run into the design of the investigation rules.

Reinganum and Wilde (1985) investigate the possibility of discretionary scheme using the first type of information: the income reported by the tax-payer. The true income liable to tax is, let us say, Y; the individual decides to conceal an amount E, reporting an amount $X \equiv Y[1 - E]$; the tax authority then has to decide whether or not to audit that report. What it does, in the Reinganum/Wilde framework, is to precommit itself to a rule which assigns a specific audit probability $p(X)$ to any amount X that is reported.[44] The *taxpayer knows full well about this rule at the time he fills out his tax return.* These authors have examined this approach for a number of very simplified tax systems and populations of tax payers and have found that a simple 'bang-bang' rule (investigate every return below a certain dollar value and no one above it) is weakly superior to a constant-probability-of-audit rule in ensuring tax compliance.

Finally let us examine a model which uses the individual's past history, suggested by Greenberg (1984).[45] Assume that everyone would cheat if it was worth his while: specifically, let p be the positive probability of detection at which every red-blooded individual would find it worthwhile taking a chance and cheating the tax man *if the game were to be played once only* (the whole point is, of course, that the game is played lots of times, so in fact the individuals also have to take into account the consequences of their future reputation as a proven cheat). The tax authority cannot afford to investigate everybody, and so, in view of the amoral selfishness of the taxpayers, it cannot hope to reduce tax evasion to nil. But can it get evasion 'low enough'? Greenberg suggests that it can using the following discretionary structure.

The tax authority announces three groups of taxpayers: those in Group 1 have a fairly small probability of being investigated p_1 (that is actually only *one half* of p); those in Group 2 have an even smaller probability of investigation p_2; the unfortunate members of Group 3 are *always* investigated. Then, year by year, tax-payers are shifted from group to group according to the method illustrated in Figure 7. If they are in Group 1 and are caught cheating they get

---

[44] The analysis is an extension of work by Townsend (1979). In Reinganum and Wilde (1984) and Graetz *et al.* (1984) audit strategies are considered where the tax authority cannot precommit itself, again using the information provided by the taxpayer's report in deciding the audit rule. Within the necessarily simplified framework that they use some interesting results emerge: e.g. within a class of taxpayers more resources should be devoted to investigating taxpayers reporting low income; higher audit costs may imply more evasion *and more auditing.*

[45] The structure of his model is similar to that of Landsberger and Meilijson (1982).

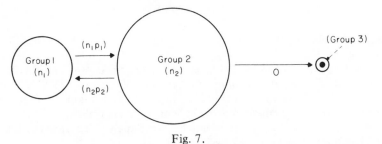

Fig. 7.

Note: If the individual is investigated he may be transferred to another group. A leftward arrow denotes what happens if he is investigated and found to be honest; a rightward arrow denotes what happens if he is caught cheating. Otherwise he stays in the same group.

shifted to Group 2; if they are in Group 2 and are investigated, they go back to Group 1 if found truthful, but off into Group 3 if found cheating; Group 3 is a black hole for habitual cheats – once in it, you stay there. If the tax-payers know about this rule then it can be shown that there is a simple equilibrium solution. Each year one finds n_1 people in Group 1, who all cheat, n_2 in the much larger Group 2, none of whom cheat and *no-one* in Group 3; it is also true that n_1 is less than the arbitrarily small 'minimum tolerable' amount of evasion and that $n_1 p_1 = n_2 p_2$, so that the groups all stay the same size. The reason that the system works is that as long as you avoid ending up in the pit of Group 3 your past sins will probably not be 'remembered' for ever by the tax authority; so it pays everybody to be 'periodically honest' in the sense that you cheat till you get caught and you are then honest until you are cleared (and are switched back to Group 1).

It is obviously easy to criticize the implified models that have been used to illustrate the discretionary image of either sort of information. Each assumes that investigation of an individual who is cheating automatically leads to conviction and in turn to a known penalty, each assumes that the individuals are thoroughly informed about the tax authority's announced policy; each assumes individuals to be rational amoral expected utility maximizers with no regard for the 'social good'. But such comments should not be taken as serious objections to the main thrust of these models. It is interesting to see demonstrated that intelligent use of information can play a central role in the design of efficient tax-enforcement policies. The above papers are a beginning, not the end.

London School of Economics

REFERENCES

Ahsan, S. M. (1974). 'Progression and Risk-Taking', *Oxford Economic Papers*, Vol. 26, pp. 318-28.

Ali, A. A. G. (1976). 'Landowners' Behavior Under Self-Assessment: Theoretical Treatment', *Journal of Development Economics*, Vol. 3, pp. 171-9.

Allingham, M. and Sandmo, A. (1972). 'Income Tax Evasion: A Theoretical Analysis', *Journal of Public Economics*, Vol. 1, pp. 323-38.

Andersen, P. (1977). 'Tax Evasion and Labour Supply', *Scandinavian Journal of Economics*, Vol. 79, pp. 375-83.

Anderson, R. W. (1976). *The Economics of Crime*, Macmillan, London.

Arrow, K. J. (1965). *Some Aspects of the Theory of Risk-Bearing*, Yrjo Jahnssonin Saatio, Helsinki.

Baldry, J. C. (1979). 'Tax Evasion and Labour Supply', *Economics Letters*, Vol. 3, pp. 53-6.

Baldry, J. C. (1984a). 'The Enforcement of Income Tax Laws: Efficiency Implications', *Economic Record*, Vol. 60, pp. 156-9.

Baldry, J. C. (1984b). 'Income, Tax Rates and Tax Evasion: Some Comments on Empirical Estimation of Tax Evasion Functions', mimeo, University of New England.

Bawly, D. (1982). *The Subterranean Economy*, McGraw-Hill, N.Y.

Becker, G. S. (1968). 'Crime and Punishment – An Economic Approach', *Journal of Political Economy*, Vol. 76, pp. 169-217.

Benjamini, Y. and Maital, S. (1985). 'Optimal Tax Evasion and Optimal Tax Evasion Policy: Behavioral Aspects', in Wenig, A. and Gaertner, W. (eds.) *The Economics of the Shadow Economy*, Springer Verlag.

Bingham, T. (1980). *Tax Evasion: The Law and the Practice*, Alexander Harden Financial Services, London.

Blades, D. W. (1985). 'Crime: What Should be Included in the National Accounts and What Difference Would it Make?' in Wenig, A. and Gaertner, W. (eds.) *The Economics of the Shadow Economy*, Springer Verlag.

Block, M. K. and Heineke, J. M. (1973) 'The Allocation of Effort Under Uncertainty: The Case of Risk-Averse Behavior', *Journal of Political Economy*, Vol. 81, pp. 376-85.

Block, M. K. and Heineke, J. M. (1975). 'Labor Theoretic Analysis of Criminal Choice', *American Economic Review*, Vol. 65, pp. 314-25.

Block, M. K. and Lind, R. C. (1975a). 'Crime and Punishment Reconsidered', *Journal of Legal Studies*, Vol. 4, pp. 241-7.

Block, M. K. and Lind, R. C. (1975b). 'Economic Analysis of Crimes Punishable by Imprisonment', *Journal of Legal Studies*, Vol. 4, pp. 47°-92.

Boidman, N. (1983). 'Tax Evasion – The Present State of Non-Compliance', *Bulletin for International Fiscal Documentation*, Vol. 37, pp. 451-79.

Bracewell-Milnes, B. (1979). *Tax Avoidance and Evasion: The Individual and Society*, Panopticum Press, London.

Carter, M. (1984). 'Issues in the Hidden Economy', *Economic Record*, Vol. 60, pp. 209-11.

Christiansen, V. (1980). 'Two Comments on Tax Evasion', *Journal of Public Economics*, Vol. 13, pp. 389-401.

Clotfelter, C. T. (1983). 'Tax Evasion and Tax Rates', *Review of Economics and Statistics*, Vol. 65, pp. 363-73.

Collard, D. (1984). 'Some Tax Investigation Rules', Mimeo, University of Bath.

Corchon, L. (1984). 'A Note on Tax Evasion and the Theory of Games', Mimeo, Madrid.

Cowell, F. A. (1975). 'Some Notes on Progression and Risk-Taking', *Economica*, Vol. 42, pp. 313-18.

Cowell, F. A. (1981a). 'Taxation and Labour Supply with Risky Activities', *Economica*, Vol. 48, pp. 365-79.

Cowell, F. A. (1981b). 'Income Maintenance Schemes Under Wage-Rate Uncertainty', *American Economic Review*, Vol. 71, pp. 692-702.

Cowell, F. A. (1985a). 'Public Policy and Tax Evasion: Some Problems', in Wenig, A. and Gaertner, W. (ed.), *The Economics of the Shadow Economy*, Springer Verlag, Berlin.

Cowell, F. A. (1985b). 'Tax Evasion with Labour Income', *Journal of Public Economics*.

Cowell, F. A. (1985c). 'The Economics of Tax Evasion: A Survey', *ESRC Programme in Taxation Incentives and the Distribution of Income*, Discussion Paper, 80.

Cross, R. B. and Shaw, G. K. (1981). 'The Evasion – Avoidance Choice – A Suggested Approach', *National Tax Journal*, Vol. 34, pp. 489-91.

Cross, R. and Shaw, G. K. (1982). 'On the Economics of Tax Aversion', *Public Finance*, Vol. 37, pp. 36-47.

Dean, P. N., Keenan, A. and Kenney, F. (1980). 'Taxpayers' Attitudes to Income Tax Evasion: An Empirical Study', *British Tax Review*, pp. 28-44.

Drèze, J. H. and Modigliani, F. (1972). 'Consumption Decisions Under Uncertainty', *Journal of Economic Theory*, Vol. 5, pp. 308-35.

Feige, E. L. (forthcoming). 'The Anatomy of the Hidden Economy', *Journal of Economic Literature*.

Feige, E. L. and McGee, R. T. (1982a). 'Supply-Side Economics and the Unobserved Economy: The Dutch Laffer Curve', *Okonomisch-statistische Berichten*, November.

Feige, E. L. and McGee, R. T. (1982b). 'The Unobserved Economy and the UK Laffer Curve', *Journal of Economic Affairs*, October.

Feige, E. L. and McGee, R. T. (1983). 'Sweden's Laffer Curve: Taxation and the Unobserved Economy', *Scandinavian Journal of Economics*, Vol. 84, pp. 499-519.

Feldman, J. and Kay, J. A. (1981). 'Tax Avoidance', in Burrows, P. and Veljanovski (eds.), *The Economic Approach to Law*, Butterworth's, London (Chap. 4).

Fishburn, G. (1979). 'On How to Keep Tax-payers Honest (or Almost So)', *Economic Record*, Vol. 55, pp. 267-70.

Fishburn, G. (1981). 'Tax Evasion and Inflation', *Australian Economic Papers*, Vol. 20, pp. 324-32.

Friedland, N., Maital, S. and Rutenberg, A. (1978). 'A Simulation Study of Tax Evasion', *Journal of Public Economics*, Vol. 8, pp. 107-16.

Garcia, G. (1978). 'The Currency Ratio and the Subterranean Economy', *Financial Analysts Journal*.

Geeroms, H. and Wilmots, H. (1984). 'An Empirical Model of Tax Evasion and Tax Avoidance', Mimio, Katholieke Universiteit Leuven.

Goode, R. (1981). 'Some Economic Aspects of Tax Administration', *International Monetary Fund Staff Papers*, Vol. 28, pp. 249-74.

Graetz, M. J., Reinganum, J. F. and Wilde, L. L. (1984). 'An Equilibrium Model of Tax Compliance with a Bayesian Auditor and Some "Honest" Taxpayers', *California Institute of Technology, Social Science Working Paper*, p. 506.

Greenberg, J. (1984). 'Avoiding Tax Avoidance: A (Repeated) Game-theoretic Approach', *Journal of Economic Theory*, Vol. 32, pp. 1-13.

Groenland, E. A. G. and van Veldhoven, G. M. (1983). 'Tax Evasion Behaviour – A Psychological Framework', *Journal of Economic Psychology*, Vol. 3, pp. 129-44.

Groves, H. M. (1958). 'Empirical Studies of Income Tax Compliance', *National Tax Journal*, Vol. 11, pp. 291-301.

Gutmann, P. M. (1977). 'The Subterranean Economy', *Financial Analysts Journal*, Vol. 33, (January/February).

Hansson, I. (1980). 'Sveriges Svarta Sektor', *Ekonomisk Debatt*, Vol. 8, pp. 595-602.

Hansson, I. (1982). 'The Unobserved Economy in Sweden', paper presented to conference on The Unobserved Economy, Wassenaar, Netherlands.

Hansson, I. (1985). 'Tax Evasion and Government Policy', in Wenig, A. and Gaertner, W. (eds.), *The Economics of the Shadow Economy*, Springer-Verlag.

Heertje, A., Allen, M. and Cohen, H. (1982). *The Black Economy*, Pan Books, London.

Heineke, J. M. (1978). *Economic Models of Criminal Behavior*, North Holland, Amsterdam.

Henry, S. (1978). *The Hidden Economy*, Martin Robertson.

Henry, S. (ed.) (1981). *Can I Have It in Cash?*, Astragal Books, London.

Herschel, F. J. (1978). 'Tax Evasion and its Measurement in Developing Countries', *Public Finance*, Vol. 33, pp. 232-68.

International Bar Association (1982). *Tax Avoidance, Tax Evasion*, Sweet and Maxwell, London.

Isachsen, A. J. and Strøm (1980). 'The Hidden Economy: The Labour Market and Tax Evasion', *Scandinavian Journal of Economics*, Vol. 82, pp. 304-11.

Isachsen, A. J., Samuelsen, S. O. and Strøm, S. (1985). 'The Behaviour of Tax Evaders', in Wenig, A. and Gaertner, W. (eds.), *The Economics of the Shadow Economy*, Springer-Verlag.

Kay, J. A. (1979). 'The Anatomy of Tax Avoidance', *British Tax Review*. pp. 354-65.

Kay, J. A. (1980). 'The Anatomy of Tax Avoidance', in Collard, D., Lecomber, R. and Slater, M. *Income Distribution: The Limits to Redistribution*. Proceedings of the Thirty First Symposium of the Colston Research Society, Scientechnica, Bristol. (A slightly revised version of Kay, 1979).

Kemp, M. C. and Ng, Y.-K. (1979). 'On the Importance of Being Honest', *Economic Record*, Vol. 55, pp. 41-6.

Kolm, S.-Ch. (1983). 'A Note on Optimum Tax Evasion', *Journal of Public Economics*, Vol. 2, pp. 265-70.

Koskela, E. (1983a). 'A Note on Progression, Penalty Schemes and Tax Evasion', *Journal of Public Economics*, Vol. 22, pp. 127-33.

Koskela, E. (1983b). 'On the Shape of the Tax Schedule, the Probability of

Detection, and the Penalty Schemes as Deterrents to Tax Evasion', *Public Finance*, Vol. 38, pp. 70–80.

Laffont, J.-J. (1975). 'Macroeconomic Constraints, Economic Efficiency and Ethics: An Introduction to Kantian Economics', *Economica*, Vol. 42, pp. 430–7.

Landsberger, M. and Meilijson, I. (1982). 'Incentive Generating State Dependent Penalty System', *Journal of Public Economics*, Vol. 19, pp. 333–52.

Laurin, U. (1983). 'Tax Evasion and Prisoner's Dilemma: Some Interview Data and a Tentative Model for Explanation', Mimeo, Department of Government, University of Uppsala.

Lewis, A. (1978). 'Perception of Tax Rates', *British Tax Review*, Vol. 6, pp. 358–66.

Lewis, A. (1979). 'An Empirical Assessment of Tax Mentality', *Public Finance*, Vol. 34, pp. 245–57.

Lewis, A. (1982). *The Psychology of Taxation*, Martin Robertson, Oxford.

Maital, S. (1982). *Minds, Markets and Money*, Basic Books, NY.

Marrelli, M. (1984). 'On Indirect Tax Evasion', *Journal of Public Economics*.

Mason, R. and Calvin, L. D. (1978). 'A Study of Admitted Income Tax Evasion', *Law and Society Review*, pp. 73–89.

McCaleb, T. S. (1976). 'Tax Evasion and the Differential Taxation of Labour and Capital Income', *Public Finance*, Vol. 31, pp. 287–92.

Mork, K. A. (1975). 'Income Tax Evasion: Some Empirical Evidence', *Public Finance*, Vol. 30, pp. 70–6.

Mossin, J. (1968). 'Taxation and Risk-Taking: An Expected Utility Approach', *Economica*, Vol. 35, pp. 74–82.

Nayak, P. B. (1978). 'Optimal Income-Tax Evasion and Regressive Taxes', *Public Finance*, Vol. 33, pp. 358–66.

O'Higgins, M. (1984). 'Assessing the Unobserved Economy in the United Kingdom', in Feige, E. (ed.), *The Unobserved Economy*, Cambridge University Press.

Pandit, V. (1977). 'Aggregate Demand Under Conditions of Tax Evasion', *Public Finance*, Vol. 32, pp. 333–42.

Peacock, A. T. and Shaw, G. K. (1982). 'Tax Evasion and Tax Revenue Loss', *Public Finance*, Vol. 37, pp. 269–78.

Pencavel, J. H. (1979). 'A Note on Income Tax Evasion, Labor Supply and Nonlinear Tax Schedules', *Journal of Public Economics*, Vol. 12, pp. 115–24.

Persson, M. and Wissen, P. (1984). 'Redistributional Effects of Tax Evasion', *Scandinavian Journal of Economics*, Vol. 86.

Polinsky, M. and Shavell, S. (1979). 'The Optimal Trade-Off Between the Probability and Magnitude of Fines', *American Economic Review*, Vol. 69, pp. 880–91.

Polinsky, M. and Shavell, S. (1984). 'Optimal Use of Fines and Imprisonment', *Journal of Public Economics*, Vol. 24, pp. 89–99.

Pratt, J. W. (1964). 'Risk-Aversion in the Small and in the Large', *Econometrica*, Vol. 32, pp. 122–36.

Pyle, D. J. (1984). *The Economics of Crime and Law Enforcement*, Macmillan, London.

Reinganum, J. F. and Wilde, L. L. (1985). 'Income Tax Compliance in a Principal-Agent Framework', *Journal of Public Economics*.

Reinganum, J. F. and Wilde, L. L. (1984). 'Sequential Equilibrium Detection and Reporting Policies in a Model of Tax Evasion', *California Institute of Technology, Social Science Working Paper*, p. 525.

Rickard, J. A., Russell, A. M. and Howroyd, T. D. (1982). 'A Tax Evasion Model with Allowance for Retroactive Penalties', *Economic Record*, Vol. 58, pp. 379-85.

Rothschild, M. and Stiglitz, J. E. (1970). 'Increasing Risk I: A Definition', *Journal of Economic Theory*, Vol. 2, pp. 225-43.

Rothschild, M. and Stiglitz, J. E. (1971). 'Increasing Risk II: Its Economic Consequences', *Journal of Economic Theory*, Vol. 3, pp. 66-84.

Sandford, C. T. (1980). 'Tax Compliance Costs, Evasion and Avoidance', in Collard, D., Lecomber, R. and Slater, M. *Income Distribution: The Limits to Redistribution.* Proceedings of the Thirty First Symposium of the Colston Research Society, Scientechnica, Bristol.

Sandmo, A. (1981). 'Income Tax Evasion, Labour Supply and the Equity-Efficiency Tradeoff', *Journal of Public Economics*, Vol. 16, pp. 265-88.

Schlicht, E. (1985). 'The Shadow Economy and Morals: A Note', in Wenig, A. and Gaertner, W. (eds.), *The Economics of the Shadow Economy*, Springer Verlag.

Schmölders, G. (1959). 'Fiscal Psychology – A New Branch of Public Finance', *National Tax Journal*, Vol. 12, pp. 340-5.

Schmölders, G. (1980). 'Der Beitrag der Schattenwirtschaft', in Mohr, J. C. B. *Wandlungen in Wirtschaft und Gesellschaft*, pp. 371-9.

Schwartz, R. D. and Orleans, S. (1967). 'On Legal Sanctions', *Chicago Law Review*, Vol. 34, pp. 274-300.

Schweizer, U. (1984). 'Welfare Analysis of Excise Tax Evasion', *Zeitschrift fur die gesamte Staatswissenschaft*, Vol. 140.

Seldon, A. (1979) (ed.). *Tax Avoision*, Institute of Economic Affairs, London.

Simon, C. P. and Witte, A. D. (1982). *Beating the System: The Underground Economy*, Auburn House, Boston, Mass.

Simons, H. A. (1938). *Personal Income Taxation*, University of Chicago Press.

Singh, B. (1973). 'Making Honesty the Best Policy', *Journal of Public Economics*, Vol. 2, pp. 257-63.

Smith, A. (1981). 'The Informal Economy', *Lloyds Bank Review*, Vol. 141.

Smithies, E. (1984). *The Black Economy in England Since 1914*, Gill and Macmillan, Dublin.

Song, Y. and Yarborough, T. E. (1973). 'Tax Ethics and Taxpayer Attitude: A Survey', *Public Administration Review*, Vol. 38, pp. 442-52.

Spicer, M. W. (1975). 'New Approaches to the Problem of Tax Evasion', *British Tax Review*, pp. 152-4.

Spicer, M. W. and Becker, L. A. (1980). 'Fiscal Inequity and Tax Evasion – An Experimental Approach', *National Tax Journal*, Vol. 33, pp. 171-5.

Spicer, M. W. and Lundstedt, S. B. (1976). 'Understanding Tax Evasion', *Public Finance*, Vol. 31, pp. 295-305.

Spicer, M. W. and Thomas, J. E. (1982). 'Audit Probabilities and the Tax Evasion Decision: An Experimental Approach', *Journal of Economic Psychology*, Vol. 2, pp. 241-5.

Sproule, R., Komus, D. and Tsang, E. (1980). 'Optimal Tax Evasion, Risk-Neutral Behaviour Under a Negative Income Tax', *Public Finance*, Vol. 35, pp. 309–17.

Srinivasan, T. N. (1973). 'Tax Evasion: A Model', *Journal of Public Economics*, pp. 339–46.

Stigler, G. J. (1970). 'The Optimum Enforcement of Laws', *Journal of Political Economy*, Vol. 78, pp. 526–36.

Stiglitz, J. E. (1969). 'The Effect of Income, Wealth and Capital Gains Taxation on Risk-Taking', *Quarterly Journal of Economics*, Vol. 83, pp. 263–83.

Stiglitz, J. E. (1982). 'Utilitarianism and Horizontal Equity', *Journal of Public Economics*, Vol. 18, pp. 1–33.

Tanzi, V. (1983). 'The Underground Economy', *Finance and Development*, December, pp. 10–13.

Taxation (1984). 'News Digest', Vol. 113, p. 325.

Townsend, R. M. (1979). 'Optimal Contracts and Competitive Markets with Costly State Verification', *Journal of Economic Theory*, Vol. 21, pp. 265–93.

Tressler, J. H. and Menezes, C. F. (1980). 'Labor Supply and Wage-Rate Uncertainty', *Journal of Economic Theory*, Vol. 23, pp. 425–37.

US Department of the Treasury, Internal Revenue Service (1979). *Estimates of Income Unreported on Individual Income Tax Returns*, Washington, D.C.

Vogel, J. (1974). 'Taxation and Public Opinion in Sweden: An Interpretation of Recent Survey Data', *National Tax Journal*, Vol. 27, pp. 499–513.

Warneryd, K. E. and Walerud, B. (1982). 'Taxes and Economic Behaviour – Some Interview Data on Tax Evasion in Sweden', *Journal of Economic Psychology*, Vol. 2, pp. 187–211.

Weiss, L. (1976). 'The desirability of Cheating Incentives and Randomness in the Optimal Income Tax', *Journal of Political Economics*, Vol. 84, pp. 1343–52.

Wertz, K. (1979). 'Allocation by and Output of a Tax Administering Agency', *National Tax Journal*, Vol. 32, pp. 143–57.

Yitzhaki, S. (1974). 'Income Tax Evasion: A Note', *Journal of Public Economics*, Vol. 3, pp. 201–2.

THE ECONOMIC ANALYSIS OF TAX
EVASION: EMPIRICAL ASPECTS

M. Marrelli *

INTRODUCTION[1]

During recent years a growing amount of economists' professional attention has been focused on the conjecture that a significant and growing hidden or underground economy exists that has eluded observation of the central Statistical Offices or, for that matter, of the economic profession in general. This conjecture, if confirmed, is rather disturbing from the point of view of traditional economic analysis: as Cowell (1985) puts it: 'much of the theory of Public Economics is based on the premise of virtually an all-knowing and all-powerful State implementing policy to maximize Social Welfare . . .'.

It is not surprising, therefore, that the issue of the 'underground economy' has provoked considerable academic controversy and a strong reaction from the agencies custodian of the economic information system: on the one hand there are some that view the existence of the underground economy as a factor which might shed new light on the current controversies in macroeconomic and public finance (Feige, 1984); on the other, the sceptics press for a more precise definition of the phenomenon and challenge the methods proposed for measurement (Porter, 1979).

It is possible to isolate a few questions that stem out of much of the economic literature on the hidden economy:

(a) what is the 'hidden' economy?
(b) how big is it?
(c) what causes it?

These questions become particularly relevant when one tries to analyse and compare different estimates, or when one tries to systematize all the pieces of literature which deal with the problem: there is a great amount of confusion as to what the term 'hidden economy' means (definitions are almost as numerous as the multitide of names

* Financial support from the CNR, Rome, is gratefully acknowledged.
[1] Since this paper was written, Smith (1986) has explored and evaluated the three major approaches to estimating the size of the black economy (for the UK) discussed here. His conclusions are that a plausible figure of household spending in the black economy is c.2½ per cent.

which have been applied to the phenomenon); furthermore many of the differences between estimates can probably be understood in terms of differences in what is being estimated. Accordingly we will subdivide this paper into four sections: in the first we shall deal with the problem of definition, and we will show how the phenomenon of tax evasion is better dealt with in the more general context of the hidden economy. In the second we will give an overview of the different methods and results of estimation procedures, and in the third section we will refer to the researches looking for its determinants.

1.   DEFINITIONAL ASPECTS

The term 'hidden' (underground, informal, irregular, black, subterranean, etc.) economy has been used by different authors to mean quite different things; 'theoretical and empirical research', however, 'requires a finer set of conceptual distinctions to clarify both the differences and the interconnections among the variety of descriptive terms presently employed by "underground economists"', (Feige, forthcoming).

In its broadest sense the hidden economy encompasses all unmeasured economic activity; Feige (1979) defines it as encompassing all those activities which 'go unreported or unmeasured by the society's current techniques for monitoring economic activity'. This definition includes those activities which are excluded from GDP by conventions, as well as those which elude the measurement process. Other economists have adopted a narrower view: for example Tanzi (1980a) and Macafee (1980) define hidden economy as the economic activity generating factor incomes which, because of unreporting and/or under-reporting is not measured by official statistics.

Following Carter (1984) we will clarify the distinction by considering the joint problems of bias and measurement (or sampling) error which any measurement process is faced with.

> Measurement begins with an idealized concept of some quantity which it is desired to measure. In an attempt to obtain an operational definition which can be implemented, the compass of the quantity to be measured is restricted somewhat. The difference between the idealized objective and the operational measure constitutes bias. Further errors are introduced in the process of actually conducting the measurement. These constitute sampling or measurement errors.[2]

In the attempt to measure aggregate output some forms of economic activity are excluded from the definition of GDP (bias); other forms,

[2] Cf. Carter (1984), p. 210, upon whose paper this part draws heavily.

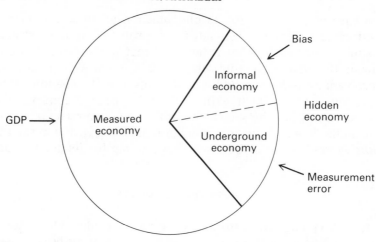

Fig. 1.

which are, on the contrary included, fail to be wholly or partially recorded because of measurement errors.

This distinction is better illustrated in Figure 1. The whole of the economic activity is represented by the whole circle; however certain aspects of it are excluded from the definition of GDP and therefore no attempt is made at measurement: these are labelled 'Informal Economy'. Examples include household production, cooperative activities, DIY, etc.[3]

On the other hand, the term underground economy encompasses all the economic activities which, although included in the definition of measurable economic activity, escape the current measurement techniques. Examples include unreported earnings, fringe benefits and the *production* of illegal goods or services.

It should be emphasized that the borderline between informal and underground economy is of uncertain nature: it is not always clear whether a given deficiency is a problem of bias or measurement error.[4] However, in the above classification both bias and measurement error constitute essential parts of the hidden economy.

Turning now more in detail to the 'underground sector', we can draw a further distinction between tax evasion and other illegal activities, and three further boundaries or borderlines. In Figure 2 the segment AB illustrates the evasion–avoidance boundary, AD the boundary between evasion and the informal economy, and BC the tax evasion–other illegal activities borderline.

---

[3] Burns (1977), Gershuny (1979), Mattera (1985) and others have drawn attention to the increasing proportion of economic activity which takes place within the household.

[4] Carter (1984) gives as an example informal production involving barter which could be excluded from GDP on two grounds: (a) because GDP is restricted to monetary exchange (bias); (b) because suitable means to assess its value are lacking (measurement error).

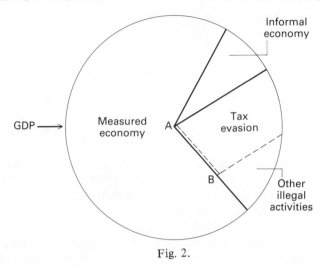

Fig. 2.

All these boundaries raise some problems: they are not merely definitional ones: several questions of economic analysis are raised.

A detailed discussion of these issues can be found in Cowell (1985); what we want to stress here is the uncertain nature of these borderlines: even if, in principle, a precise definition of tax evasion or tax avoidance, etc., can be found, there are strong reasons to believe that a certain number of economic activities go across the previously defined boundaries and, furthermore, there are strong reasons to believe that, due to the existing structure of legal or social institutions, phenomena taking place in one sector of the economy (e.g. the informal sector) produce relevant effects on the other sectors (e.g. the underground one).

An example can help to clarify this point: consider the case of a household which, because of the costs imposed through taxation and regulation, would not want to employ a decorating contractor. The household can either employ a decorator for cash on which tax will be evaded, or can undertake the decorating task personally; in the former case we are in the presence of underground activity, while in the latter the activity takes place in the informal economy. The choice between the two will obviously depend on the results of a usual maximization problem whose parameters are given by social or legal institutions.

The division of the hidden economy into informal and underground economies, and the further subdivision of the underground economy, provide a useful conceptual categorization; however it must be emphasized that the uncertain nature of the boundaries, and especially the strong interdependence between activities taking place in different sectors, do not allow one to consider the phenomenon of tax evasion on its own; the above-mentioned phenomenon is better dealt with in the more general context of the hidden economy.

2. SIZE OF THE HIDDEN ECONOMY

2.1. Estimation methods

The size of the hidden economy is quantified in three different ways:

(1) Figures proposed on the basis of *pure speculation*; examples are the figures provided by De Grazia (1980) for West Germany based on calculations of the Zentralverband des Deutschen Handwork (hidden economy comprises 2 per cent of German GNP), or Intersocial (1980) for Japan (1 per cent).

(2) *Educated guesses*. The best known and widely quoted example is Sir William Pile's (former chairman of the Inland Revenue Service of the UK) figure that Britain's hidden economy plausibly amounts to 7–5 per cent of GNP. Other examples are provided by Kaiser (1976), Katz (1973) and, Grossman (1977) for the USSR.

(3) Estimates based on *defined methods*. In what follows we will obviously concentrate upon this last type of measurement. Two possible approaches provide a rationale for this last type of measurement:

(a) although hidden, hidden activity leaves traces in measured activity through which it can be assessed indirectly;

(b) the amount of hidden income directly discovered in intensive (official or unofficial) investigations of small samples of taxpayers can be grossed up to obtain an estimate of the extent of the underground economy.

Accordingly one can categorize estimation methods as indirect and direct ones.

In general, direct methods are carried out at the micro-level, while indirect ones are more used at macro-level; on the other hand it should not be surprising that different methods of estimation do not necessarily take into account the same aspect of the hidden activities.

DIRECT METHODS

There are at least two methods which try to estimate directly the size of the hidden economy:

(a) projections based on the results of an intensive audit of a sample of taxpayers;

(b)   projections based on the results of surveys of people's economic activities and attitudes.

Both these methods (and particularly (a)) concentrate on the 'tax evasion' aspect of the hidden economy and, if carefully pursued, can provide a relatively reliable, if conservative, estimate of the size of the hidden economy.

Method (a) consists in projecting the results of an intensive audit of a sample of taxpayers over the population at large; this method, by its own very nature, can only be carried out by the taxing authorities and, as such, imposes upon itself certain limitations, since a tax authority can only be expected to report on these violations of tax laws over which it has direct jurisdiction.

Method (b), on the other hand, is likely to run into the difficulties of non-response, evasiveness or, even more, misrepresentation due to the need to supply answers which are consistent with tax forms, although this can be mitigated if the questionnaire used in the survey focuses mainly on other activities, so that the extent of tax evasion may be inferred indirectly.

INDIRECT METHODS

Indirect methods are, in general, classified according to the behaviour of the various decision-makers who generate the traces on the basis of which the hidden economy's size is estimated. Four general approaches can be distinguished, the first three of which are distinguished on the basis of where the traces of the hidden economy appear; the fourth on the basis of the causes which give rise to the hidden economy:

(c)   Methods which investigate traces in the form of discrepancies between *income and expenditures,* or *different measures of income* both at macro- or micro-level;
(d)   Methods based on the traces appearing in *monetary aggregates;*
(e)   Methods based on traces visible in the *labour market;*
(f)   Causal (or soft-modelling) methods.

(c)   THE DISCREPANCY APPROACH

This consists mainly of two methods.

(c.1)   *The expenditure–income discrepancy method*   This method relies on the assumption that while some *income* earned by an individual may go unreported or under-reported, much of it, in the form of *expenditure,* will eventually show up somewhere. If this is true, then the discrepancy between income and expenditure gives a clue to the size of the hidden economy.

(c.2) *The method based on the discrepancy between different measures of income*   This method generally assumes that hidden incomes may also be reflected by the difference between calculations of aggregate income on the basis of tax returns (once legal avoidance has been taken care of) and on the basis of the distribution side of the national accounts (Petersen (1982) for Germany; Visco (1984) for the personal income tax in Italy). The limitations are obvious: (1) *both* components in the difference are subject to measurement error so that one runs the risk of confounding this measurement error with the real phenomenon of the hidden economy; (2) there are errors due to the differences in the statistical coverage; (3) the national income estimates are not always completely independent on the tax base income estimates, i.e. income not captured by tax authorities may also not appear in the national income data (Macafee, 1980; Frey and Pommerehne, 1982).

(d) THE MONETARY AGGREGATE APPROACHES

These approaches concentrate on the traces left by the existence of the hidden economy in the monetary sphere. Three approaches can be distinguished.

(d.1) *Denomination of currency*   This is based on the assumption that when the size of the underground economy increases (and so, therefore, does the need for currency) the number of large-denomination banknotes in circulation must be expected to increase as well, in order to facilitate payments.

In the USA from 1960 to 1970, the stock of smaller denomination notes ($1 to $10) rose 37 per cent, while big bills increased more than 75 per cent;[5]; from the end of 1966 to mid-1978 the value of $100 bills in circulation rose by more than 250 per cent (Ross, 1978, p. 93). In the UK the ratio value of £10 and £20 bills to all other notes in circulation rose from 7 per cent in 1967 to 47.6 per cent in 1979 (Macafee, 1980, p. 87).

The emphasis on the large-denomination notes phenomenon appeared most clearly in the work of Henry (1976), which is, to our knowledge the only attempt to derive an estimate of the size of the underground economy by using this approach. Using an equation that linked the demand for large-denomination notes to 'legal' fac-

---

[5] 'The Growing Appetite for Cash', *Business Conditions* (Federal Reserve Bank of Chicago), April 1971, p. 16.

tors (e.g. price level, personal consumption expenditures, etc.), Henry calculated the extra demand for big bills that resulted from tax evasion; the proposed measure of tax evasion (by assuming that $50 bills or higher were used for this purpose) was about $30 billion a year, to which he added another $30 billion due to profit-motivated crime. There is no need to go further into this particular measurement approach, with its rather obvious shortcomings.

(d.2) *Currency/demand deposit ratio*   This approach assumes that the size of the underground economy is reflected in the ratio of currency relative to demand deposits held with banking institutions; it relies on there being a stable relationship between cash held by the private sector and the total monetary base. Fixing a particular baseline date at which the underground economy is assumed to be neglectable then enables one to determine the size of the underground economy by observing the growth of currency in excess of the monetary base. This approach, first used by Cagan (1958) and made popular by Gutmann (1977), has been widely used after much-needed improvements (Tanzi, 1980a; Commercial Bank of Australia, 1980; Klovland, 1980; O'Higgins, 1980; Feige, 1980b). Since the original papers by Cagan and Gutmann it has been recognized that there are a great many factors influencing the relationship between currency and other monetary magnitudes (be it demand deposits or some measure of it), in addition to the size of the hidden economy. The need to control for such influences has led to a new generation of models to estimate the size of the hidden economy. In particular a series of papers, pioneered by Tanzi (1980a), are aimed at estimating the relationship between currency and explanatory variables other than the size of the hidden economy. The unexplained residual or the tax variable coefficient is then taken to be an indicator of the size of the hidden economy.

The results of this approach, however, depend crucially on the choice of the base period, and on the assumption made with regard to the currency velocity in the underground and in the measured economy.

(d.3) *Transactions approach*   This approach stems from the proposition that all market-economic activities (whether measured or underground) are transacted in money terms, and that this relationship is constant. This method is based on the demand for money equation, either in its quantity form ($MV = PT$, where V = velocity of money, P = price level and T = volume of transaction) or in more sophisticated forms (Bhattacharyya *et al.* 1986); as the size of the total stock of money (M) is observable, and by feeding into the equation the 'appropriate' values of V, it is possible to deduce the size of *total* product. Deducting from it the official estimate of GNP gives the size of the underground economy as a residual in terms of GNP (Feige, 1979).

(e) METHODS BASED ON TRACES VISIBLE IN THE LABOUR MARKET

These methods are based on the assumption that a low official labour force participation rate (compared with other periods or other similar countries) can be partially explained by the existence of the hidden economy. Once an estimate of the 'actual' participation rate has been obtained (through interviews, proxy variables like energy consumption, projection of past employment rate, etc.), the difference between this and the official participation rate allows an estimate of the size of the irregular labour force, and, therefore, of the hidden sector. This method has mainly been used for Italy (Contini 1981b; Fuà 1977), but some applications have also been attempted for other countries (OECD, 1978b, 1979, 1980b).

By definition this approach captures both monetary and bartering income-creating activities, so that what is being estimated is both the underground and part of the informal economy. However, the limitations are obvious: measurement errors can be present in both participation rates, and the survey-based method suffers the same limitation as any such method.

(f) CAUSAL (SOFT MODELLING) METHODS

This approach (Weck-Hanneman and Frey, 1985; Frey, Weck and Pommerhene, 1982), attempts to reverse the usual procedure of constructing an econometric model: having once identified the possible explanatory variables of the hidden economy, various assumptions about their relative coefficients are made, and these are 'fed in' to the model (or the equation) and the size of the hidden economy is then read off on the left side of the equation.

By appropriately specifying the explanatory equation it is possible, with this method, to estimate tax evasion only, or the underground economy, or even the whole of the hidden economy. However this procedure is likely to be quite sensitive to the model specification and the assumption made on the size of the relative coefficients; since, in general, these are estimated from available evidence from other countries, the results crucially depend on the similarity between the country in question and the countries on which the estimated parameters are based.

2.2. Estimation results

DIRECT METHODS

Among the attempts to measure the extent of unreported income, by grossing up the results of intensive auditing over a sample of tax-payers, one of the most ambitious has been that of the US Internal Revenue Service (1979, 1983). Since 1963 the IRS has relied on the Taxpayer Compliance Measurement Program (TCMP) to extend the detection of unreported income beyond what is routinely discovered through quick checks of all returns and auditing of ones with suspicious claims. The TCMP involves intensive auditing of about 50,000 taxpayers, randomly chosen, where tax returns are matched against information reports that are supposed to be filed by business and individuals when substantial payments are made for services, interest payments, dividends, etc. A general problem with all tax compliance programmes is that people not reporting at all are often left out of the account; in order to overcome this problem the IRS combined TCMP data with estimates of unreported income received by approximately five million people who are believed to file no return at all.[6]

Because the IRS, especially in the 1983 report, limited itself to estimating taxable income, the agency did not compare its figures to the overall official GNP; however, it is worth noting that the estimate of $250 billion in unreported income for 1981 was equal to more than 8 per cent of GNP. By a similar procedure the Swedish Riksskatteverk extrapolate tax audits results to the whole taxable population (Hansson, 1980, p. 598); the results (relative to the late 1970s) range from 8 per cent to 15 per cent of taxable income.

A number of other studies use method (b) above to estimate the size of the hidden economy for different countries[7] and a representative sample of direct methods and relative results is provided in Table 1.

INDIRECT METHODS

(c) *Discrepancy approach* As already mentioned, this approach consists in evaluating the differences between either (1) the amount of income in the national accounts and the income estimates based on adjusted tax returns, or (2) income and expenditure of private

---

[6] This last set of data has been estimated by the General Accounting Office (GAO, 1979), while previously the IRS had found only 0.6 million nonfilers for the same year (1972).

[7] See, for example, Brown et al. (1984) for the UK, Isachsen and Strøm (1985), Isachsen, Klovland and Strøm (1982), SIFO (1981) in Hansson (1982) also for Norway.

TABLE 1
Size of Unreported Incomes

Direct methods

Country	Measure	Method	Source	Year	Estimate (%)
USA	% GNP	(a)	IRS (1983)	1981	8
Sweden	% Taxable Income	(a)	Rikskattevek in Hansson (1982)	late 1970s	8-15
UK	% Earned Income	(b)	Brown et al. (1984)	1980	0.5
Norway	% GNP	(b)	Isachsen, Klovland and Strøm (1982)	1979	2.3
Sweden	% GNP		SIFO in Hanson (1982)	1979	0.5

households. Park (1979), for the USA, found the first discrepancy to be about 5.5 per cent in 1968; Sweden's Statistika Centralbyran estimated, for 1978, a residual error of the first type of 4.7 per cent of officially measured GNP (Hansson, 1980, p. 597 *et seq*), and so did the Danish Council of Economic Experts whose result for 1977 was 6 per cent of GNP (Økonomische Rad, 1977). On the other hand, for other countries, various reports give a much higher estimate: Albers (1974) for Germany arrives at a discrepancy of 9 per cent for 1968; Frank (1972) calculates somewhat less than 20 per cent of Belgian GNP (1970); Roze (1971) calculates an even larger figure for France: the estimate of missing factor incomes is computed at roughly 23 per cent of GNP for 1965. Finally Visco (1983), for Italy, estimated the gap between earned income estimated from tax returns (after avoidance had been taken account of) and wage income from the national accounts at about 10 per cent for employees in 1980 and at about 23 per cent for the self-employed.

Turning now to the income–expenditure discrepancy, there are a number of studies which calculate expenditure income discrepancies for specific types of households, occupational groups, income classes, etc., and compare them with the disaggregated residual on the macro-level. O'Higgins (1980), Ofer and Vinokur (1980), Macafee (1980) and Dilnot and Morris (1981) constitute good examples of how this has been done. Table 2 shows a sample of the estimates achieved by using the discrepancy approach.

(d) *Monetary aggregate approach* Both the currency/demand deposit ratio and the transaction approach have had widespread

TABLE 2
Discrepancy Approach

Country	Measure	Method	Source	Year	Estimate (%)
Germany	% GNP	c. 2	Petersen (1982)	74	5
	% GNP	c. 2	Albers (1974)	68	8.9
Belgium	% GNP	c. 2	Frank (1982)	78	11
	% Tax base	c. 2	Frank (1982)	78	19
France	% GNP	c. 2	Roze (1971)	66	23
Italy	% Tax Base	c. 2	Visco (1983)	80	10 (employees) 35 (self-employed)
UK	% GNP	c. 1	Macafee (1980)	78	2.5-3
	% GNP	c. 1	Dilnot and Morris (1981)	79	3
	% GNP	c. 2	O'Higgins (1980)	78	3
Sweden	% GNP	c. 2	Hanson (1980)	78	4.5
Denmark	% GNP	c. 2	Økonomische Rad (1977) in Frey and Pommerehne (1982)	67-77	12-6
USA	% GNP	c. 2	Park (1979)	68-77	5.5-4
	% GNP	c. 1	Molefski (1982)	78	4.5
Israel	% GNP	c. 1	Ofer and Vinokur (1980)	73	6.7

application: after the first attempts by Cagan (1958) and Gutmann (1977) a number of more sophisticated approaches appeared in the literature.

In particular Tanzi (1980a) for the USA, and Klovland (1980) for Sweden and Norway, estimated currency demand equations which, in general, show that the out-of-sample predictions of currency holdings are smaller than actual holdings if the effects of taxation on demand are not taken into account. By relating this 'excess' demand for currency, attributable to taxation, to the output of the hidden economy via the velocity of circulation of currency in the hidden sector (assumed to be equal to that of the official sector) estimates of the size of the hidden economy are obtained. In particular Tanzi (1980a) obtains for the USA in 1976 an estimate of between 8.1 and 11.7 per cent of the GNP, while Kovland (1980, see also Isachsen, Klovland and Strøm, 1982) estimates the size of the hidden economy in Sweden and Norway for 1978 to be 13.2 per cent and 9.2 per cent of GDP respectively. The same crucial assumption on the velocity of money is at the base of the transaction approach (Feige, 1979); in both cases the results crucially depend on the assumption made with respect to the velocity of circulation in the official and underground sectors. Furthermore for some countries, such as USA or Switzerland, no satisfactory approach has been found to deduct that part of the total stock of money which is used for purely financial purposes, and/or which is held in the hands of foreigners and therefore plays no part in the hidden economy. (The US dollar is used as the national currency unit in Liberia and Samoa, it is used freely alongside the official currency in the Bahamas, Bermuda, Panama, etc., and in many parts of South America it is as acceptable as national currency.)

In order to avoid the problem of assuming a value for the currency velocity in the hidden economy, Bhattacharyya et al. (1986) estimate a series of values for the hidden economy which are conditional upon the chosen values of the velocity of circulation (expressed in elasticity terms); then they choose that particular value which leaves the estimated hidden economy unchanged before and after the inclusion in the model of the correct dynamic structure. They therefore estimate two series of the size of the hidden economy for the UK and the USA from 1960 to 1984, which ranges from 3.6 to 10.6 per cent of GNP and from 2.9 to 16.2 per cent of GNP respectively.

Table 3 summarizes some of the results obtained by the monetary aggregate methods.

LABOUR MARKET APPROACH

As already mentioned, such a method has mainly been used for Italy; in Italy (OECD, 1978b) one observes a lower rate of participation in the labour market than in other industrial countries of the West. However, to attribute the differences in participation rates to the existence of the hidden economy confronts various rather obvious difficulties.

The participation rate for a particular country and period is influenced by many different factors: it is therefore very doubtful to assume a *constant* participation rate as benchmark. The identification of what constitutes 'participation' in the labour market implies

TABLE 3
Monetary Aggregate Approach

Country	Measure	Method	Source	Year	Estimate (%)
Germany	% GNP	d. 2	Kirchgassner (1983)	1955-80	8-12
	% GNP	d. 2	Langfelt (1982)	1980	4-13
		d. 3	Langfelt (1982)	1980	16-24
Belgium	% GNP	d. 2	Mont (1982)	1980	15
		d. 2	Geeroms (1983)	1980	3.8-12.7
USA	% GNP	d. 2	Gutmann (1977)	1976	10-14
		d. 2	Tanzi (1980a)	1976	8-11
		d. 2	Feige (1980)	1979	28
		d. 2	Bhattacharyya et al. (1986)	1979-84	10-15
		d. 2	Molefski (1982)	1980	14
		d. 2	Feige (1979, 1980b)	1979	33; 27
UK	% GDP	d. 2	Dilnot and Morris (1981)	1979	7.2
		d. 2	Bhattacharyya et al. (1986)	1960-84	3.6-8
		d. 3	Feige (1981)	1979	15
Sweden	% GDP	d. 2	Klovland (1980)	1978	13.2
Norway	% GDP	d. 2	Klovland (1980)	1978	9
Switzer- land	% GNP	d. 2	Weck-Hanneman and Frey (1985)	1980	3.7
Canada	% GNP	d. 3	Mirus and Smith (1981)	1964-80	5-8
		d. 3	Mirus and Smith (1981)	1976	22

a difficult measurement problem, in order to overcome which a special interview technique has been devised to discover the 'true' participation. While the overall participation rate of 1975 is 35.5 per cent, the interviews undertaken by DOXA (Censis, 1976) have come to an estimate of 39.5 per cent; on this basis more than 10 per cent of the total working population is ascribed to the underground economy. The estimates, however, differ substantially in size; for example Contini (1981a,b) comes to somewhat more than 17 per cent and L. Frey (1978) reaches 25 per cent if multiple job-holders are included.

In order to obtain an estimate of the size of the underground economy it is necessary to know labour productivity in the hidden sectors; under different assumptions the following sample of estimates are reached:

ISTAT (in Martino, 1980)	1975–79	10% of GNP (minimum)
De Grazia (1980)	1975–79	10–25%
Martino (1980)	1975–79	25–33%
Contini (1981)	1977	14–20%

Franz (1982, in Skolka, 1985), using a similar approach for Austria, reaches an estimate of 3.45 per cent of GNP.

CAUSAL METHODS

The approaches discussed so far endeavour to measure the size and development of the hidden economy by looking at various indicators or traces left behind. Only the modified currency demand estimation approach partially takes causes or determinants into account, in particular only in the form of taxes.

Once the causes of the hidden economy are identified it is possible to derive the relative size of the hidden economy by assigning weights to the various causes (soft modelling technique); this technique does

TABLE 4

Participation Rates (%) for Males Between 15 and 64 in Various Countries, 1975

Switzerland	97.2	F.R. Germany	85.7
UK	91.7	France	84.1
Sweden	89.2	Italy	83.5
USA	85.3		

Source: OECD, Labour Force Statistics.

TABLE 5

Causal Approach
% of GNP 1978

Sweden	13.2 (base)	F.R. Germany	8.6
Belgium	12.1	USA	8.3
Denmark	11.8	UK	8.0
Italy	11.4	Finland	7.6
Netherlands	9.6	Ireland	7.2
France	9.4	Spain	6.5
Norway	9.2 (base)	Switzerland	4.3
Austria	8.9	Japan	4.1
Canada	8.7		

not allow one to state what the size of the shadow economy is as a percentage of official GNP; indeed in order to do this one would have to know the absolute values of the coefficients of the explanatory variables, and not only their weighting system. However, by this approach it is possible to derive relative sizes of shadow economies of different countries; these relative measures may be transformed into absolute measures (shares of official GNP) if some countries' size of hidden economy is estimated according to some other method. In their most recent work, Weck-Hanneman and Frey (1985) isolate six explanatory variables: burden of taxation, burden of regulation, tax immorality, participation rate of the labour force, working time per week, and share of foreign workers in the economy. The system of weights attached to them is such that: burden of taxation $\geqslant$ tax immorality $\geqslant$ burden of regulation $\geqslant$ participation rate = working hours $\geqslant$ foreign workers.

Accordingly a combined cross-section and time series analysis of 17 OECD countries is made over the period 1960–78, then taking as reference points the currency demand based estimates by Klovland (1980) for Sweden (13.2 per cent of GNP) and Norway (9.2 per cent) for the year 1978, they transform the relative measures already obtained into estimates of absolute measures of the hidden economy. Table 5 shows their results. This method rests on the assumption that the relevant causal variables have been correctly identified, and that the weighting scheme is reasonable. Furthermore, the results crucially depend on the goodness of the estimates used as a base.

3. THE SEARCH FOR DETERMINANTS

Due to chronic data unreliability or non-availability, empirically based models are very rare in the literature; this has led Frey and Weck-Hanneman to comment that 'compared to mere estimation of the size of the hidden economy, little emphasis is placed on analyzing the causes leading to the existence and growth of an underground sector' (1983a, p. 823).

However a certain number of attempts have been made. In the first place, when there are available data, one may construct an *econometric model* of evasion. Three such models have been put forward, by Clotfelter (1983), O'Higgins (1985) and Isachsen, Samuelson and Strøm (1985). Clotfelter, using data from the IRS's TCMP, identifies as explanatory variables net income, marginal tax rates, wages and salaries as a proportion of adjusted gross income (AGI), and interest and dividends as a proportion of AGI to take account of different possibilities of detection, plus a series of dummy variables to reflect marital status, age and region. He finds that the marginal tax rate is positively correlated with evasion, that there is a significant difference in evasion behaviour between recipients of various types of income: personal taxpayers have a low value of the income-elasticity of underreporting (0.292) compared with that of farm business income (0.656) and that of non-farm business income (0.62). Furthermore, married people evade more than single persons; younger people more than old.[8]

O'Higgins, on the other hand, using time-series data for Canada, Germany, USA and UK, obtained by different estimation methods, identifies GNP, the unemployment rate and the rate of price inflation as explantory variables of the hidden economy.

GNP is found to have a positively significant coefficient, prices are positive and highly significant in both North American countries but insignificant elsewhere, while unemployment is significant only in the USA. His results suggest that conclusions from one country should not be uncritically adopted as being valid for others. In both models there could be multicollinearity amongst some of the regressors; general problems of model specification are discussed in Baldry (1984).

Finally Isachsen *et al.* have estimated a model with endogenous labour supply based on interview data; the dependent variables are labour in the black economy and in the official economy, and tax under-reported. Among the independent variables are the marginal tax rate, the probability of detection, the penalty rate, gross income, sex, age, location and education.

Black labour market activity is greater among craftsmen, those in mid-life cycle, those with non-working spouses; evasion increases with marginal tax rates and decreases with income.

When data are not available, or non-reliable, a way around the problem has been to resort to *attitude surveys*, in which one attempts to analyze people's views as to their tax liability.

Among others, Dean *et al.* (1980), Groenland and van Veldhoven (1982), Laurin (1983), Lewis (1978, 1979, 1982) and Schmolders (1980) have attempted to formalize notions of taxpayers' perceptions of the equity of the structure of taxation, their views on opportunities for avoidance and notions of tax morality.

In general, young age, greater perceived opportunities for evasion, perceived inequity of the tax system, and lower degree of tax morality predispose individuals towards tax evasion; on the other hand, tax rates and income have an ambiguous effect on tax evasion, as does the price variable.

---

[8] Crane and Nourzad (1985), using similar data, obtained a positive correlation between the proportion of income unreported and the cost of money as expressed by the rate of interest.

The study of Geeroms and Wilmots (1984) is particularly important since it attempts to incorporate tax avoidance, which is found to be a close substitutive to tax evasion, as the theory predicts.

Finally, another way through the problem is the *experimental approach*; this is a variant of the economic approaches based on experimental psychology. The problems with this type of approach are self-evident; extreme caution is called for in designing the experiment; people may act in a special way simply because they know it is an experiment. However, if properly designed, such experiments might be able to confirm or refuse certain theoretical predictions which 'hard' data, if available, would be unlikely to test.

Friedland *et al.* (1978), Schwartz and Orleans (1967), Spicer and Becker (1980), Spicer and Thomas (1982) and Benjamini and Maital (1985) have all carefully adopted this method, and come out with some convincing answers. Among these: large fines may be more effective than a high probability of audit; tax evasion is high among those who perceive substantial inequities in the tax system; higher tax rates lead to more evasion.

Baldry (1985) reaches the conclusion that the 'standard', theoretical, model of income tax evasion is probably inadequate to explain some of the behaviours which the experimental evidence suggests. In particular: (1) the fact that moral compunctions seem to have some effect in reducing the number of dishonest taxpayers; (2) total tax burden (and therefore average more than marginal tax rate) plays a role in explaining tax evasion behaviour.

CONCLUSIONS

The hidden economy is a profound phenomenon of our times; however measured, however defined, one conclusion is common to all the authors who attempted to deal with it: the problem of the hidden economy cannot be dismissed as quantitatively trivial. Much of the work that has been done is not very satisfactory, but some of the results of the empirical analyses should lead theoretical economists to re-examine the standard model of tax evasion. If economists do not re-examine statistics and theory, probably wrong analysis, wrong conclusions and wrong policy prescriptions will be the result.

University of Naples

REFERENCES

Adler, H. J. and Hawrylyshyn, O. (1978). 'Estimates of the Value Household Work: Canada, 1961 and 1971', *Review of Income and Wealth*, Vol. 24, pp. 333-55.

Albers, W. (1974). 'Umverteilungswirkungen der Einkommensteuer' in *Oeffentliche Finanzwritschaft und Verteilung* II, W. Albers (ed.), Berlin: Duncker & Humblot, pp. 69-144.

Alden, J. and Saha, S. (1978). 'Analysis of Second Jobholding in the EEC', *Regional Studies*, Vol. 12.

Baldry, J. C. (1984). 'Income, Tax Rates and Tax Evasion: Some Comments on Empirical Estimation of Tax Evasion Functions', Mimeo, University of New England, Australia.

Baldry, J. C. (1985). 'Income, Tax Rates and Income Tax Evasion: Experimental Evidence, Mimeo, University of New England.

Bawley, D. (1982). *The Subterranean Economy*, New York: McGraw-Hill.

Benjamini, Y. Maital, S. (1985). 'Optimal Tax Evasion and Optimal Tax Evasion Policy: Behavioral Aspects' in Wenig and Gaertner (1985).

Bhattacharyya, D. K., Karavitis, N. E. and Tsouhlou, A. (1986). 'A Robust Method of Calculating the Size of the Hidden Economy: Quarterly Estimates for the UK and the USA', Mimeo, University of Leicester.

Bingham, T. (1980). *Tax Evasion: The Law and the Practice*, London: Alexander Harden Financial Services.

Blades, D. W. (1985). 'Crime: What Should be Included in the National Accounts and What Difference Would it Make?' in Wenig and Gaertner (1985).

Board of Inland Revenue (1981). *One Hundred and Twenty Third Report*, Cmnd 8160, London: HMSO.

Boidman, N. (1983). 'Tax Evasion – The Present State of Non-Compliance', *Bulletin for International Fiscal Documentation*, Vol. 37, pp. 451-79.

Bracewell-Milnes, B. (1979). *Tax Avoidance and Evasion: The Individual and Society*, London: Panopticum Press.

Brown, C. V., Levin, E. J., Rosa, P. J. and Ulph, D. T. (1984). 'Tax Evasion and Avoidance on Earned Income: Some Survey Evidence *Fiscal Studies*, Vol. 5, pp. 1-22.

Burns, S. (1977). *The Household Economy*, Boston: Beacon Press.

Business Week (1978). 'The Fast Growth of the Underground Economy Business Week, 13 March, pp. 73-7.

Cagan, P. (1958). 'The Demand for Currency Relative to Total Money Supply' (National Bureau of Economic Research, Occassional Paper 62, NY) *Journal of Political Economy*, Vol. 66, pp. 303-29.

Camera di Commercio, Industria, Artigianato di Torino (1978). 'L'Occupazione Irregolare in Piemonte', *Collana Ricerche e Documentazione*, No. 9, Torino.

Campa, G. and Visco, V. (1972). 'Una stima del gettito teoretico per classe di reddito familiare dell'imposta di ricchezza mobile sui redditi da lavoro dipendente nel 1968' *Tributi*, Vol. 75, pp. 127-43.

Cannullo, G. and Montanari, M. G. (1978). 'Lavoro regolare e lavoro nero in alcuni comuni delle Marche' in *Lavoro regolare e lavoro nero*, P. Alessandrini (ed.), Bologna: Il Mulino, pp. 147-82.

Cantelli, P. (1980). *L'economia sommersa*, Roma: Editori Riuniti.

Capodaglio, G. (1979). 'Lavoro nero o anacoretismo economico?' *Rivista Internazionale di Scienze Economiche e Commerciali*, Vol. 26, pp. 629-33.

Carter, M. (1984). 'Issues in the Hidden Economy', *Economic Record*, Vol. 60, pp. 209-11.

Censis (1976). *L'Occupazione occulta – Caratteristiche della partecipazione al lavoro in Italia*, Rome: Fondazione Censis.

Chassaing, P. (1979). 'L'economie souterraine', *L'economie*, Vol. 369, pp. 7-23.

Chopra, O. P. (1982). 'Unaccounted Income – Some Estimates', *Economic and Political Weekly*, Vol. 17, pp. 739-44.

Clotfelter, C. T. (1983). 'Tax Evasion and Tax Rates', *Review of Economics and Statistics*, Vol. 65, pp. 363-73.

Coen, A. (1980). 'I dati reperibili sulla opportunita e propensione al lavoro in rapporto alla occupazione ed alla educazione delle forze di lavoro marginale' Rome, Istituto di Studi per la Programmazione Economica.

Collard, D. (1984). 'Some Tax Investigation Rules', Mimeo, University of Bath.

Commercial Bank of Australia (1980). 'The Underground Economy in Australia' Commercial Bank of Australia Economic Review, September, 1980, pp. 8-12 (also in Tanzi (ed.) (1982b), Ch. 18).

Contini, B. (1979). *Lo sviluppo di un'economia parallela: La segmetazione del mercato del lavoro in Italia e la crescita del settore irregolare*, Milan: Edizioni di Comunita.

Contini, B. (1981a). 'Labor Market Segmentation and the Development of the Parallel Economy – The Italian Experience', *Oxford Economic Papers*, Vol. 2, pp.

Contini, B. (1981b). 'The Second Economy of Italy', *Taxing and Spending*, Vol. 4 (also in *Journal of Contemporary Studies*, Vol. 4, reprinted in Tanzi (ed.) (1982b)).

Contini, B. (1981c). 'The Anatomy of the Irregular Economy', Mimeo, Berkely, University of Torino and University of California.

Cowell, F. A. (1985). 'The Economics of Tax Evasion: A Survey', ESRC Programme in Taxation Incentives and the Distribution of Income, Discussion Paper 80.

Crane, S. E. and Nourzad, F. (1985). 'Time Value of Money and Income Tax Evasion Under Risk Averse Behaviour: Theoretical Analysis and Empirical Evidence, *Public Finance*, Vol. 40, pp. 381-94.

Dean, P. N., Keenan, A. and Kenney, F. (1980). 'Tax-payers' Attitudes to Income Tax Evasion: An Empirical Study', *British Tax Review*, pp. 28-44.

De Grazia, R. (1980). 'Clandestine Employment: A Problem of Our Time' *International Labour Review*, Vol. 119, pp. 549-63.

Dilnot, A. and Morris, C. N. (1981). 'What Do We Know about the Black Economy?' *Fiscal Studies*, Vol. 2, pp. 58-73.

Feige, E. L. (1979). 'How Big Is the Irregular Economy?' *Challenge*, Vol. 22, pp. 5-13.

Feige, E. L. (1980a). 'Den dolda sektorns tillvaxt-70-talets ekonomiska problem i nytt ljus', *Ekonomisk Debatt*, Vol. 8, pp. 570-89.

Feige, E. L. (1980b). 'A New Perspective on Macroeconomic Phenomena: The Theory and Measurement of the Unobserved Sector of the United States: Causes, Consequences, and Implications' Mimeo, Wassenaar: Netherlands Institute for Advanced Study, August.

Feige, E. L. (1981). 'The UK's Unobserved Economy: A Preliminary Assessment', *Journal of Economic Affairs*, Vol. 1, pp. 205-12.

Feige, E. L. (1984). 'Macroeconomics and the Unobserved Economy', in W. Block and M. Walker (eds.) *Taxation: an International Perspective*, The Fraser Institute.

Feige, E. L. (forthcoming). 'The Anatomy of the Hidden Economy', *Journal of Economic Literature*.

Feige, E. L. and McGee, R. T. (1982a). 'Supply-Side Economics and the Unobserved Economy: The Dutch Laffer Curve', *Okonomisch-statistiche Berichten*, November.

Feige, E. L. and McGee, R. T. (1982b). 'The Unobserved Economy and the UK Laffer Curve', *Journal of Economic Affairs*.

Feige, E. L. and McGee, R. T. (1983). 'Sweden's Laffer Curve: Taxation and the Unobserved Economy', *Scandinavian Journal of Economics*, Vol. 84, pp. 499-519.

Fishburn, G. (1979). 'On How to Keep Tax-payers Honest (or Almost So)', *Economic Record*, Vol. 55, pp. 67-70.

Fishburn, G. (1981). 'Tax Evasion and Inflation', *Australian Economic Papers*, Vol. 20, pp. 324-32.

Frank, M. (1972). 'La sous-estimation et la fraude fiscale en Belgique: ampleur et remedes', *Cahiers Economiques de Bruxelles*, Vol. 53. pp. 5–46.

Frank, M. (1976). 'Fraude des revenus soumis a l'impot des personnes physiques et perte d'impot qui en resulte pour le Tresor-etude methodologique', *Public Finance*, Vol. 31, pp. 1-30.

Frank, M. (1982). 'Essay on the Unobserved Economy by the Fiscal Approach and its Incidence on Income and Wealth Distribution, Mimeo, University of Brussels.

Frank, M. and Dehejser-Meulders, D. (1977). 'A Tax Discrepancy Coefficient Resulting from Tax Evasion or Tax Expenditure, *Journal of Public Economics*, Vol. 8, pp. 67-78.

Frank, M., Delcourt, E. and Roselle, E. (1973). 'Problemes methodologiques et statistiques relatifs a l'evaluation de la sous-estimation et de la fraude fiscale' in *L'exacte perception de l'impot*, Brussels, Bruylant.

Freud, D. (1979). 'A Guide to Underground Economics', *Financial Times*, 9 April.

Frey, B. S. and Pommerehne, W. W. (1982). 'Measuring the Hidden Economy: Though this be Madness, there is Method in it', in Tanzi (ed.) (1982b).

Frey, B. S. and Weck, H. (1981). 'Bureaucracy and the Shadow Economy: A Macro Approach', in *Anatomy of Government Deficiency*, H. Hanusch (ed.), Detroit: Wayne State University Press.

Frey, B. S. and Weck, H. (1982). 'The Hidden Economy as an Unobserved Variable' Mimeo, University of Zurich, May.

Frey, B. S. and Weck, H. (1983a). 'What Produces a Hidden Economy? An International Cross-section Analysis', *Southern Economic Journal*, Vol. 49, pp. 822-32.

Frey, B. S. and Weck, H. (1983b). 'Estimating the Shadow Economy: A Naive Approach', *Oxford Economic Papers*, Vol. 35, pp. 23-44.

Frey, B. S., Weck, H. and Pommerehne, W. (1982). 'Has the Shadow Economy Grown in Germany? An Exploratory Study', *Weltwirtshaftliches Archiv*, Vol. 118, pp. 499-524.

Frey, L. (1978). *Il lavoro nero in Italia nel 1977: Tendenze dell'occupazione*, Torino: Fondazione Ceres, June.

Friedland, N., Matal, S. and Rutenberg, A. (1978). 'A Simulation Study of Tax Evasion', *Journal of Public Economics*, Vol. 8, pp. 107-16.

Fuà, G. (1977). 'Employment and Productive Capacity in Italy', Banca Nazionale del Lavoro, *Quarterly Review*, Vol. 122, p. 215.

Gao (US General Accounting Office) (1979). Who's Not Filing Income Tax Returns?, Report to the Congress of the US by the Compt roller General, Washington DC: US Government Printing Office, July.

Garcia, G. (1978). 'The Currency Ratio and the Subterranean Economy', *Financial Analysts Journal*.

Geeroms, H. (1983). 'De ondergrondse economie in Belgie', *Tijdschrift voor Economie en Management*, Vol. 28, pp. 77-90.

Geeroms, H. and Wilmots, H. (1984). 'An Empirical Model of Tax Evasion and Tax Avoidance', *Public Finance*,

Gershuny, J. I. (1979). 'The Informal Economy: Its Role in Post-Industrial Society' *Futures*, Vol. 11, pp. 3-15.

Groenland, E. A. G. and van Veldhoven, G. M. (1983). 'Tax Evasion Behaviour – A Psychological Framework', *Journal of Economic Psychology*, Vol. 3, pp. 129-44.

Grossman, G. (1977). 'The Second Economy of the USSR', *Problems of Communism*, Vol. 26, pp. 25-40 (also in Tanzi (ed.) (1982b)).

Groves, H. M. (1958). 'Empirical Studies of Income Tax Compliance', *National Tax Journal*, Vol. 1, pp. 291-301.

Gutman, P. M. (1977). 'The Subterranean Economy', *Financial Analysts Journal*, Vol. 33 (Jan/Feb).

Hansson, I. (1980). 'Sveriges Svarta Sektor', *Ekonomisk Debatt*, Vol. 8, pp. 595-602.

Hansson, I. (1982). 'The Unobserved Economy in Sweden', Paper Presented to Conference on The Unobserved Economy, Wassenaar, Netherlands.

Hansson, I. (1985). 'Tax Evasion and Government Policy', in Wenig, A. and Gaertner, W. (eds.) (1985).

Heertje, A., Allen, M. and Cohen, H. (1982). *The Black Economy*, London, Pan Books.

Henry, J. (1976). 'Calling in the Big Bills', *Washington Monthly*,

Henry, S. (1978). *The Hidden Economy*, Oxford: Martin Robertson.

Henry, S. (ed.) (1981). *Can I have it in Cash?*, London: Astragal Books.

Herschel, F. J. (1978). 'Tax Evasion and its Measurement in Developing Countries', *Public Finance*, Vol. 33. pp. 232-68.

Internal Revenue Service (1979). Estimates of Income Unreported on Individual Income Tax Returns, Washington DC: Government Printing Office.

IRS (1983). Income Tax Compliance Research: Estimates for 1973-81, Washington, DC: Government Printing Office.

Intersocial, (1980). 'Le travail au noir en Europe et aux Etats Unis', *Intesocial*, Vol. 61, pp. 3-16.

Isachsen, A. J. and Strøm, S. (1980). 'The Hidden Economy: The Labour Market and Tax Evasion', *Scandinavian Journal of Economics*, Vol. 82, pp. 304-11.

Isachsen, A. J. and Strøm, S. (1985). 'The Size and Growth of the Hidden Economy in Norway', *Review of Income and Wealth*, Vol. 31, pp. 21-38.

Isachsen, A. J., Klovland, J. T. and Strøm, S. (1982). 'The Hidden Economy in Norway', Ch. 13 of Tanzi (ed.), (1982b).

Isachsen, A. J., Samuelsen, S. O. and Strøm, S. (1985). 'The Behaviour of Tax Evaders', in Wenig and Gaertner (eds.) (1985).

Kaiser, R. G. (1976). *Russia: The People and the Power*, New York: Pocket Books.

Kay, J. A. (1979). 'The Anatomy of Tax Avoidance', *British Tax Review*, pp. 354-65.

Katz, Z. (1973). 'Insights from Emigrés and Sociological Studies on the Soviet Union', in *Soviet Economic Prospects for the Seventies*, Washington, DC, Joint Economic Committee, pp. 87-94.

Kenadjian, B. (1982). 'The Direct Approach to Measuring the Underground Economy in the United States: IRS Estimates of Unreported Income', Ch. 5 of Tanzi (ed.) (1982b).

Kendrick, J. W. (1979). 'Expanding Imputed Values in the National Income and Product Accounts', *Review of Income and Wealth*, pp. 349-63.

Kirchgassner, G. (1983). 'Size and Development of the West German Shadow Economy, 1955-80', *Zetschrift fur die Gesamte Staatswissenschaft*, Vol. 139, pp. 197-214.

Klovland, J. T. (1980). 'In Search of the Hidden Economy: Tax Evasion and the Demand for Currency, Norway and Sweden', Mimeo, Norwegian School of Economics and Business Administration, Discussion Paper 18/80.

Klovland, J. T. (1983). 'Tax Evasion and the Demand for Currency in Norway and Sweden; is there a Hidden Relationship?' Norwegian School of Economics and Business Administration, Discussion Paper 07/83.

Langfelt, E. (1982). 'The Unobserved Economy in the Federal Republic of Germany: A Preliminary Assessment', Mimeo, University of Kiel.

Laurin, U. (1983). 'Tax Evasion and Prisoner's Dilemma: Some Interview Data and a Tentative Model for Explanation', Mimeo, Department of Government, University of Uppsala.

Lewis, A. (1978). 'Perception of Tax Rates', *British Tax Review*, Vol. 6, pp. 358-66.

Lewis, A. (1979). 'Am Empirical Assessment of Tax Mentality', *Public Finance*, Vol. 34, pp. 245-57.

Lewis, A. (1982). *The Psychology of Taxation*, Oxford, Martin Robertson.

Long, S. B. (1981). 'The Internal Revenue Service: Measuring Tax Offence and Enforcement Response', Bureau of Social Science Research.

Macafee, K. (1980). 'A Glimpse of the Hidden Economy in the National Accounts', *Economic Trends*, Vol. 316, pp. 81–7 (also in Tanzi (ed.) (1982b)).

Maital, S. (1982). *Minds, Markets and Money*, New York, Basic Books.

Martino, A. (1980). 'Another Italian Economic Miracle', Mimeo, Mont Pelerin Society, Stanford Conference.

Mason, R. and Calvin, L. D. (1978). 'A Study of Admitted Income Tax Evasion', *Law and Society Review*, pp. 73-89.

Mattera, P. (1985). *Off the Books*, London, Pluto Press.

Matthews, K. G. P. (1982). 'Demand for Currency and the Black Economy in UK', *Journal of Economic Studies*, Vol. 9. pp. 3-22.

Matthews, K. G. P. (1983). 'National Income and the Black Economy', *Economic Affairs*, pp. 261-7.

Miller, R. (1979). 'Evidence of Attitudes to Evasion from a Sample Survey', in Seldon (ed.), (1979), pp. 115-25.

Mirus, R. and Smith, R. S. (1981). 'Canada's Irregular Economy', *Canadian Public Policy*, Vol. 7, pp. 444-53 (also in Tanzi (ed.) (1982b).

Molefski, B. (1982). 'American Underground Economy', in Tanzi (ed.) (1982b).

Mont, J. (1982). 'De zwarte activiteiten in Belgie: oorzaken, ombagen and implicaties', *Tijdschrift voor Economie en Management*, Vol. 27, pp. 259-73.

Mork, K. A. (1975). 'Income Tax Evasion: Some Empirical Evidence', *Public Finance*, Vol. 30, pp. 70-6.

OECD (1978a). 'Methods Used To Estimate the Extent of Tax Evasion', Mimeo, CFA (78)6, Paris.

OECD (1978b). 'Unrecorded Unemployment: The Experience of the Italian "Istituto centrale di statistica" in Investigating Non-institutional Work', Mimeo, MAS/WP7(78)1, Paris.

OECD (1979). 'Unrecorded Employment', Mimeo MAS/WP7(79)6, Paris.

OECD (1980a). 'Une etude sur l'exactitude des declarations des revenues en France', Mimeo, DAF/CFA/WP8/80.4, Paris.

OECD (1980b). 'Measuring the Volume of Unrecorded Employment', Mimeo, MAS/WP7(80)3, Paris.

Ofer, G. and Vinokur, A. (1980). *'Private Sources of Income of the Soviet Urban Household'*, Santa Monica, Rand Corp.

O'Higgins, M. (1980), *Measuring the Hidden Economy: A Review of Evidence and Methodology*, Outer Circle Policy Unit.

O'Higgins, M. (1981a). 'Aggregate Measures of Tax Evasion: an Assessment-I', *British Tax Review*, pp. 286-302.

O'Higgins, M. (1981b). 'Tax Evasion and the Self-employed – An Examination of the Evidence-II', *British Tax Review*, pp. 367-78.

O'Higgins, M. (1984). 'Assessing the Unobserved Economy in the United Kingdom', in Feige, E. (ed.), *The Unobserved Economy*, Cambridge: Cambridge University Press.

O'Higgins, M. (1985). 'The Relation between the Formal and Hidden Economies: An Exploratory Analysis for Four Countries' in Wenig and Gaertner (eds.) (1985).

Okonomiske Rad (1967). Den personlige indkomstfordeling og indkomstudjaevningen over de offentlige finanser, Statens Trykningskontor, Copenhagen.

Okonomiske Rad (1977). Dansk okonomi, Statens Trykningskontor, Copenhagen.

Park, T. (1979). 'Reconciliation between Personal Income and Taxable Income 1947-77', Mimeo, Bureau of Economic Analysis, Washington, DC.

Pestieau, P. (1984). 'Belgium's Irregular Economy', in Wenig and Gaertner (eds.) (1985).

Petersen, H. G. (1982). 'Size of the Public Sector, Economic Growth and the Informal Economy: Development Trends in the Federal Republic of Germany; *Review of Income and Wealth*, Vol. 28, pp. 191-215.

Porter, R. (1979). 'Some Notes on Estimating the Underground Economy', Mimeo, Federal Reserve.

Rey, M. (1965). 'Estimating Tax Evasion: The Example of the Italian General Sales Tax', *Public Finance*, Vol. 20, pp. 3-14.

Ross, I. (1978). 'Why the Underground Economy is Booming', *Fortune*, 9 October, pp. 92-8.

Roze, H. (1971). 'Prestations sociales, impot direct et cellule revenus', *Economie et Statistique*, Vol. 20, pp. 3-14.

Schmolders, G. (1959). 'Fiscal Psychology – A New Branch of Public Finance', *National Tax Journal*, Vol. 12, pp. 340-5.

Schmolders, G. (1980). 'Der Beitrag der Schattenwirtschaft', in Mohr, J. C. B., *Wandlungen in Wirtschaft und Gesellschaft*, pp. 371-9.

Schwartz, R. D. and Orleans, S. (1967). 'On Legal Sanctions', *Chicago Law Review*, Vol. 34, pp. 274-300

Seldon, A. (ed.) (1979). *Tax Avoision*, London, Institute of Economic Affairs.

SIFO (1981). Svartbetalare och svartjobare, Mimeo, SIFO, Stockholm.

Simon, C. P. and Witte, A. D. (1982). *Beating the System: The Underground Economy*, Boston, Mass., Auburn House.

Skolka, J. (1985). 'The Parallel Economy in Austria', in Wenig and Gaertner (eds.) (1985), pp. 60-75.

Smith, A. (1981). 'The Informal Economy', *Lloyds Bank Review*, Vol. 141.

Smith, S. (1986). *Britain's Shadow Economy*, Institute for Fiscal Studies, Oxford.

Song, Y. and Yarborough, T. E. (1973). 'Tax Ethics and Tax-payer Attitude: A Survey', *Public Administration Review*, Vol. 38, pp. 442-52.

Spicer, M. W. and Becker, L. A. (1980). 'Fiscal Inequity and Tax Evasion – An Experimental Approach', *National Tax Journal*, Vol. 33, pp. 171-5.

Spicer, M. W. and Thomas, J. E. (1982). 'Audit Probabilities and the Tax Evasion Decision: An Experimental Approach', *Journal of Economic Psychology*, Vol. 2, pp. 241-5.

Tanzi, V. (1980a). 'The Underground Economy in the United States: Estimates and Implications', *Banca Nazionale del Lavoro, Quarterly Review*, Vol. 135, pp. 427-53 (also Ch. 4 in Tanzi (ed.)).

Tanzi, V. (1980b). 'Underground Economy Built on Illicit Pursuits is Growing Concern of Economic Policy Makers', *IMF Survey*, pp. 34-37.

Tanzi, V. (1982a). 'The Underground Economy in the United States: Annual Estimates, 1930-80', *IMF Staff Papers*, pp. 283-305.

Tanzi, V. (1982b). *The Underground Economy in the United States and Abroad*, Lexington, Mass., D. C. Heath.

Tanzi, V. (1983). 'The Underground Economy', *Finance and Development*, December, pp. 10-13.

Tucker, M. (1980). 'The Underground Economy in Australia', *Commercial Bank of Australia Economic Review*.

Visco, V. (1983). 'L'evasione dell'imposta sul reddito delle persone fisiche in Italia', *La crisi della imposizione progressiva sul reddito*, Gerelli, and Valiani, (eds.), F. Angeli, Milan.

Vogel, J. (1974). 'Taxation and Public Opinion in Sweden: An Interpretation of Recent Survey Data', *National Tax Journal*, Vol. 27, pp. 499-513.

Warneryd, K. E. and Walerud, B. (1982). 'Taxes and Economic Behaviour – Some Interview Data on Tax Evasion in Sweden', *Journal of Economic Psychology*, Vol. 2, pp. 87-211.

Weck-Hanneman, H. and Frey, B. S. (1985). 'Measuring the Shadow Economy: The Case of Switzerland', in Wenig and Gaertner (eds.) (1985).

Wenig, A. and Gaertner, W. (eds.) (1985). *The Economics of the Shadow Economy*, Berlin: Springer Verlag.

INDEX

229

*Index compiled by
Joyce Kerr*